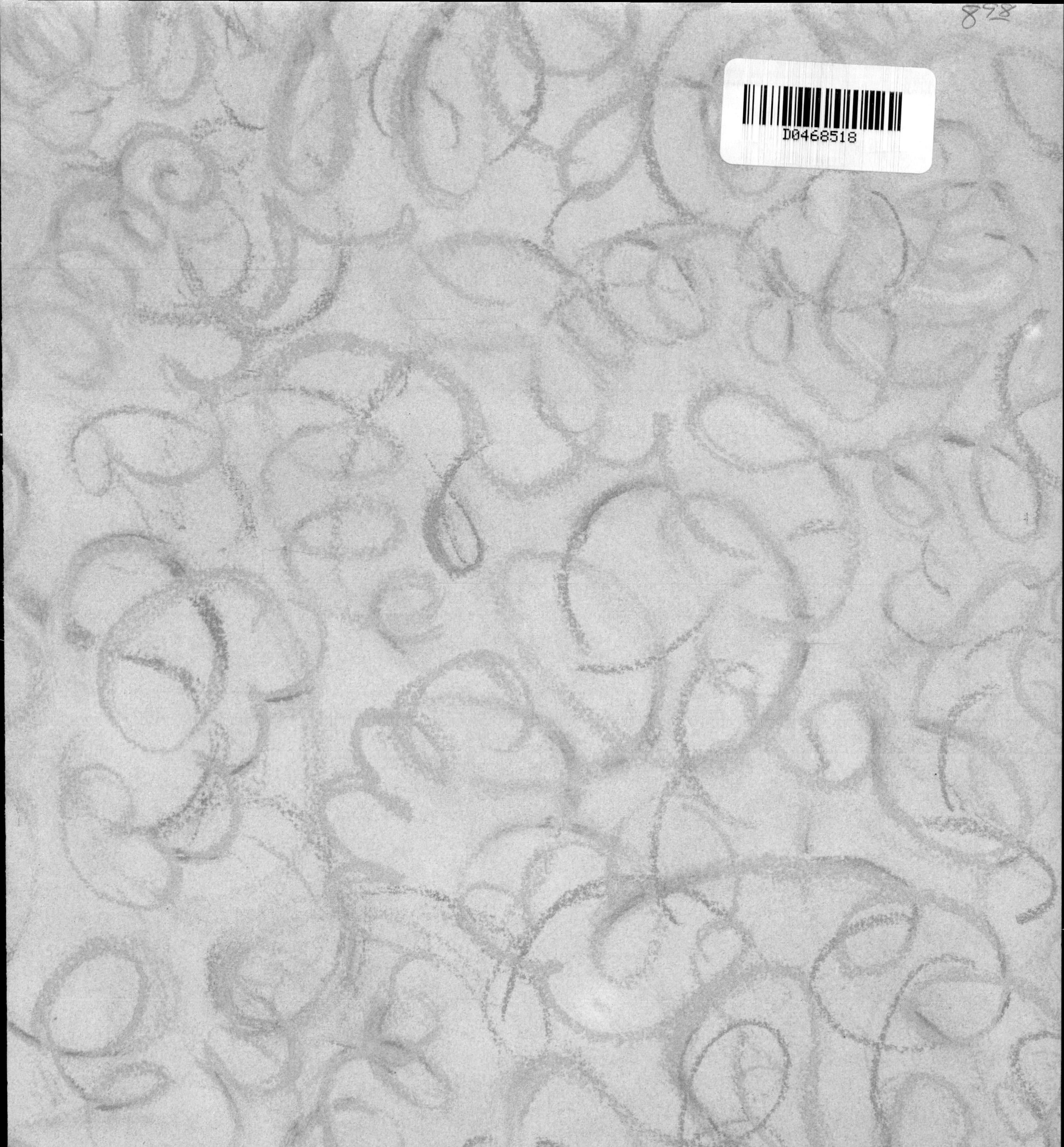

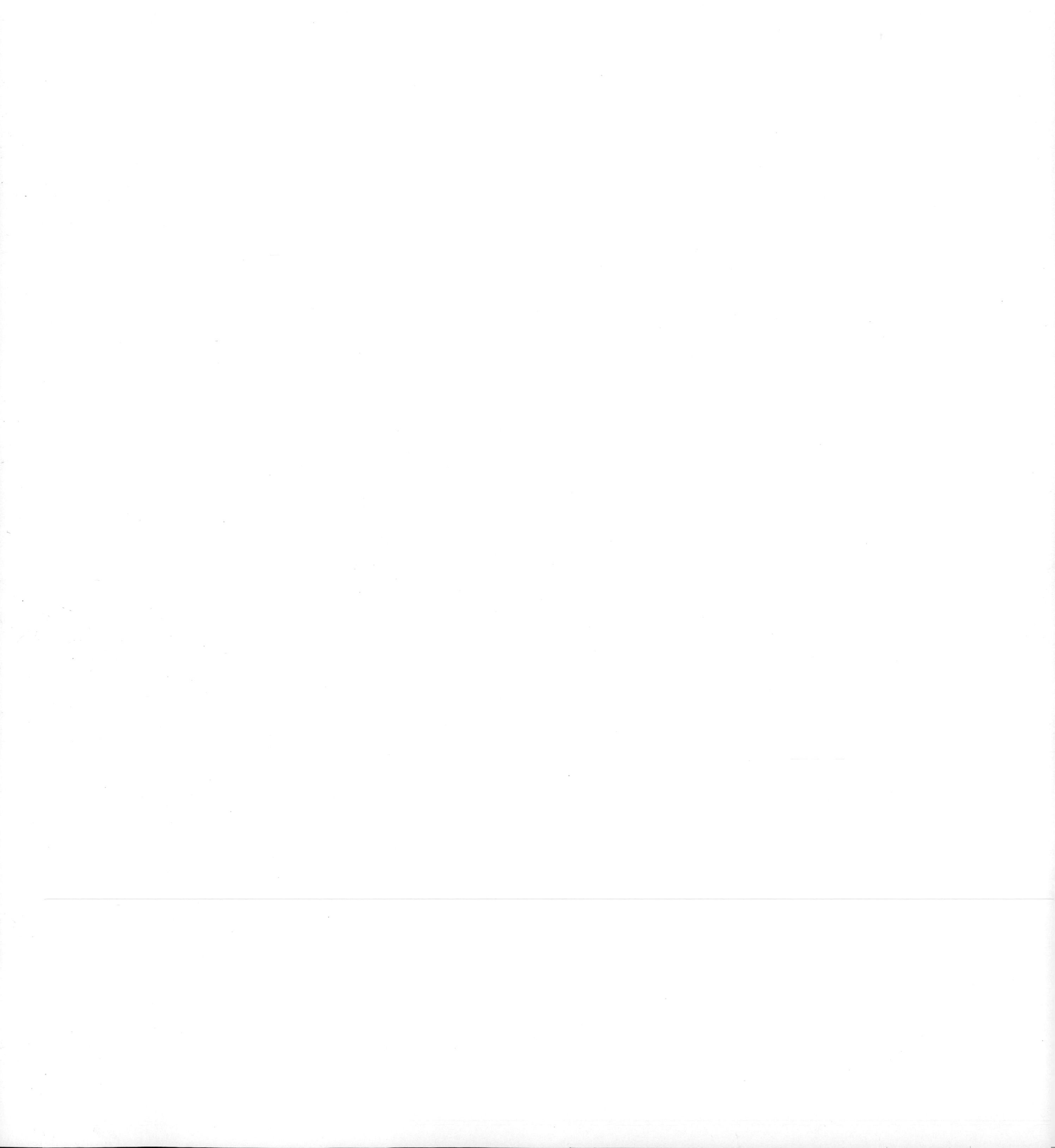

CREATIVE DESIGN

PARTY & TABLE DECORATIONS

CREATIVE DESIGN

PARTY & TABLE DECORATIONS

Suzie Major • Karen Lansdown • Susy Smith

GALLERY BOOKS
An Imprint of W. H. Smith Publishers Inc.
112 Madison Avenue
New York City 10016

52 Bedford Row,
London WC1R 4LR,
United Kingdom.

ISBN 0-8317-8605-1

This edition published in 1989 by Gallery Books,
an imprint of W.H. Smith Publishers, Inc.,
112 Madison Avenue, New York 10016.

Gallery Books are available for bulk purchase for sales promotion and premium use. For details write or telephone the Manager of Special Sales, W.H. Smith Publishers, Inc., 112 Madison Avenue, New York, New York 10016. (212) 532-6600.

CREDITS

Editor-in-chief: Jilly Glassborow

Assistant editor: Lisa Dyer

Designer: Kathy Gummer

Photographers: Steve Tanner and Terry Dilliway

Line artwork: New Leaf Designs

Typeset by: The Old Mill, London

Color separation by: Fotographics Ltd, London — Hong Kong

Printed in Italy

CONTENTS

Garlands and Hanging Decorations **6**

Table Centrepieces **28**

Tablecloths and Napkins **44**

Place Cards and Placemats **60**

Hats and Masks **72**

Gifts and Favours **80**

Index **95**

INTRODUCTION

Whatever the event — be it Christmas, Easter, Thanksgiving, a child's birthday party or a special dinner party — an array of colourful decorations will always add to the occasion. This stylish book is packed with over 150 decorations that are both simple and fun to make, from traditional paper chains and fun-loving party hats to sophisticated table centrepieces and elegant napkin folds.

Throughout *Party and Table Decorations* you will find a variety of ways to add a touch of originality to your entertaining. For easy reference, the book is divided into sections, each dealing with a different aspect of party and table preparation. If you intend to devise an overall theme for your celebration, a little thought and planning is necessary. For optimum effect, reflect one specific theme in all the decorations you create. The designs in this book are versatile and may be easily adapted to suit your own taste by using a different colour or material. Each design is accompanied by colourful step-by-step photographs and easy-to-follow instructions showing you how to put the finished article together from basic materials. And, where necessary, templates for shapes that might prove difficult to draw freehand have been supplied on pages 90-92.

You know your guests, and your own individual style, so experiment a little with our suggestions to create your own unique effects.

 GARLANDS AND HANGING DECORATIONS 

Attractive decorations, hanging on the walls or from the ceiling, will add sparkle to any festive occasion. This section covers all kinds, from garlands to wreaths and mobiles, and uses a wide range of materials including fresh flowers and foliage as well as paper, fabric, ribbon, tinsel and foil. These designs are suitable for adults or children to make, and will fit your chosen party theme, whether it is a holiday celebration, a birthday, wedding or graduation.

FRESH FROM THE GARDEN

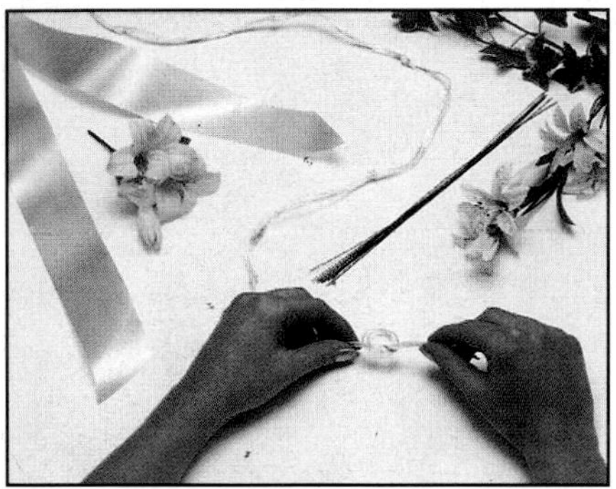

This beautiful garland can be made any time of the year; just use whatever foliage is in season and either real or silk flowers. Take three lengths of string and knot them together at regular intervals of about 20-25cm (8-10in). Using contrasting thread or paper clips, mark the points from which the garland will be hung and to which ribbon will be attached.

Tie short lengths of florist's wire to small bunches of foliage. Then start twisting the foliage onto the string, working from both ends so that the garland looks symmetrical. Intersperse the foliage with wired bunches of flowers. A delicate balance is needed to make this design look as full as possible while taking care not to make the foliage too heavy for the string.

Wire on lengths of wide satin or gift wrap ribbon as you come to the marked points. Keep on adding small wired bunches of fresh foliage, silk flowers and ribbon from both ends, until they meet in the middle.

GRADUATION GARLAND

BOOTEE GARLAND

If a young member of the family has just graduated from college or university, throw a party for him or her, and hang a graduation garland of mortarboards on the wall. First cut out 20cm (8in) squares from foil cardboard or ordinary cardboard covered in foil paper. Stick shiny tape around the edges of each square.

Next turn each square over and mark two diagonal pencil lines across it as shown. Where they meet in the centre, pierce a small hole. Push a tassel (see page 93 for instructions) through the front, and tape it in place. Now make a hole in one corner and attach each mortarboard to a length of tinsel, tying it with a small piece of gold-covered wire.

Pin this clever garland to the front of the table at a christening party. First cut bootee shapes from pink and blue towelling fabric (terrycloth) — two for each bootee. Next, cut strips of pink and blue spotted ribbon to fit the top edge of each bootee shape. Press them in half and then pin and tack (baste) them to the tops of the bootees. Stitch them in place.

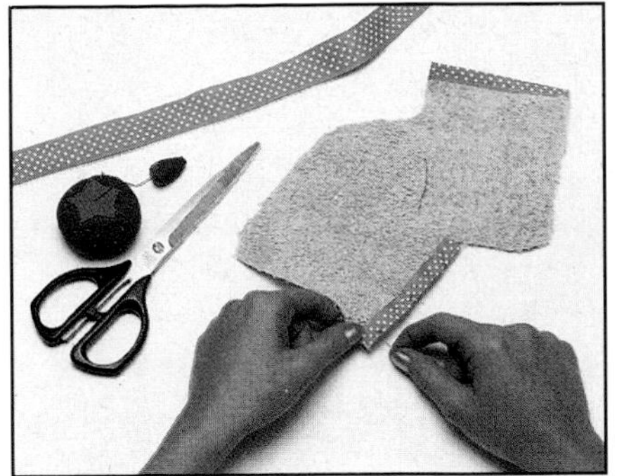

Now sew the front and back of each bootee together, around the edge, with right sides facing. Trim the seam and turn the bootee right side out. Attach a bow in matching ribbon.

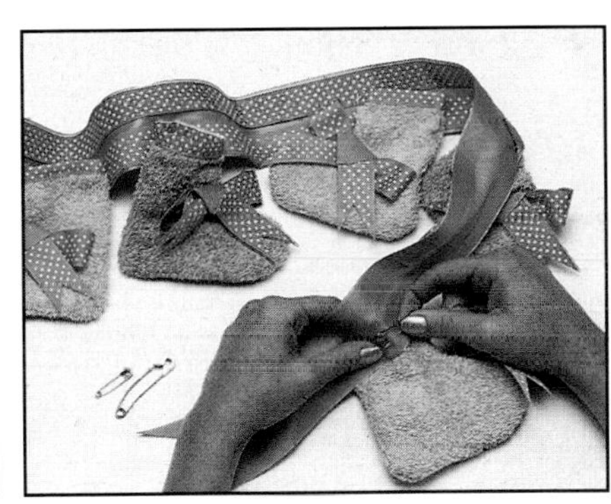

Cut a length of wide ribbon and trim it with pink and blue spotted ribbon using double-sided tape. Pin the bootees to the ribbon as shown To hang the garland, fix a large safety pin at each end, so that you can pin or hook it in place.

HIGHLAND HOLLY

HOT LIPS

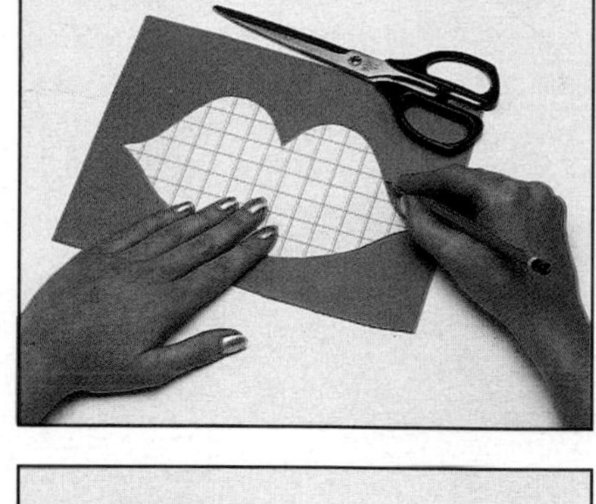

Luscious lips to show your sweetheart how much you love him on Valentine's Day or your anniversary. You will need a piece of fluorescent pink craft paper 76 by 12.5cm (30 by 5in). You should be able to get four strips this size out of a standard sheet of craft paper. Draw a lips shape (using folded paper will ensure symmetry) and cut it out in cardboard.

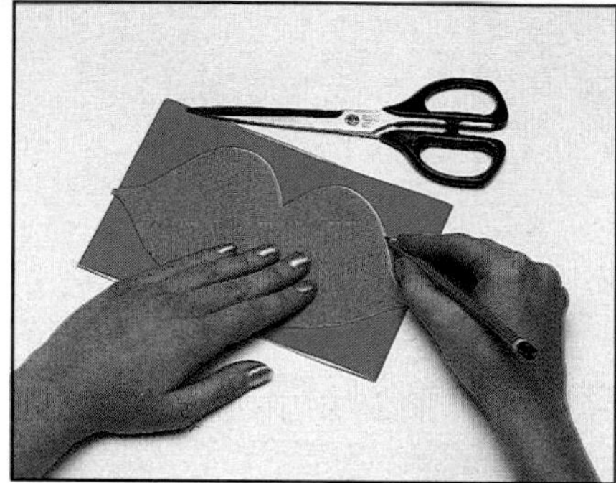

Fold the paper in half from right to left, and then from right to left again. This will give you four sets of lips. Place the pattern on top and draw round it, making sure that the pattern meets each side; otherwise the lips won't hold together.

Deck the hall with sprigs of holly, made from felt and suspended from a tartan ribbon. First, make a holly pattern from paper and use this to cut out two pieces of green felt and one of wadding for every sprig. Place two felt pieces together, with the wadding in between, and pin in place. Now, with three strands of green embroidery thread, overstitch neatly all around the edges.

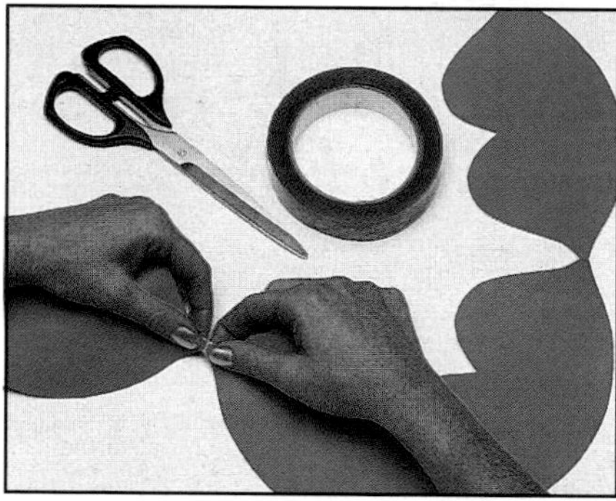

Cut out the shape using sharp scissors. Join each set of lips together at the ends to make one long garland.

Thread your sewing machine with green cotton thread and stitch 'veins' onto each holly leaf — one down the centre and the rest sloping from the centre to the points. Next, take four red wooden or plastic beads for each leaf and sew them in place, close to the inside edge, using six strands of red embroidery thread.

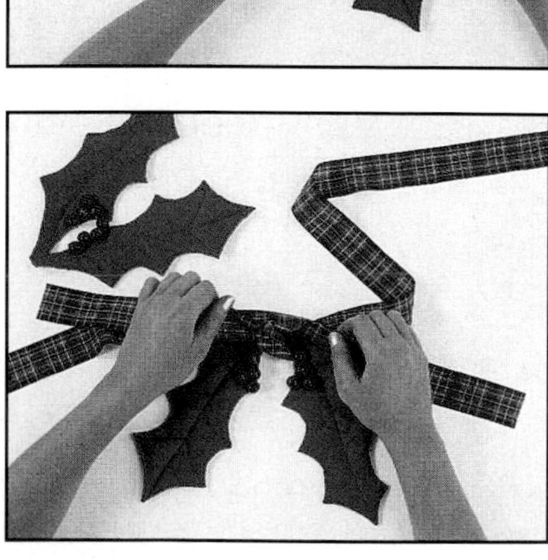

Measure out a length of tartan ribbon from which to hang the holly; the length will depend on the number of sprigs you are making. Now cut shorter lengths of ribbon — one per sprig — to make the bows. Tie the sprigs to the garland with the short lengths of ribbon, finishing off with a bow. Finally, cut a V shape in the tails of the bows and hang your garland in place.

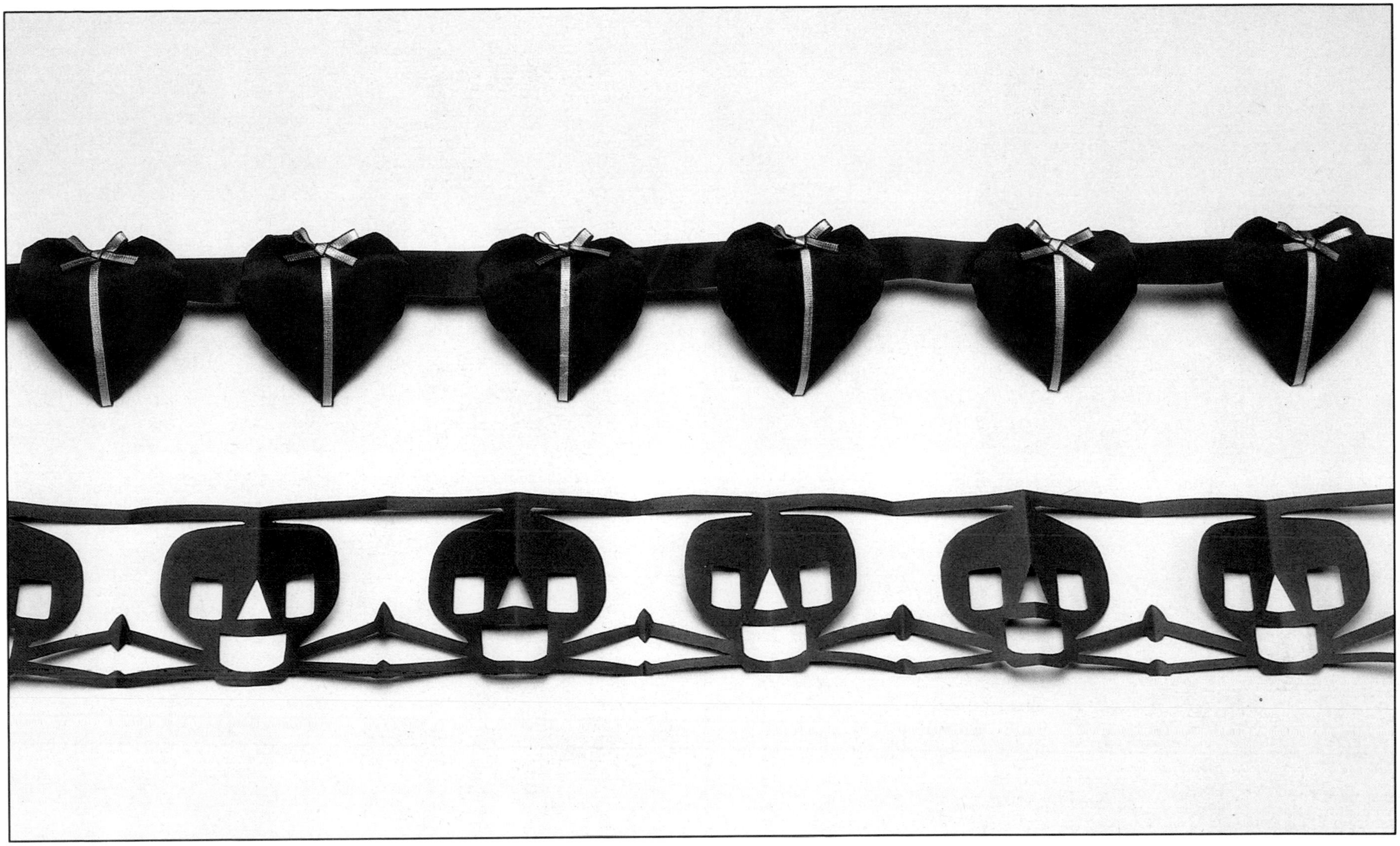

HEARTS DELIGHT

For each heart cut out two shapes in scarlet satin, using the template on page 90. Placing right sides together, sew around the edges, taking only a very small seam allowance and leaving a small gap at the top for turning it right side out.

Turn the heart right side out and stuff it carefully with polyester filling. Then neatly sew up the gap. Trim each heart with a strip of silver ribbon down the middle and a silver bow on the top. Attach the hearts to a strip of wide red satin ribbon.

SKULL AND CROSSBONES

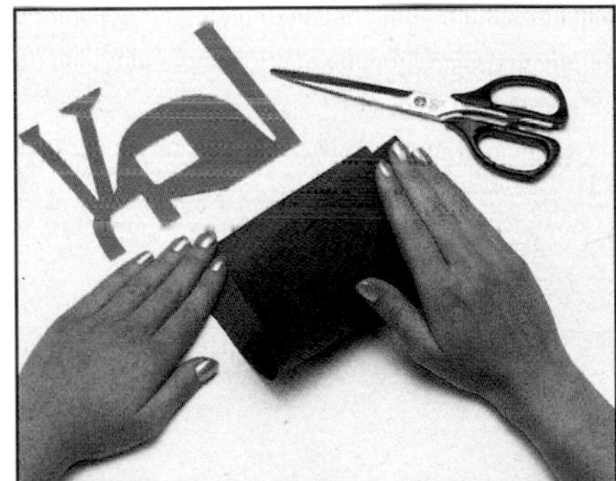

This garland is easy to make for a Halloween or fancy dress party. First take long strips of black paper, measuring 105 by 75cm (40 by 30in) each. You may need to buy a roll of paper to get the length you require. Fold each strip in half from right to left, three times.

Trace and cut out the template given on page 90 and use it to trace the shape onto the folded strip. Cut out the shape carefully with sharp scissors. Open out the strip, and join each strip to the next with a little sticky tape at the edges.

SCALLOPED SQUARES

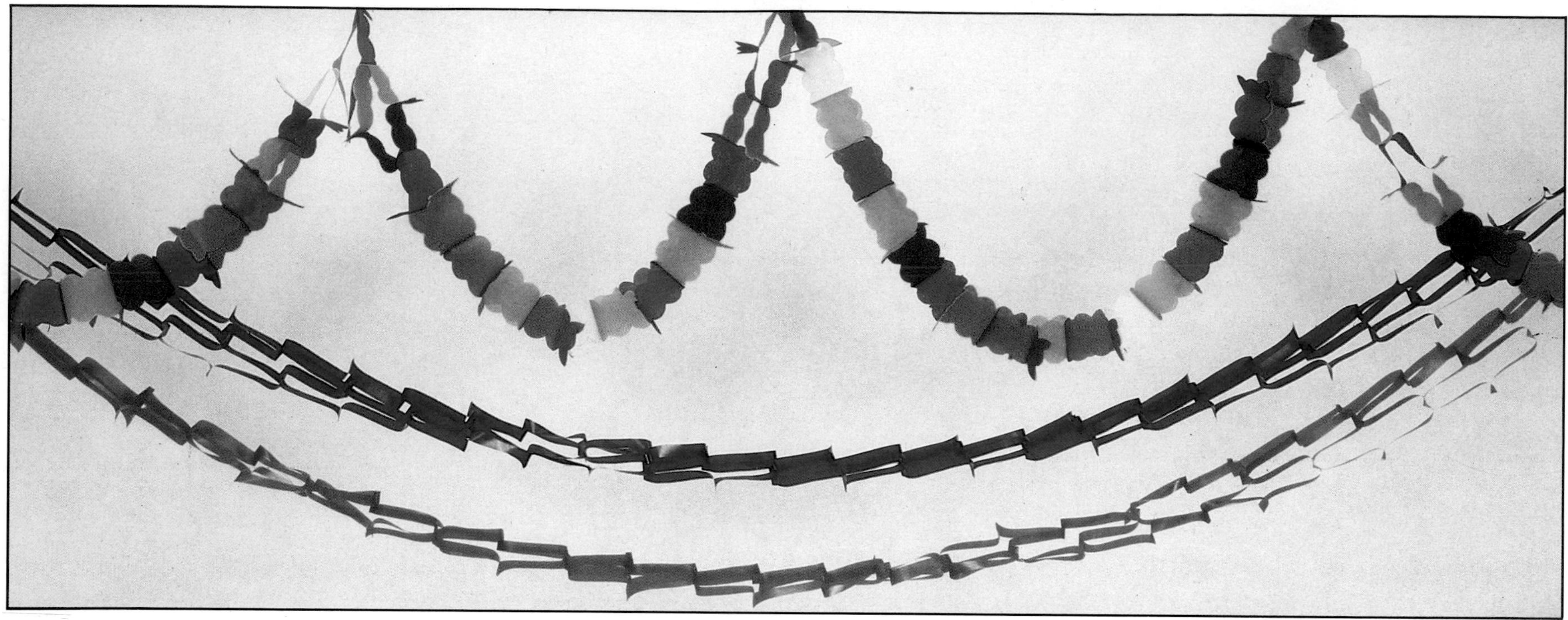

This variation on the standard pull-out chain is rectangular and has scalloped edges. It is very simple to make, though. Using the template on page 90, cut out lots of tissue shapes in different colours and mix them up for a random, multi-coloured effect.

All you need to do now is glue them together. Take the first two and stick them centre to centre.

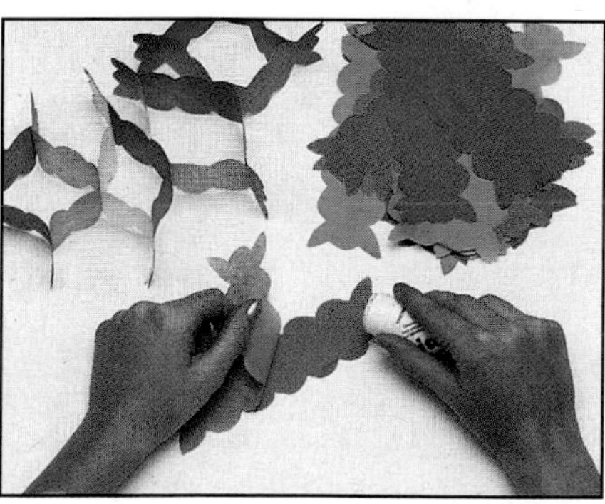

Now take another piece and glue it to one of the first pieces at each end. Continue gluing, alternately centre-to-centre and end-to-end, until the chain is the required length.

EXPANDING CHAIN

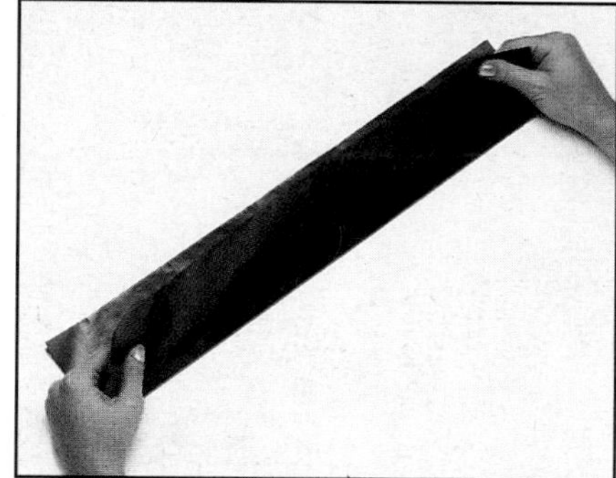

This traditional Christmas paper chain is easy to make and is shown cut from a waxed paper, which is stronger than ordinary tissue. First take a sheet of paper measuring about 50 by 35cm (20 by 14in) and fold it into four lengthwise.

Now make evenly spaced cuts all along one edge, stopping about 1.5cm (½in) from the other side. Turn the paper around and make additional cuts between the first set, again stopping short of the edge.

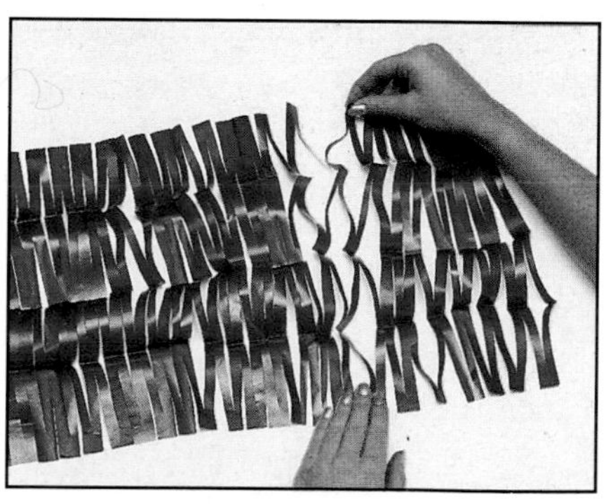

Open the chain out carefully. If you wish, you can glue the ends of two chains together to make a longer one. If your chain sags too much, string some thread through the top links to hold it together.

SHINY FOIL CHAIN

CREPE PAPER CHAIN

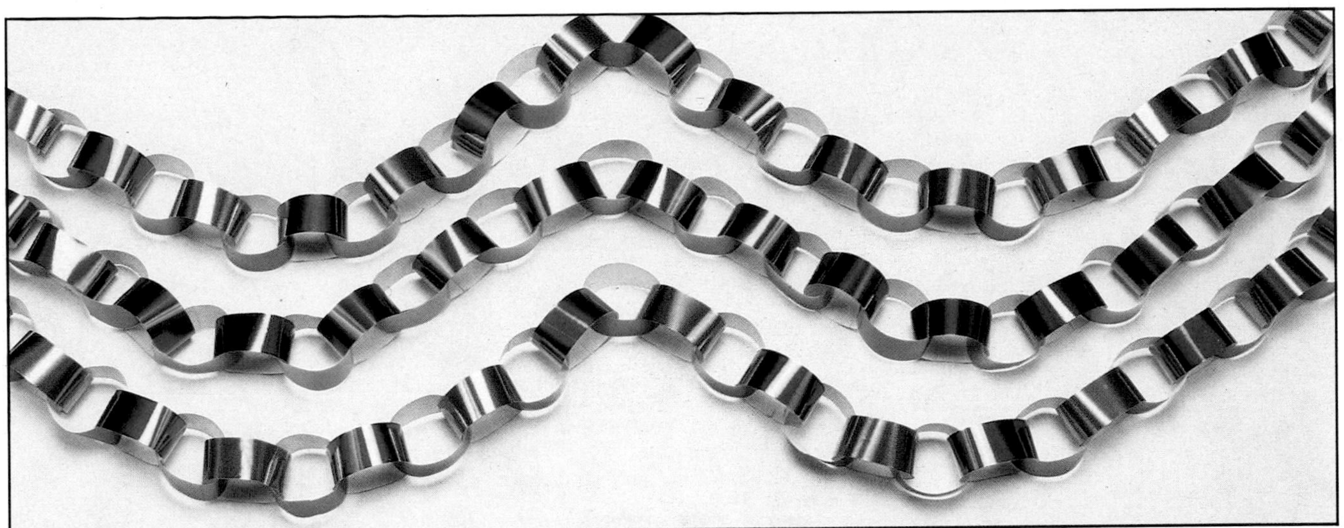

This simple paper chain takes only a few minutes to make. All you need are two different-coloured crepe papers and a touch of glue. Cut 7.5cm (3in) off the end of each crepe paper roll. Place the strips at right angles to each other, and glue one end over the other as shown.

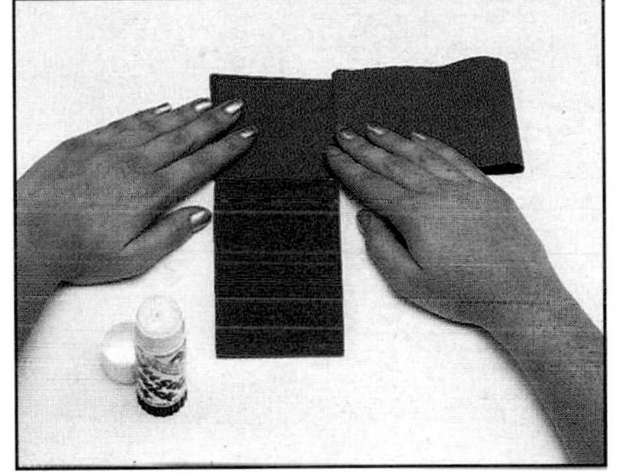

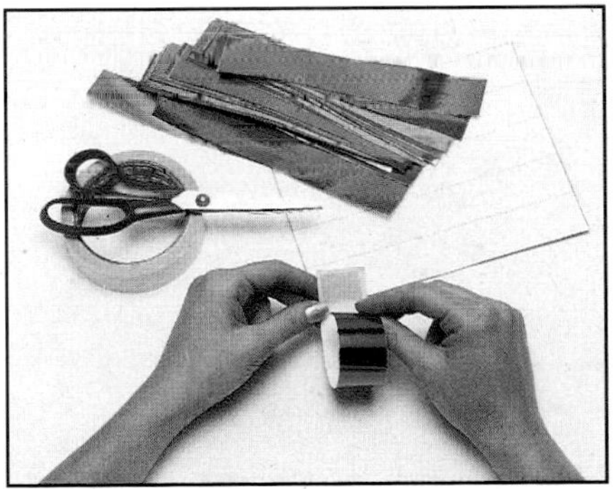

Bright-coloured foil paper makes a festive version of the simple link chain. Begin by cutting lots of strips about 18 by 3cm (7 by 1¼in). Stick the ends of the first strip together with double-sided tape (neater and quicker than glue) to make a link.

Now simply thread the next strip through and stick the ends together. Continue in this way, alternating the colours, until the chain is as long as you want it.

Bring the lower strip up and fold it over the other, then fold the right-hand strip over to the left as shown.

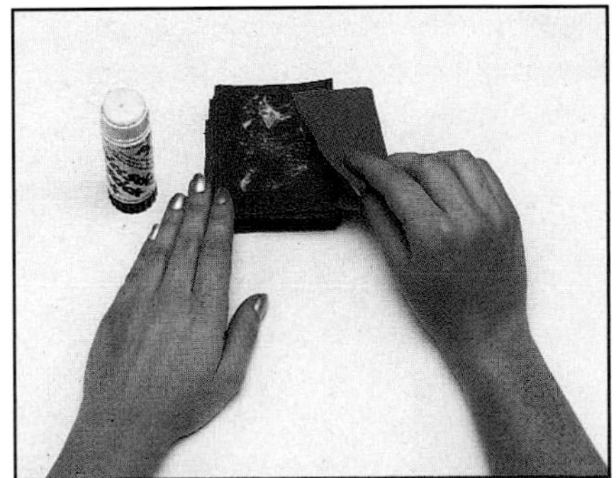

That's all there is to it; just keep folding the strips over each other alternately until you reach the end. Glue them together at the ends and trim off any extra bits.

SWEETS GALORE

For those with a sugary tooth, here is a garland covered in brightly wrapped sweets — to be enjoyed long after the party is over. Cut a length of ribbon about 135cm (54in) long and mark the centre. Next cut three 112cm (45in) lengths of ribbon and make them up into three bows, stapling the loops into an open position as shown and trimming the ends into points.

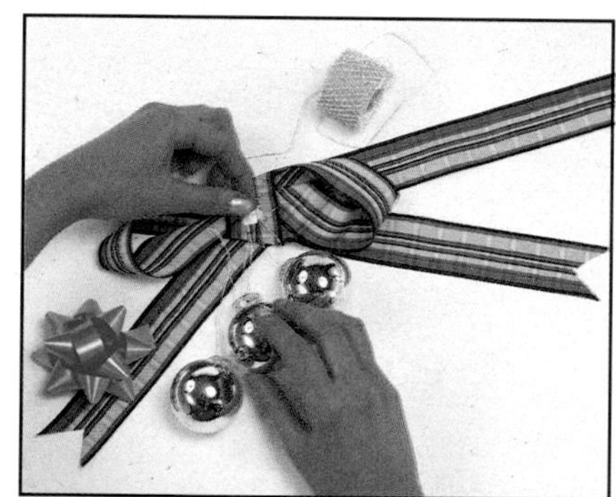

Tape the bows onto each end and onto the centre of the main ribbon length. Then use silver thread to hang clusters of baubles from the centre of the bows. (Hang the baubles at varying lengths for the best effect.) Glue the threads to the centre of the bows and cover them up with an adhesive ribbon rosette.

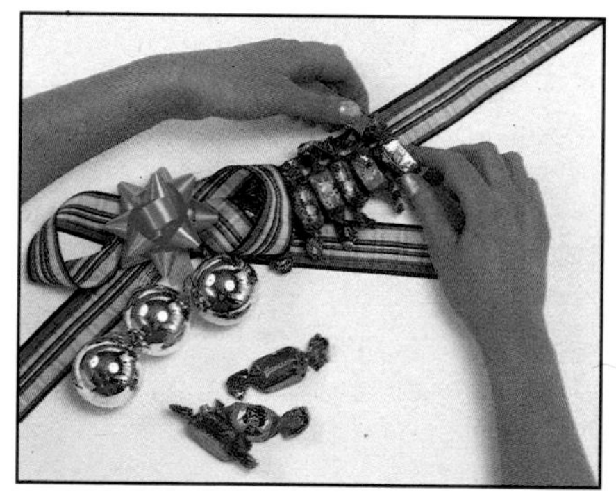

Decorate some sweets with silver stars and staple them along the top edge of the ribbon between the bows. Use double-sided tape to attach the underside of the sweets to the ribbon. Finally, sew curtain rings onto the back of the ribbon for hanging the garland.

For the rosettes, cut a circle of silver cardboard, 10cm (4in) across. Take a piece of ribbon 80cm (32in) long, fold it in half and staple it to the centre of the circle. Trim the ribbon ends into points. Staple the sweets in a circle around the cardboard as shown, then stick a ribbon star in the centre. Using sticky tape, attach a curtain ring to the back of the circle for hanging up the rosette.

SWAGS OF NET

This is a lovely decoration for a wedding table and makes the most of a crisp white tablecloth. Begin by taking some large white wooden rings — the kind used on curtain poles — and winding ribbon around them as shown.

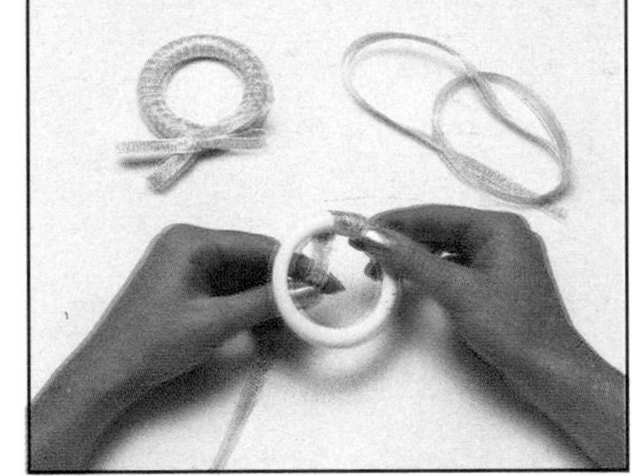

Tie a bow at the top to hide the little metal ring, then pin each one to the front overhang of the tablecloth, spacing them evenly. Thread through a length of net, bunching it between the rings to make a good swag.

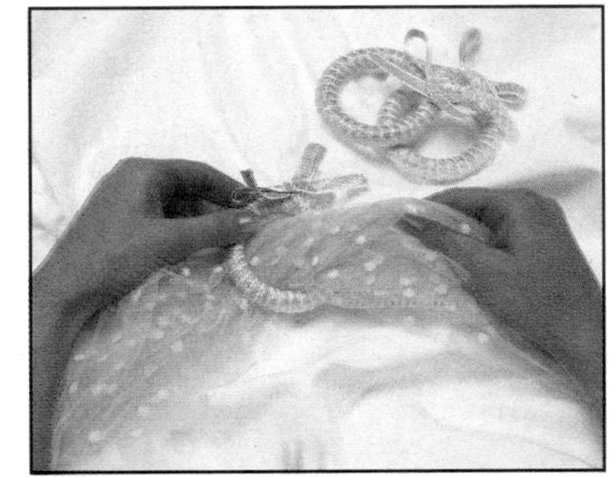

When the net is evenly arranged, attach strips of curling gift wrap ribbon to the lower edge of each ring as a finishing touch. Curl the ribbon by running the blunt edge of a pair of scissors along it.

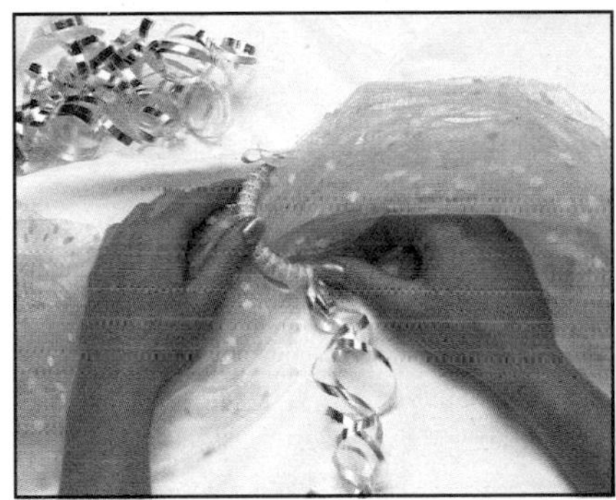

CANDY CRACKERS

The paper used for these crackers is similar in texture to curling gift wrap ribbon and has a lovely shiny satin finish. Cover empty toilet paper rolls or cardboard tubes with white sticky-backed plastic, which prevents the colour from showing through. Now cut pieces of shiny paper, twice as long as the tubes, and wide enough to go easily around them.

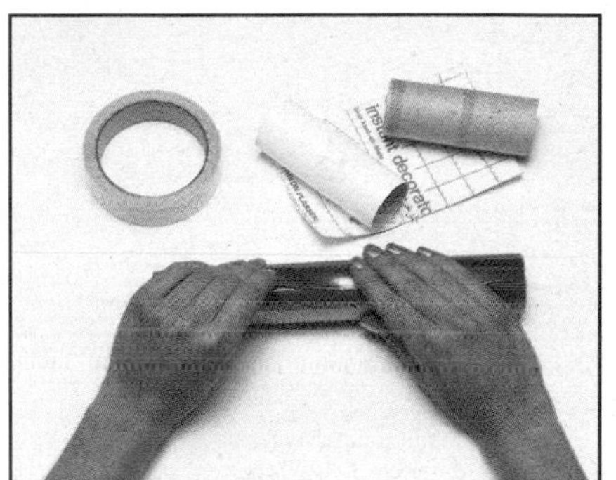

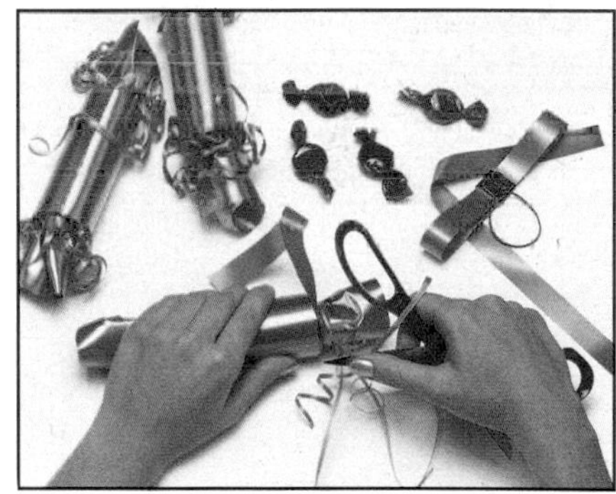

Wrap the tube in the paper and fix in place with double-sided tape. Don't twist the ends; scrunch them in with elastic (rubber) bands, which you can then cover with strips of curling ribbon. Decorate the crackers with boiled sweets (hard candies), stuck on with double-sided tape. Staple the crackers onto a strip of tinsel and trim the garland with sweets and baubles.

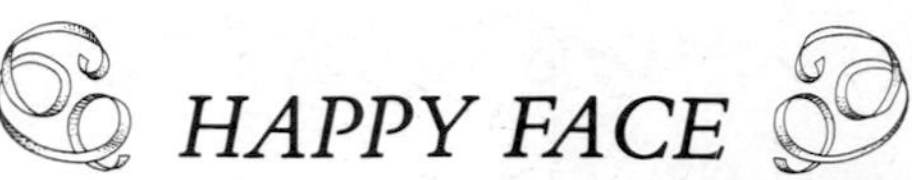

HAPPY FACE

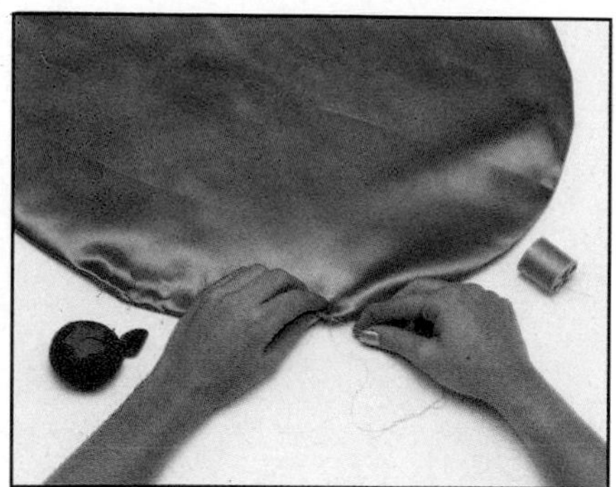

This jolly wall hanging can be folded up in a drawer and brought out every Halloween. Cut out two satin shapes, using the template on page 90. Place right sides together, and sew around the edge, leaving the flat part at the bottom open. Turn the shape right side out, slip in a piece of medium-weight wadding (batting), and slipstitch the gap together.

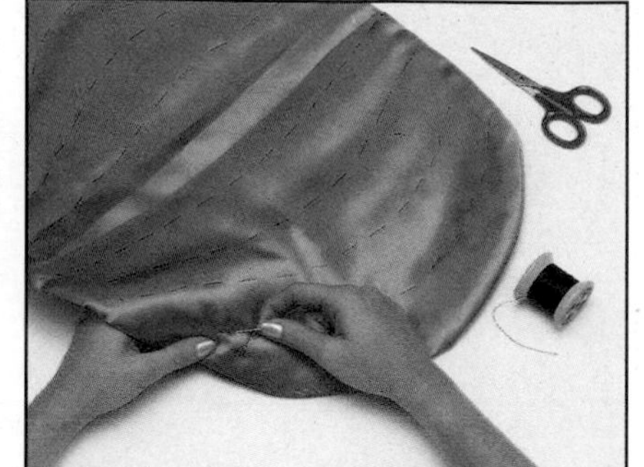

Mark the quilting lines with tacking (basting) stitches using dark thread. Now machine quilt, using a small zigzag stich and orange thread. If you haven't got a machine, a small backstitch will be fine. Remove the tacking when you have finished.

Cut out the eyes, mouth and stem in black and green felt, using the templates on page 90. The loop is another piece of felt, about 13cm (5in) long, which you sew under the edge of the stem. All the felt pieces are sewn on with a machined satin stitch using orange thread.

COLOURFUL KITE

The frame for this kite is made from garden sticks. Mark off the lengths specified, and stamp on them where you want them to break! Take one stick 60cm (24in) long and another 40cm (16in) long, and tie them together with twine so that the three upper arms are equal. Next add two top pieces, 28cm (11½in) long, and the two lower side pieces 45cm (18½in) long. Tie all these in place.

Now take two large sheets of brightly coloured tissue paper. Tear one in half lengthwise and lay one half over the large sheet. Lightly glue it along the edges to keep it in place. Turn the paper over. Now lay the frame over the tissue, and cut around the shape, leaving a 5cm (2in) border all around.

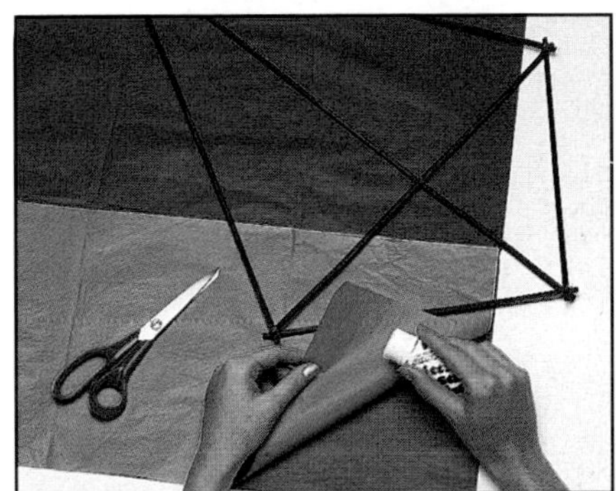

Apply glue to the outside frame of the kite, and fold the edges of the tissue over it. Finish by adding a red rosette and a paper ribbon tail with bows strung along it. After use on the big day, this can be transferred to the wall of the children's room. It has to be handled carefully, but once hung up will last for ages.

PRETEND BALLOONS

These are just as colourful as real balloons, but they won't pop, or even gently expire! Cut out balloon shapes from coloured cardboard or stiff paper, then cover them on one side with spray-on glitter.

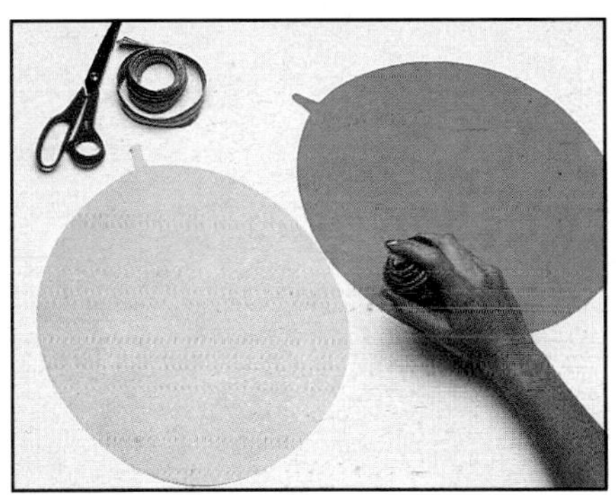

Two balloon shapes can be glued together at the edges, or they can all be strung up separately. Tape the balloons to a length of colourful striped ribbon.

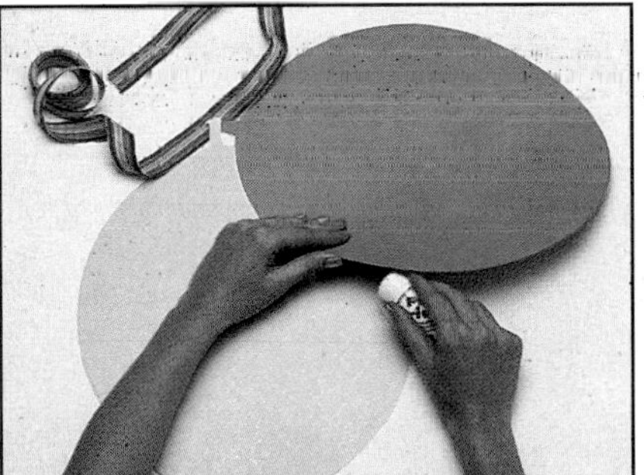

Lastly, use more of the same ribbon to make up some bows, and fix them to the balloons with some double-sided tape.

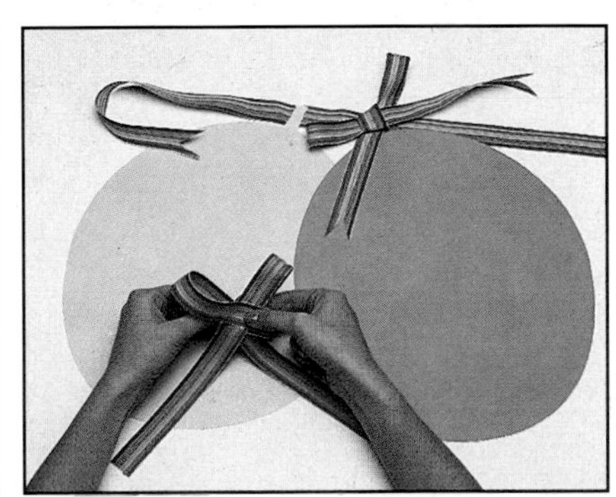

OUTLOOK FINE

If the day outside is gloomy, try brightening the outlook with some 'stained glass window' pictures. These are cut from black art paper and backed with coloured tissue. First cut pieces of art paper 38 by 30cm (15 by 12in). Mark a 3.5cm (1½in) border all the way round. Now draw your design, taking care that it is always connected in some way to the outer border.

Next cut away any parts of the picture that you want to be coloured, taking care not to detach the black areas from the frame.

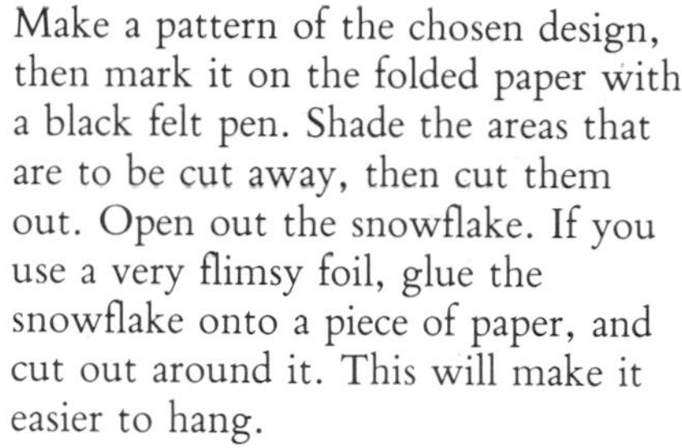

Now glue tissue paper to the back. For your first attempt use just one colour; then as you feel more confident, you can build up pictures using three or more different coloured tissues. When the picture is finished, affix it lightly to the windowpane, then watch what happens when the light shines through it.

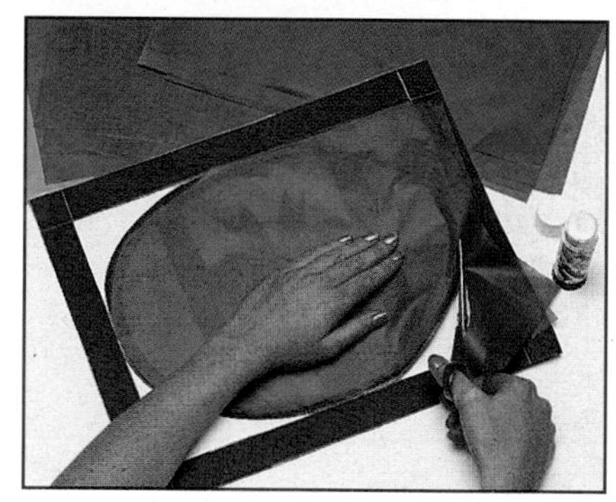

SNOWFLAKE

You can always have snow at Christmas, even when the sun is shining outside. Make this snowflake in foil or in plain white paper and hang it over a window-pane. First take a square of paper, fold it into quarters, then in half diagonally, then lastly back on itself as shown.

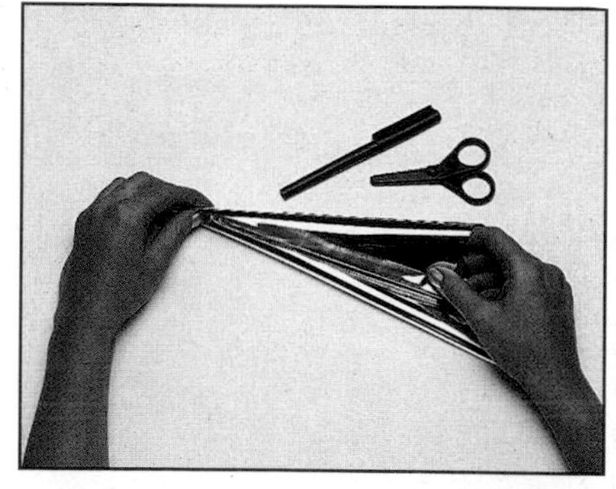

Make a pattern of the chosen design, then mark it on the folded paper with a black felt pen. Shade the areas that are to be cut away, then cut them out. Open out the snowflake. If you use a very flimsy foil, glue the snowflake onto a piece of paper, and cut out around it. This will make it easier to hang.

Finally, decorate the snowflake with sequins in bright jewel colours. The more patience you have, the more sequins you will use and the better it will look!

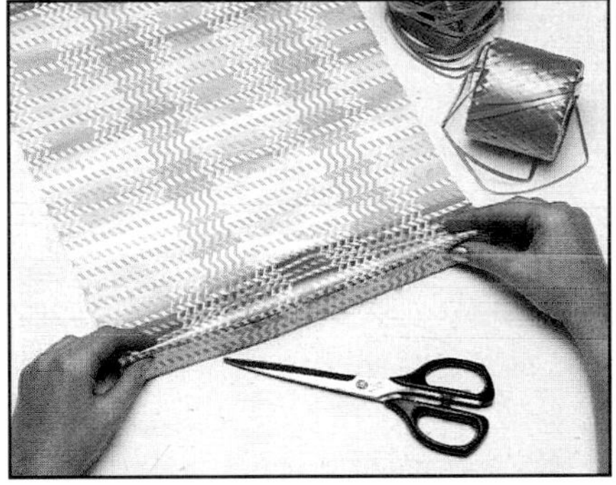

What could be simpler than these crisply-pleated paper fans, trimmed with curling ribbons? To begin, take a strip of printed wrapping paper and pleat it crosswise as shown.

When you have finished the folding, hold the fan together by stapling it at one end. Cut some strips of gift wrap ribbon and run them along the edge of a ruler, or over a scissors blade, so that they curl.

Slip the ends of the ribbons between the folds of the fan and staple them in place. Finish by fixing a ribbon rosette over the stapled end.

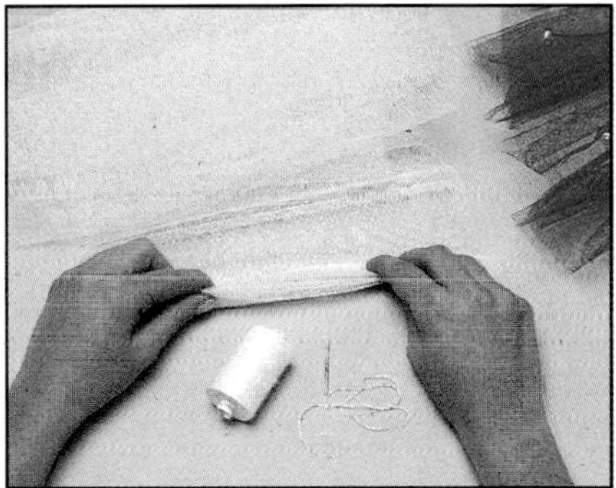

Hang these pretty net fans on the wall or on the corner of a mirror, or use them to decorate a tablecloth. They are made from strips of net about 30cm (12in) wide and 1 metre (40in) long. Cut two strips of each colour and concertina-fold them crosswise, treating the two layers as one. When you have finished pleating, make a few stitches through the net at one end to hold it together.

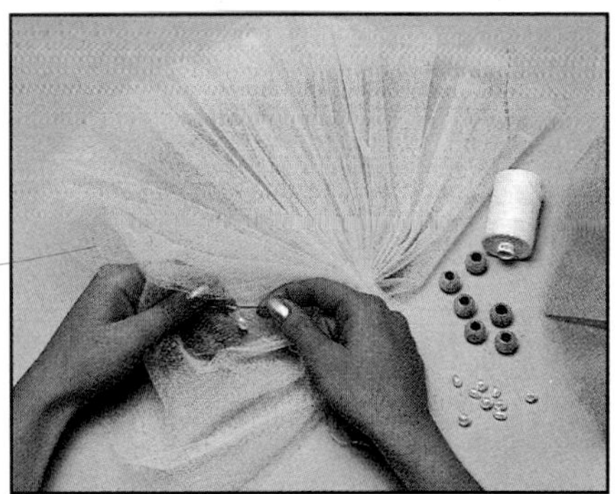

Sew little pearl beads or silver sequins onto the net to decorate it. Trim away any rough edges on the outside of the fan.

Finish off by spraying some round wooden beads with silver paint and sewing them to the centre of the fan to cover the pleating.

HEART STRINGS

For this mobile cut out 40 hearts in thin pink cardboard and 40 in blue, using the template on page 90. Glue one side of a blue heart, lay the end of a long piece of nylon thread on it, and place a pink heart on top; press them firmly together. Now glue another two hearts together, with the thread between them, leaving a gap of about 4cm (1½in) between this and the first heart.

Add three more hearts to the thread. Cut off the thread about 20cm (8in) above the top heart. Make seven more heart strings. Cut two circles of cardboard using a dessert plate as a pattern. In one make eight tiny holes, about 2.5cm (1in) from the edge. Insert the strings and tape them in place. In the other circle insert four threads and tie them to a curtain ring. Glue the two circles together.

SWAYING PALMS

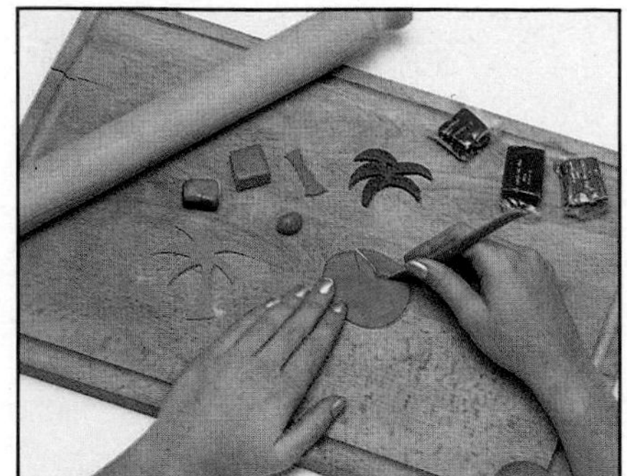

This tropical-style mobile is made of coloured modelling clay, the kind you can bake. You simply mould it, bake it in the oven, glue the pieces together and varnish it for a lovely shiny finish. You need eight palm trees for the mobile. Roll out the clay with a rolling pin and cut out the shape of the tree using the template on page 90.

If using more than one colour, cut the trunk and branches separately. Remember to make a hole in the top to hang each one. Also cut out a ring of clay about 15cm (6in) in diameter, with eight holes on the outer edge and four on the inner. Bake the shapes as instructed; when they are cool, glue the trunks and branches together. Varnish them on both sides.

To string them, use a strong nylon or waxed cord. The first should be 5cm (2in) long, the second 10cm (4in) and so on, with 5cm (2in) added to each length. This will give the impression that the trees fall in a spiral. Slip them through the holes in the support and knot them onto a bead above. Knot four more strings through the inner edge, and attach them to a ring to hang the mobile.

CHEEKY CHICKS

These little fluffy chicks make a charming mobile. For each chick you need two pom-poms (see page 93 for instructions). For the larger pom-pom use cardboard circles, 6cm (2½in) in diameter with 2.5cm (1in) holes. The small circles are 5cm (2in) across with the same size hole. When the larger one is ready to be cut away, push a pipe cleaner through the hole to form the legs and feet.

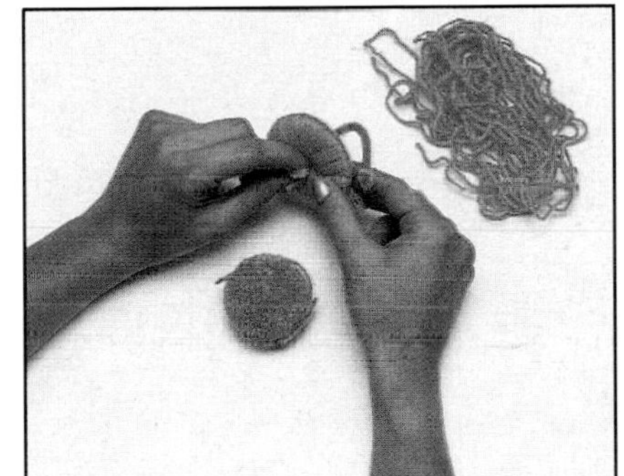

Now cut and tie the pom-poms, joining the head and body together by tying the spare yarn tightly. Make one or two stitches through the head and body to hold them in place.

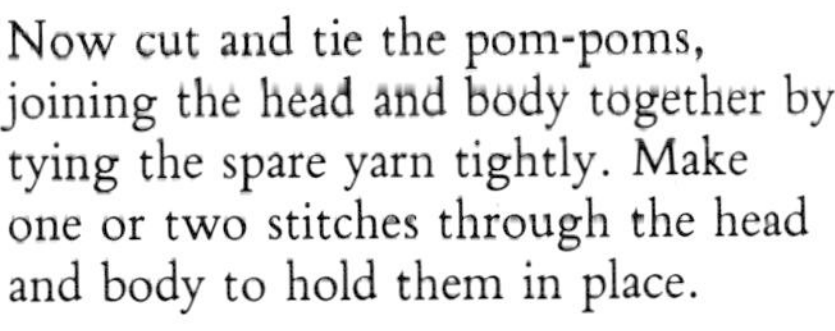

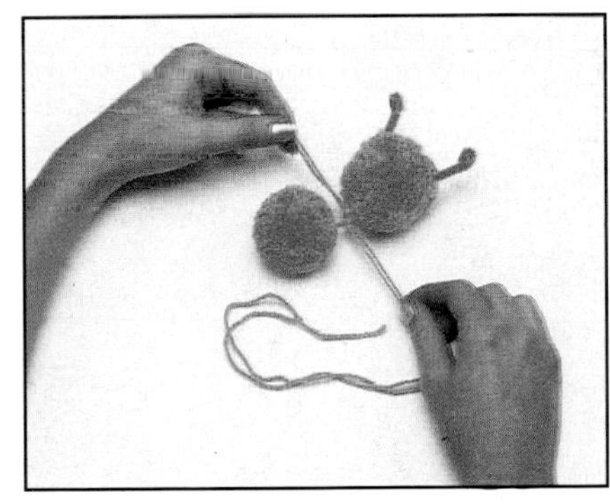

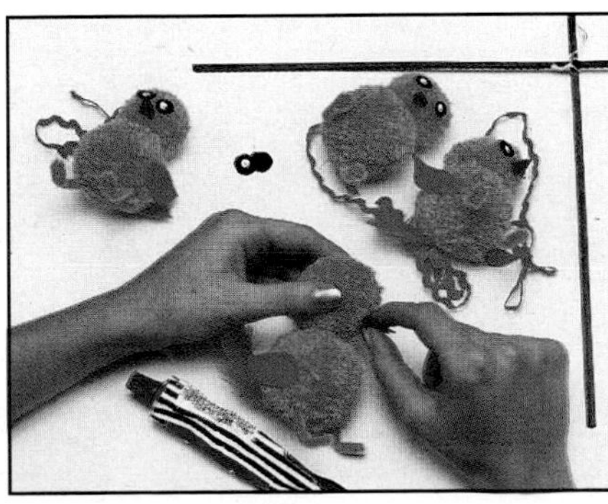

Trim each chick with a felt beak, eyes and wings, and a feather for the tail, sticking them on with a dab of glue. Tie a piece of shirring elastic around the neck, and use this to attach a piece of rickrack or ribbon to the chick. Then hang it onto two crossed sticks, tied together. Glue the rickrack in place to prevent the chicks from slipping off.

BIRDS ON THE WING

This mobile is made from cardboard (or construction paper) bird shapes with tissue paper fanned wings and tails. For each bird cut two bird shapes, using the template on page 90. Glue the two pieces together, placing thread between them, in line with the wings, to hang the bird from. Mark where the wings will fit, and cut a slit.

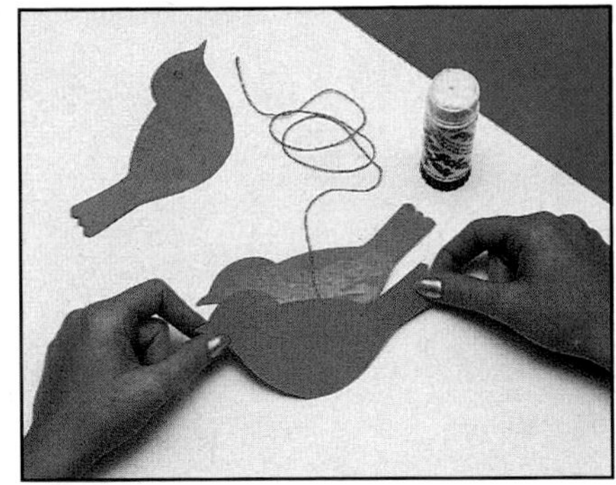

For the fanned wings take a piece of tissue paper 35 by 22cm (14 by 9in) and concertina-fold it lengthwise. Round off the edges and push the folded paper through the slit in the bird, so that there is an equal amount on each side. Glue the inside edges upward to the sides of the bird to make the wings fan out.

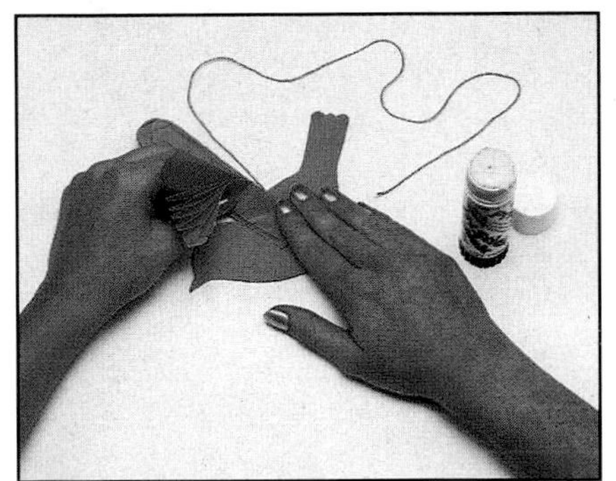

For the tail use a piece of tissue paper 35 by 12cm (14 by 5in), and concertina-fold it widthwise. Round off the edges, then slip one end over the tail of the cardboard bird; glue it in place as shown. Finish off with sequins for the eyes. Hang the birds from two crossed sticks, tied or glued together.

EIGHT-POINTED STAR

A large foil star to hang in the centre of the ceiling or over the fireplace. Try it out on a piece of ordinary paper first, as it is a little fiddly. Cut a piece of foil paper about 45cm (18in) square. Fold it in half from corner to corner, then in half twice again, making a small triangle.

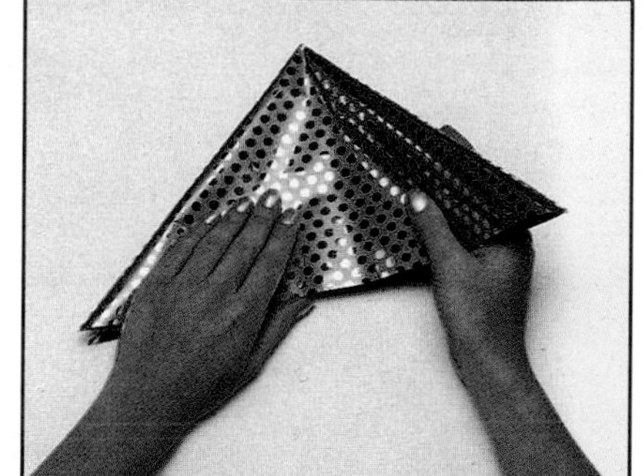

Bend the single-fold edge over to the edge with three folds. Open it out, and rule two lines from the corners at the base of the triangle to the centre crease. Cut along these two lines.

Refold the crease and rule two more lines, forming a small triangle as seen here. Cut this out. Now snip the point off and open the star out. Glue it to another piece of thicker foil paper for backing and cut the star out carefully when the glue has dried. Finish it off with a ribbon rosette in the centre.

TWINKLE TWINKLE

This simple star can be hung on the wall or from the ceiling. First make the pattern for the star. Using a ruler and protractor, draw an equilateral triangle (each angle is 60°). Cut out the triangle and use it as a pattern to make another one. Then glue one triangle over the other to form the star. Use this pattern to cut a star from foil paper.

Fold the star in half three times between opposite points. Next fold it in half three times between opposite angles as shown. Every angle and point should now have a fold in it.

The star will now easily bend into its sculptured shape. Make a small hole in its top point with a hole punch or a skewer, then put some thread through the hole to hang it up.

FANCY FOIL

Make these shiny decorations from foil wrapping paper. Cut out eight circles in each of the following diameters: 9cm (3½in), 7.5cm (3in) and 6cm (2¼in). Then from cardboard cut out four circles 2cm (¾in) in diameter and two of 1.5cm (½in) for the centres. Fold the largest foil circles into quarters and staple four of them onto a large cardboard circle.

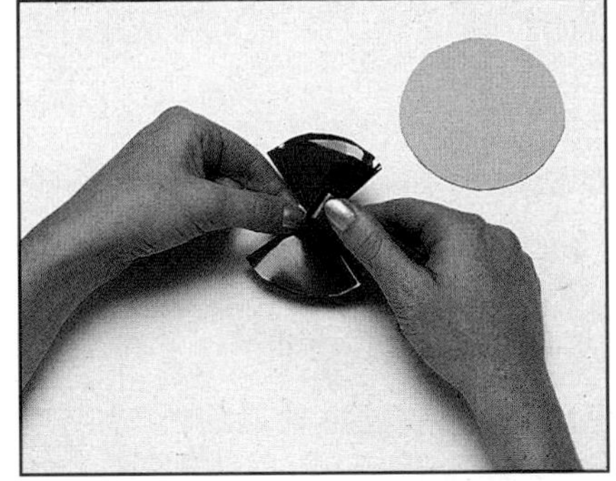

In the same way, staple the other four foil circles to another cardboard circle. Glue the two cardboard circles together with a string between them. Leave a long piece hanging below for the other two balls. Fluff out the edges of foil to make a good shape.

Now make the other two balls in the same way, using the smaller cardboard circles for the tiniest. Fix the balls to the string as you go.

GRACEFUL BELLS

This decoration can be made with tissue paper, coloured aluminium foil, thin cardboard or construction paper. Cut between six and twelve bell shapes (depending on the thickness of the paper you use). Fold each shape in half and then open it out again.

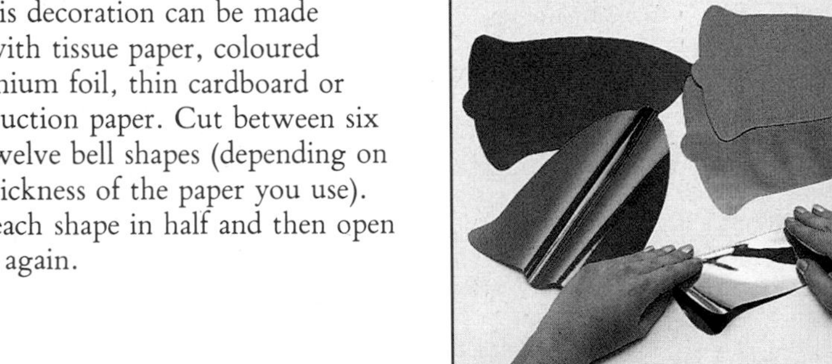

Lay the cut-outs carefully on top of each other with all the creases in the centre. Now take a needle and thread, and starting at the top, make three long stitches down the middle. Bring the needle up and over the bottom to secure the shapes in place. Next make a small stitch between each long stitch. At the top, knot the two ends together.

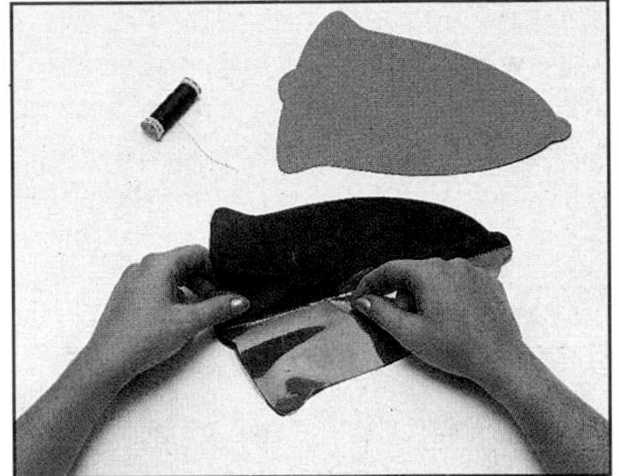

Ease the bell open, piece by piece, until it forms a rounded shape. You could easily do exactly the same thing with other shapes such as a heart, ball or tree.

This makes an ideal Christmas wall hanging, particularly if you haven't room for a real tree. First make a paper pattern of a tree, about 75cm (30in) high and 59cm (23½in) wide at the widest point across the bottom branches. Also cut a pattern for the pot, about 25cm (10in) high. Make it about as wide as the base of the tree, with a slightly wider, 8cm (3in) deep 'rim' at the top as shown.

Cut out two pieces of green felt from the tree pattern and two pieces of red for the pot. Also cut out a piece of wadding (batting) for each. The wadding for the pot should be about 4.5cm (1¾in) shorter, since the rim of the pot will be turned down. On the front of the tree mark diagonal lines for the branches as shown.

Place the tree pieces together, with wadding on top. Pin, tack (baste), then stitch 1cm (⅜in) from the edge, leaving the lower edge open. Clip the corners and turn tree right side out. Stitch along marked lines. Make up the pot, sewing up to 4cm (1½in) from the top. Turn it right side out and slip the tree inside; sew it in place. Sew the upper sides of the pot together and turn the rim down.

To decorate the tree cut out little pockets of red felt and sew them in place as shown. Insert little gifts — either real ones or gift-wrapped cardboard squares.

Finish off by adding plenty of ribbons and bells. Curtain rings also look good covered in ribbon and sewn on. Sew a loop to the top of the tree to hang it by.

 *EVERLASTING WREATH* 

This is a very effective fabric wreath, which can be brought out for Christmas year after year. All you need are three strips of fabric, in red, green and white, about 150cm (60in) long and 18cm (7in) wide. Sew them into tubes, right side facing, leaving one end open.

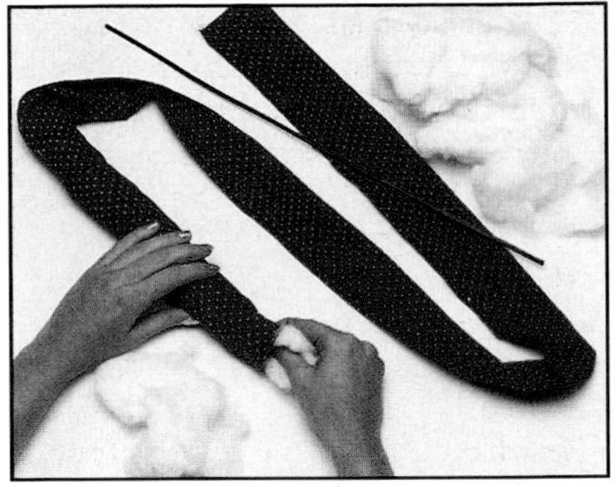

Turn each tube right side out and stuff it with polyester filling, polystyrene beads or old tights (pantyhose) cut into strips. Have a stick handy to help push the stuffing down the tube. Turn in the raw edges and sew them together.

Wind narrow red ribbon around the green tube, sewing it in place at each end to secure. When you have made all three tubes, plait them together loosely and join the ends together. Cover the point where they join with a large bow made from net, and add three small net bows around the ring.

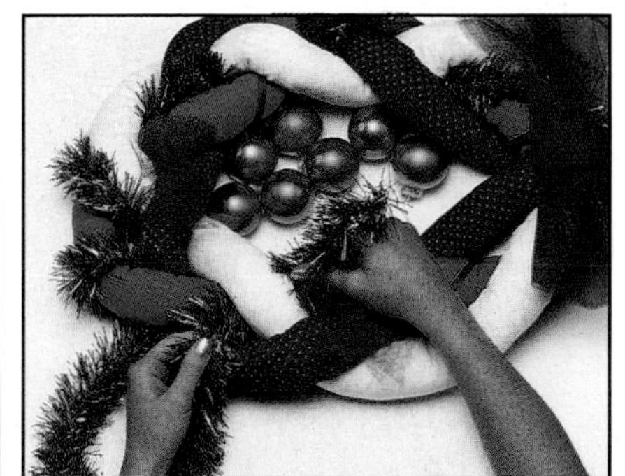

Thread tinsel through the wreath, and decorate with golden baubles, tied on with thread at the back. To finish, add some curly strands of gold gift wrap ribbon. Curl the ribbon by running the blunt edge of a pair of scissors along it.

HOOP-LA!

This Christmas wreath is based on a child's plastic hoop, and makes a delightful decoration for the wall or mantelpiece. First of all you need a plastic hoop; any size will do. Cut long strips of wadding (batting) and wind them around the hoop, holding the edges in place with sticky tape. We gave it two layers of medium-weight wadding.

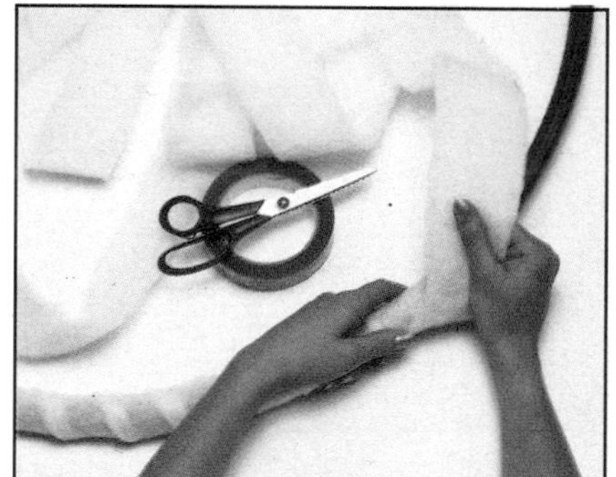

Next take some 8cm- (3in)-wide ribbon and wind it firmly around the hoop, in the opposite direction to the wadding. Make sure the wadding is entirely covered. Take a contrasting ribbon, about 6cm (2in) wide, and wrap it over the first ribbon, leaving equal spaces between the loops. Repeat with a third ribbon, 4cm (1½in) wide.

Make sure each ribbon starts and finishes in the same place so that all the joins are together. This will be the top of the hoop. Wind tinsel around the hoop, over the ribbons. Pin or staple a wide piece of ribbon over all the joins at the top. Tape a cluster of ribbon, tinsel, baubles and bells at the top and add a large bow to finish off.

WARM WELCOME

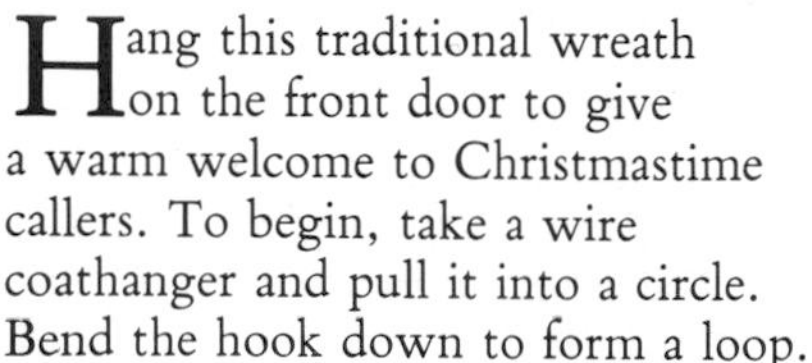

Hang this traditional wreath on the front door to give a warm welcome to Christmastime callers. To begin, take a wire coathanger and pull it into a circle. Bend the hook down to form a loop.

Now wire together small bunches of holly, spruce and other foliage. Then attach each bunch to the circle. Be careful when handling the holly; you can get a bit scratched, and some people can come out in a rash from it. Keep going in one direction until the whole circle is covered.

On top of this add some wired pine cones and, for extra colour, some curly red ribbon. (Use curling gift wrap ribbon for this, running the blunt edge of a pair of scissors along it to make it curl.) Red holly berries look great if you can get hold of them, but they tend to drop very quickly, so they would need replacing often. Finish off with a big red satin bow.

 # HANGING EVERGREEN WREATH 

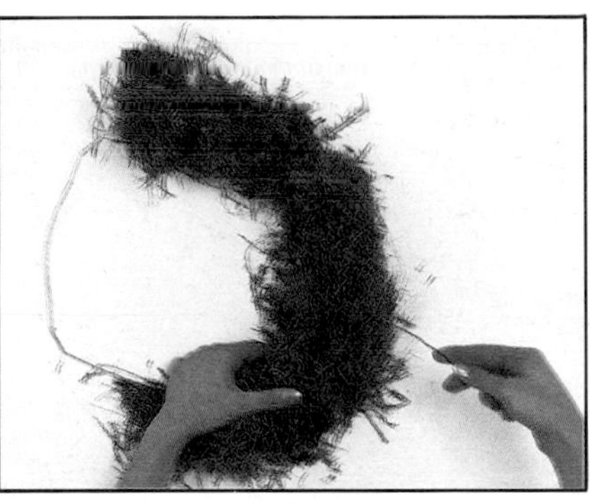

This festive wreath looks very effective suspended from a hook screwed into the ceiling. Use wire cutters to snip the hook off a coat hanger. Bend the hanger into a circular shape. Bunch damp sphagnum moss around the wire to a thickness of about 5cm (2in), using gardener's wire around it to hold it in place.

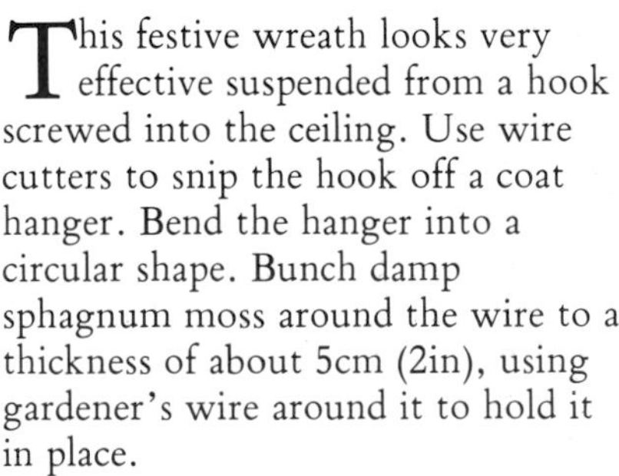

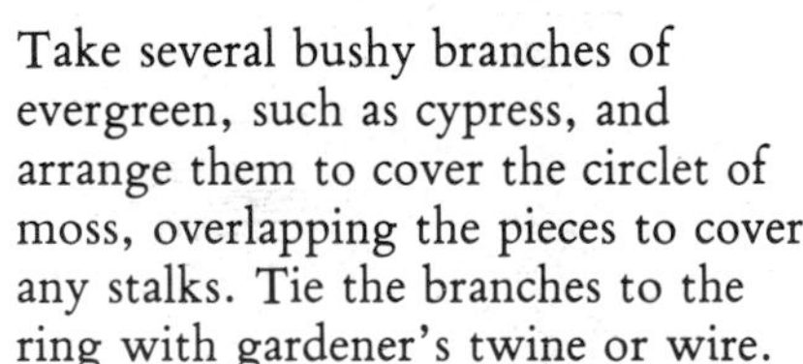

Take several bushy branches of evergreen, such as cypress, and arrange them to cover the circlet of moss, overlapping the pieces to cover any stalks. Tie the branches to the ring with gardener's twine or wire.

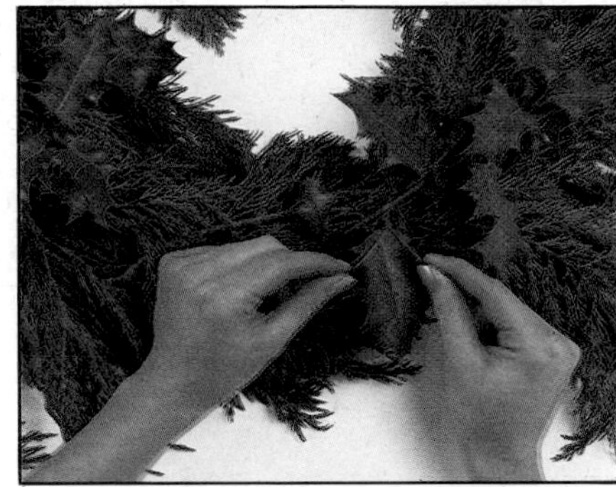

Add several sprigs of holly, again securing them with wire. If the holly is a bit short of berries, you can add some fake berries at this point.

To hang the wreath you will need two lengths of satin ribbon. Each piece should be twice the length of the drop from the ceiling to your hanging height, plus an extra 20cm (8in) for tying around the wreath. Tie each of the four ends opposite one another around the wreath so that the two lengths cross in the centre.

Make four bows from the same colour ribbon and pin them to the wreath over the four tying-on points.

Gently push a length of florist's wire through each of four red wax candles, approximately 1.5cm (½in) above the bases, as shown.

Position each candle halfway between two bows, and twist the wire around the wreath to hold it in place. To hang the wreath, tie another length of ribbon around the two main ribbons where they cross, make a loop to go over the hook, and tie the ends in a bow.

LITTLE CRACKERS

These miniature crackers can be hung on the Christmas tree or on the wall. First take a piece of cartridge (drawing) paper or light cardboard about 8cm (3in) wide and long enough to roll into a tube. Hold it together with a little sticky tape.

Cut a piece of crepe paper or foil twice as long as the tube, and roll the tube in it. Stick the edges together with double-sided tape. Squeeze the paper together at both ends, and tie some thread around them. Fluff out the ends and make small cuts in them to make a fringe.

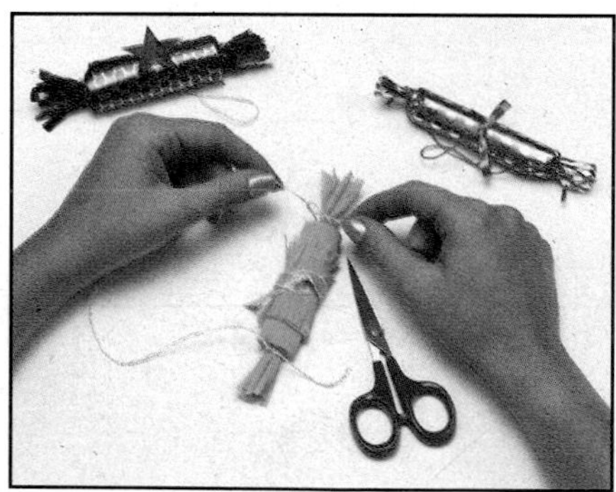

To decorate the cracker, cut some extra, narrow pieces of crepe paper or foil, fringe them at the edges and wrap them around the tube as before. Alternatively, tie a bow round the cracker or stick a silver star in the middle. Tie a length of ribbon or sparkly twine to the ends by which to hang the cracker.

LITTLE BOXES

These little boxes make charming tree decorations. If you haven't got any suitable ones that you can wrap for the tree, you can easily make your own from cardboard. For a cube, you need to mark out a Latin cross shape. The lower arm of the cross should be twice as long as the top and side arms. Also add a 1.5cm (½ in) border to all arms except the top one for gluing the cube together.

Fold along all the lines as shown, then bring the cube together, gluing all the sides in place.

Now simply wrap the box in attractive paper, and tie it with ribbons and bows to look like a parcel. Pop it on or under the tree.

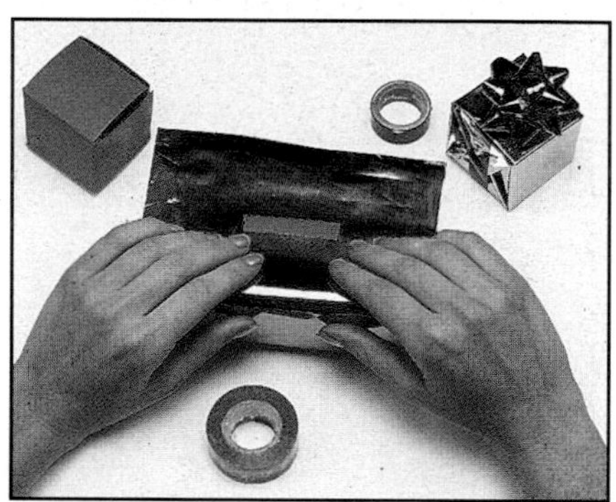

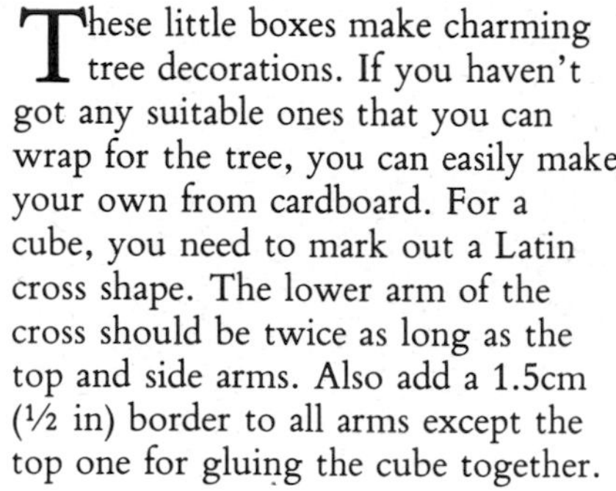

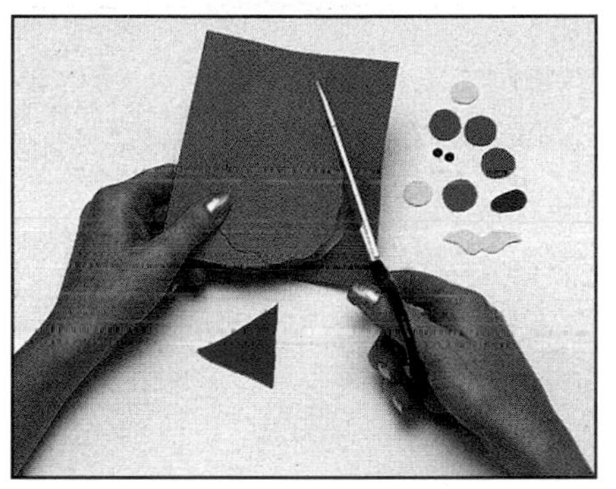

These jolly Santa faces will add Christmas cheer to the tree. Cut out all the pieces in felt, using the template on page 91. Glue the main face piece to a piece of cardboard. When it is dry, cut around it.

All you have to do now is glue on all the other pieces. The nose and cheeks are affixed before the moustache, which goes on top.

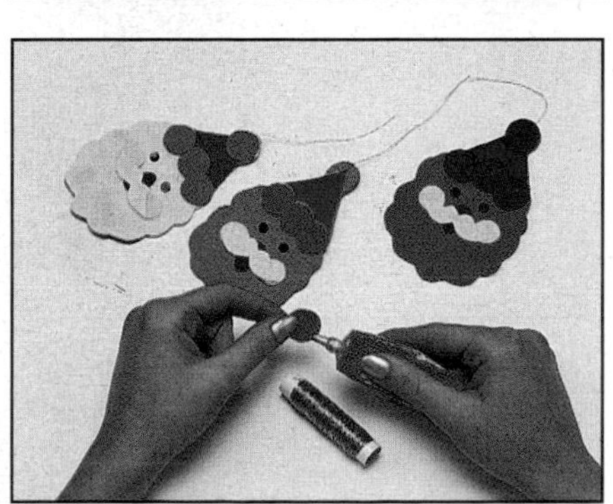

Place a loop of thread under the circle on the top of the hat, to hang up the face. Glue on two dark sequins to represent the eyes.

Make a pattern for a Christmas stocking using the template on page 91, and cut it out double in one piece by placing the pattern on the fold of the felt. Cut a strip of fake fur to fit the stocking, about 5cm (2in) deep. Catch the fur to the felt, top and bottom, by hand, with small stitches.

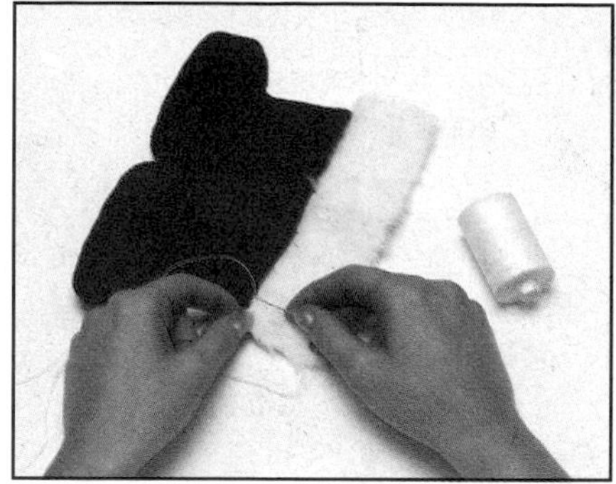

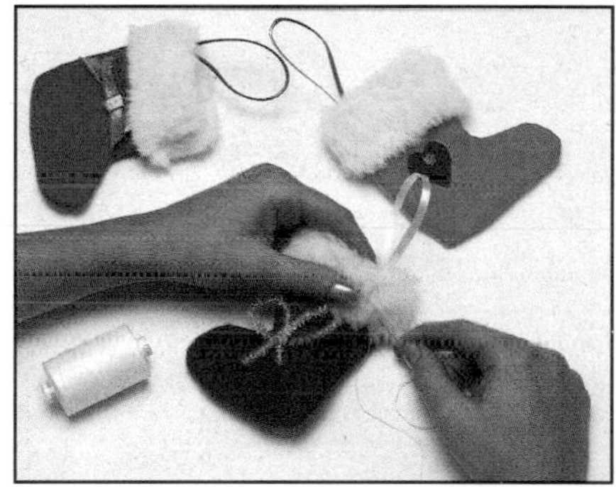

Now overcast the two sides of the stocking together, starting at the ankle and working around the foot and up the front. Turn the stocking right side out.

Turn the fur down about 2.5cm (1in) to the right side, catching it down around the edge. Decorate the stocking with sequins, bows, etc., and sew a loop of ribbon just inside the edge to hang it from the tree.

TABLE CENTREPIECES 

Every table needs a focal point, and this is, more often than not, in the centre. The usual choice for a centrepiece is a flower arrangement or a bowl of fruit, but occasionally it is fun to dream up something a little more unusual or exotic. The important thing to remember is that although a centrepiece should be large enough to make a statement, it should never take over the table, leaving little room for anything else and forcing your guests to peer around it to talk to one another! In this section you will discover how to make a wide range of centrepieces, some purely decorative and some edible.

Although designed for a wedding reception, this table setting would also be suitable for a special dinner party. The look is pretty and lacy, and the centrepiece picks up the apricot and white colour scheme. The apricots can be eaten at the end of the meal, provided they are kept separate from the poisonous ivy leaves by a paper doily.

APRICOTS AND CREAM

A mound of luscious apricots, flowers and leaves makes a pretty centrepiece for a summer buffet or dinner party. Place a white doily on a glass or china cake stand. Carefully push ivy leaves underneath the edge of the doily. The leaves should be washed and can be wiped with cooking oil for extra shine.

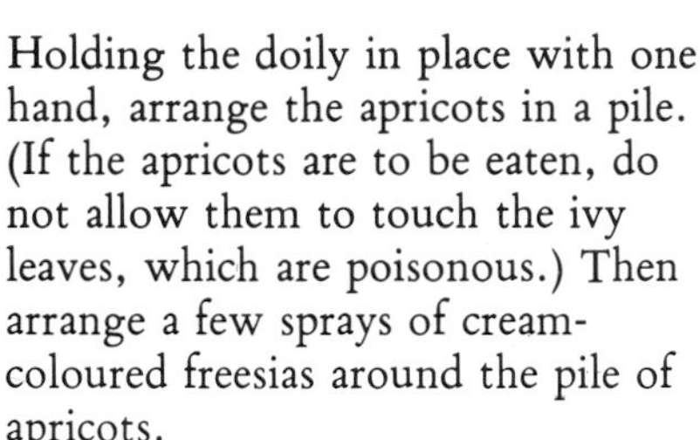

Holding the doily in place with one hand, arrange the apricots in a pile. (If the apricots are to be eaten, do not allow them to touch the ivy leaves, which are poisonous.) Then arrange a few sprays of cream-coloured freesias around the pile of apricots.

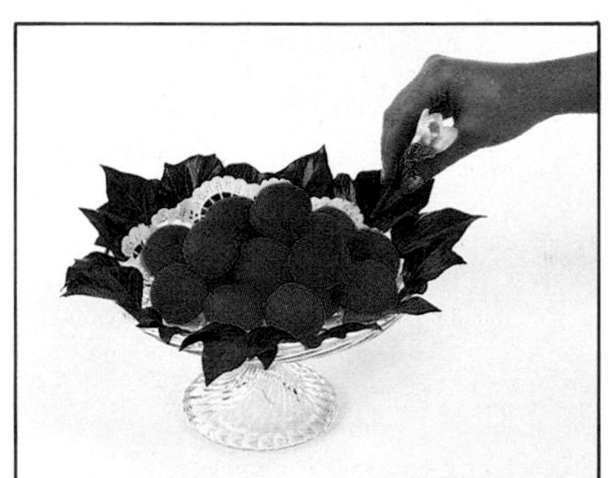

Finally, slot flowers into the gaps between the apricots — any small cream or white flowers will do; those used here are narcissi. Check with your florist that the flowers you choose are not poisonous.

NEST OF EGGS

For an unusual Easter centre-piece fill a rustic basket with a selection of different eggs. The basket shown contains a mixture of hen's eggs, tiny speckled quail's eggs (which can be eaten as an hors d'oeuvre), and carved wooden eggs. Half fill the basket with paper to form a base for the eggs, then add a layer of packing straw.

Arrange your selection of eggs in the packing straw to show off their different colours and patterns. Tie a ribbon around the handle of the basket to provide a finishing touch.

LAYERED FRUIT SALAD

This colourful fruit salad not only makes an eyecatching centrepiece but also can be served for a refreshing dessert. Set aside the best-looking fruit to decorate the edges of the container — in this case, kiwi fruit and several large strawberries. Cut up the remaining strawberries, and peel and section the tangerines.

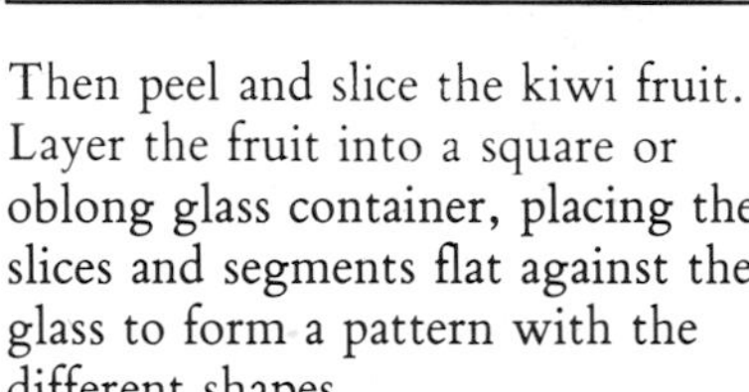

Then peel and slice the kiwi fruit. Layer the fruit into a square or oblong glass container, placing the slices and segments flat against the glass to form a pattern with the different shapes.

Peel and thickly slice the remaining kiwi fruit into three pieces, and then slice again down the centre, stopping halfway. Slice the strawberries down the middle, stopping 1 cm ($^{3}/_{8}$in) short of the stalk. Slide the fruit onto the edge of the glass, either in two rows as shown or alternating all the way around.

ETCHED MELON FRUIT BOWL

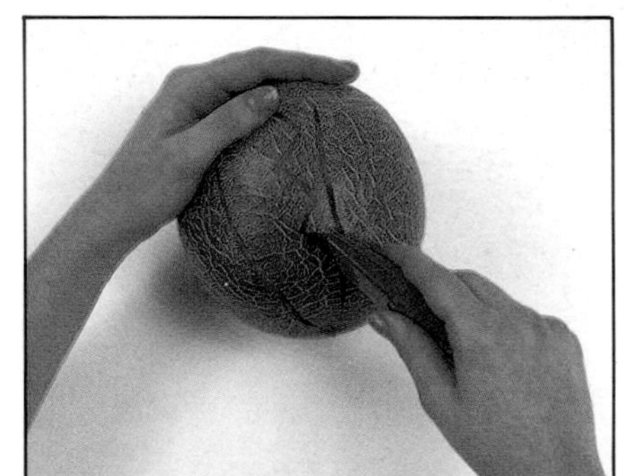

This clever centrepiece not only looks scrumptious but can be served for dessert at the end of the meal. Using a sharp knife, cut strips out of the melon skin to create a pattern all over it. Take care not to cut too deeply into the skin. Discard the cut-out pieces.

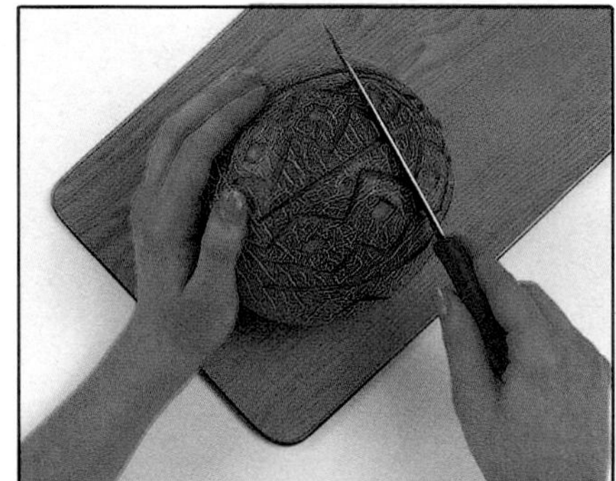

Having completed the design, place the melon on a chopping board. With a sharp kitchen knife slice the top off the melon; set it aside.

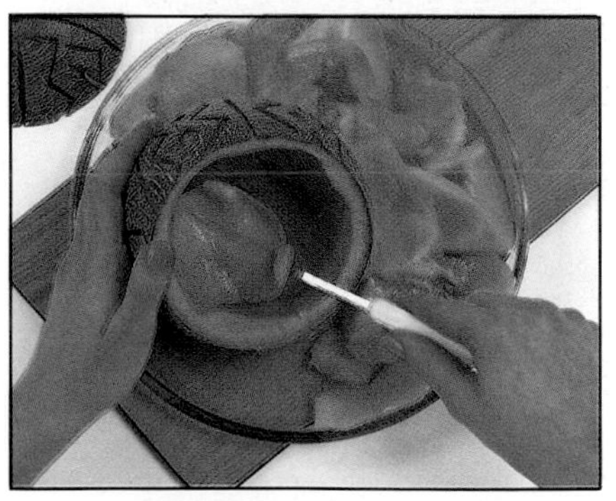

Scoop out the flesh of the melon onto a plate. Discard the seeds and slice or cube the melon flesh. Mix this with other fruits to create a salad, and return it to the melon bowl. Garnish it with mint leaves. Place the melon on a plate, and surround it with a selection of other fruits.

For a summer table centrepiece nothing can surpass the beauty of flowers. The tall jug contains a mixture of anemones, ranunculus, kaffir lily *(Schizostylis)* and white September flowers, the mixture of shapes providing variety. The smallest vase contains a tiny narcissus, ranunculus and anemones with a few sprigs of love-in-a-mist *(Nigella).*

This fat, rounded jug has a fairly wide neck and is therefore ideal for full-blown roses, which look good clustered together to form a close, rounded shape. Delicate stalks of white September flowers (aster) and a few heads of love-in-a-mist show up well against the pale pink roses and give more definition to the arrangement.

FROSTED FRUIT

This stunning centrepiece looks grand enough to grace the most formal dinner party, and yet is very simple to make. Using a pastry brush, coat each piece of fruit with egg white.

Working over a large plate, sprinkle granulated sugar over the fruit so that it adheres to the coating of egg. Alternatively, the fruit can be dipped into a bowl of sugar, although this tends to make the sugar lumpy.

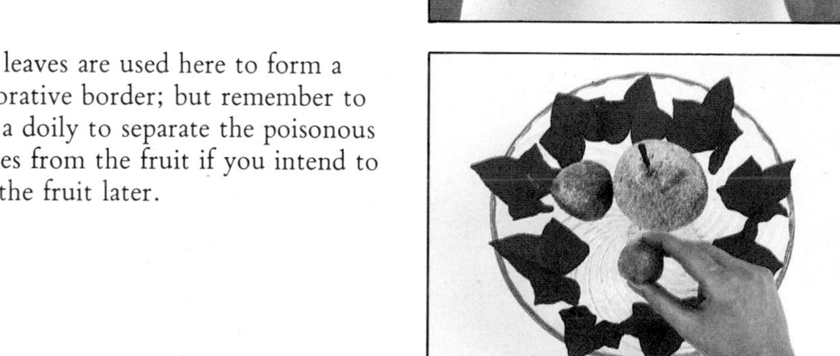

Ivy leaves are used here to form a decorative border; but remember to use a doily to separate the poisonous leaves from the fruit if you intend to eat the fruit later.

HAND-PAINTED FRUIT BASKET

Fruit is often used as a centrepiece, and here an attractive effect has been created by hand-painting a plain wicker basket to match the colour of the fruit. Paint the basket inside and out with a water-based paint in the background colour, using a small decorating brush. Leave the basket to dry.

Dip a sponge into a saucer containing the contrasting colour of paint. Dab the sponge a few times on a piece of scrap paper to remove any excess. Then sponge all over the outside of the basket, replenishing your paint supply when necessary.

Arrange the fruit in the basket as shown, adding a few leaves for contrast. Clementines are shown here, but apples, bananas and other fruit could be added for variety.

CONE CANDLE STAND

IVY CANDLE-RING

Believe it or not, this arrangement is quite simple once you get the hang of folding the cones. You need two colours of foil paper. Cut out lots of boat shapes 16.5cm (6½in) along the top and 12.5 (5in) along the bottom and about 6cm (2½in) deep. Glue one colour to another, back-to-back.

Form each boat into a cone and glue it in place. The first few you make may not look too professional, but it doesn't matter; these can go on the outside of the stand and will be partially covered. You will soon get the hang of folding the cones. Bend the bottoms under; it helps to hold the shape and looks tidier.

When you have several cones made, start gluing them around the edge of a 20cm- (8in-) diameter silver cake board. Place another two layers inside the first, leaving room for a chunky candle in the middle.

This elegant candle-ring is the ideal centrepiece for a special dinner party at any time of the year. A circular cake base serves as the foundation for the arrangement. Begin by attaching strands of ivy to the edge of the base, securing them with drawing pins.

Build up the ring by adding more strands and bunches of leaves until only a small space remains in the centre. Push stems of freesia among the ivy leaves to provide colour contrast.

Use a mixture of white and green candles of varying heights to form the centre of the arrangement. Secure each candle to the base with a blob of glue or Plasticine (modelling clay).

CANDLE CLUSTER

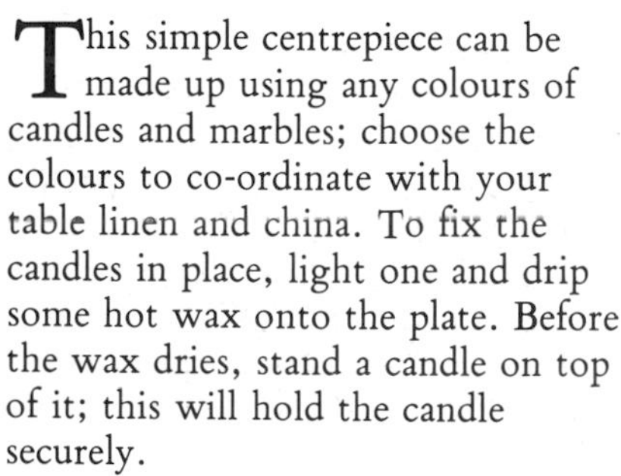

This simple centrepiece can be made up using any colours of candles and marbles; choose the colours to co-ordinate with your table linen and china. To fix the candles in place, light one and drip some hot wax onto the plate. Before the wax dries, stand a candle on top of it; this will hold the candle securely.

When all the candles have been arranged in a group, surround them with a 'sea' of marbles. Take care to put the marbles in place gently, for they may crack the plate if dropped onto it.

CO-ORDINATED CANDLESTICKS

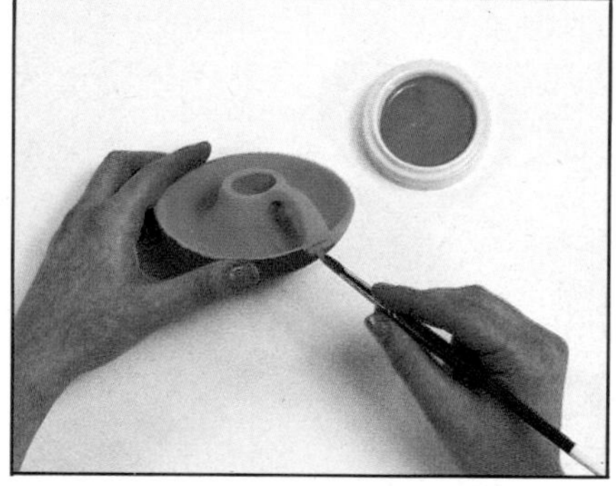

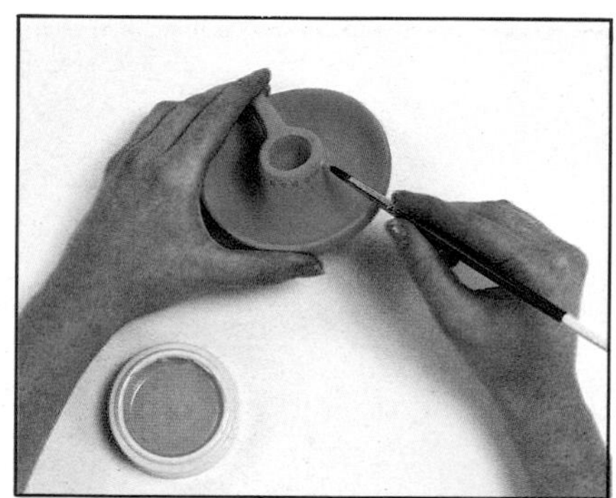

Candles can always be relied on to lend atmosphere to any occasion. For a co-ordinated effect, paint plain terracotta or glazed candlesticks to match your colour scheme. You will need water-based paint for terracotta candlesticks and ceramic paint for glazed ones. Give the candlestick two coats of base colour, using a soft, narrow artist's paintbrush.

Use one or more contrasting colours to decorate the holder. If using a lighter colour on a dark base, paint the design in white first and colour in afterwards. Sponging or spattering the base coat with a contrasting colour would look equally attractive.

HARLEQUIN PARTY MASK

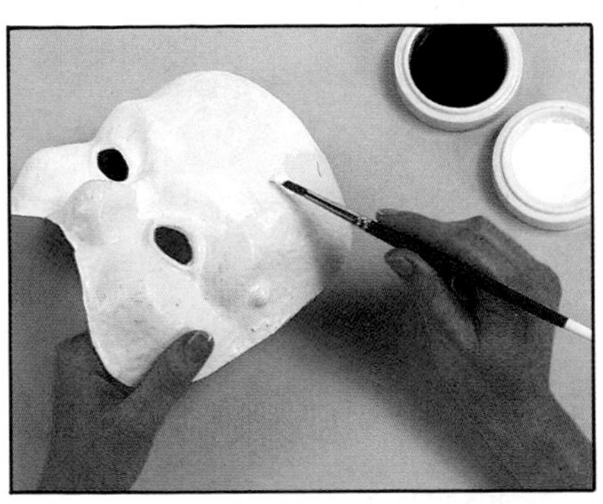

These unusual harlequin masks form the perfect party centrepiece, especially when co-ordinated with a black and white table setting, as shown on page 60. The masks can be bought or home-made from papier mâché. Paint each mask white.

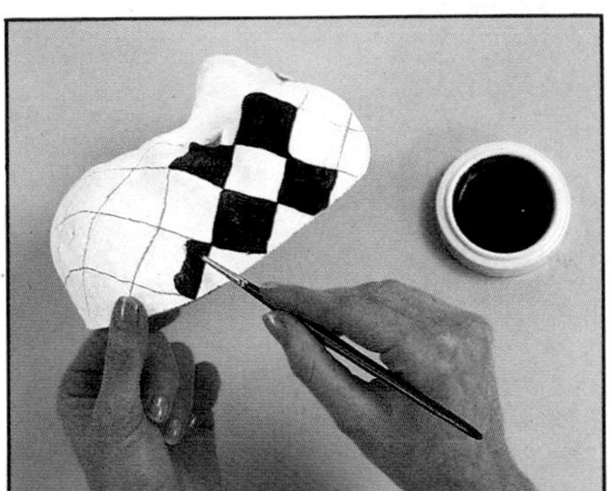

With a pencil draw diagonal lines across the mask to create a grid. Don't worry if the squares are not exactly symmetrical. Paint alternate squares black.

Glue a length of black lace or net around the edge of the mask. Add coloured feathers and ribbons for the finishing touches. Stand the masks back to back so that one is facing each side of the table.

RIBBONS AND CURLS

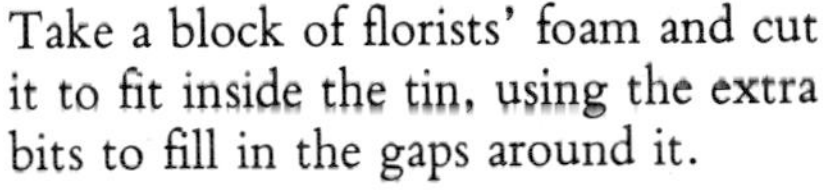

What could be prettier than this profusion of ribbons and flowers? The one shown is pink and white, but you should choose whatever matches your décor. First of all you will need a biscuit or cake tin. Cover the outside with silver foil paper, allowing a little extra at the top to turn over and glue. (This will be easier if you snip down to the tin.) Decorate it with strips of ribbon.

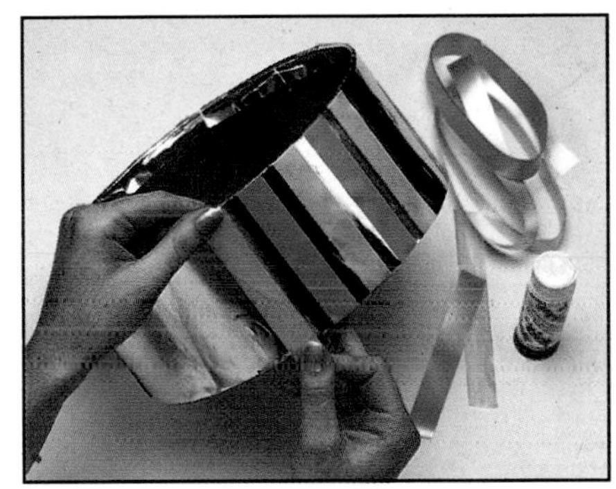

Take a block of florists' foam and cut it to fit inside the tin, using the extra bits to fill in the gaps around it.

Now wire up pieces of gift wrap ribbon, little baubles, strips of crepe paper and silk flowers. Curl the ribbon by running the blunt edge of a pair of scissors along it. Push the wires into the foam, arranging them until the tin is totally full. Use strips of ribbon around the outside, and let them fall over the side of the tin.

JACK-O'-LANTERN

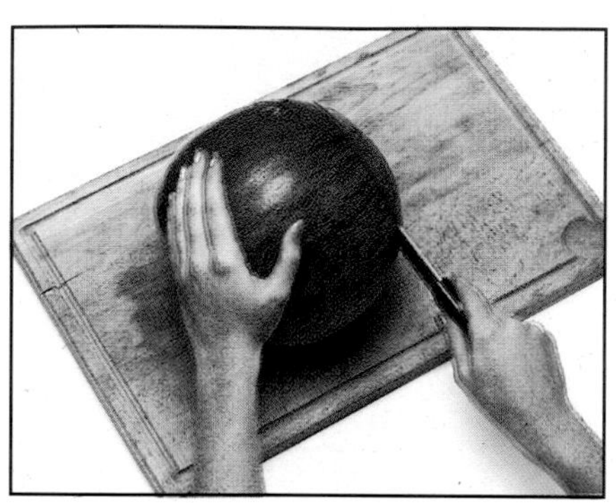

A pumpkin is a versatile vegetable; use one to make this jolly Halloween lantern and some good things to eat also. First take a ripe pumpkin and cut a slice off the top. You will need a very sharp knife, as pumpkins can be very tough — so be careful of your fingers.

Scoop out the insides, leaving a good 1 to 2.5cm (½ to 1in) rind. Use the flesh to make a pumpkin pie. The seeds also can be eaten. Wash and dry them, then place them on a baking tray and sprinkle them with salt. Bake them in the oven until they are dry and crunchy.

Now mark the eyes, nose and mouth on the front of the pumpkin with a black felt pen.

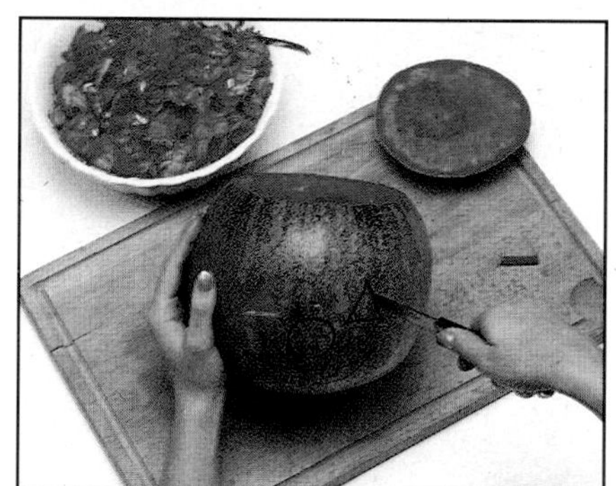

Cut carefully around the lines, and then push the features out from the inside. Rinse out the inside of the pumpkin, and dry it thoroughly with paper towels.

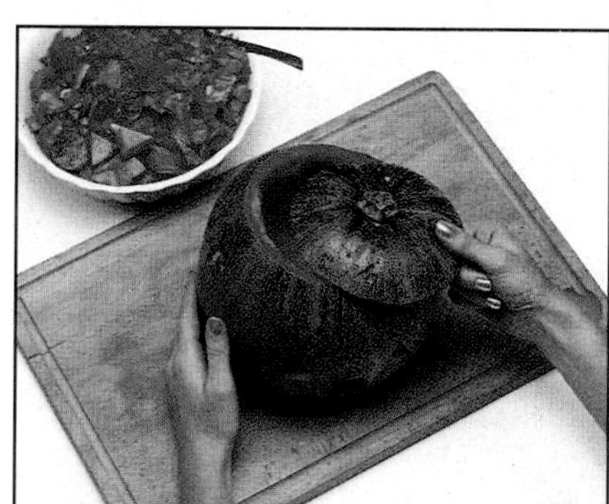

Finally, pop a couple of night lights or small candles inside, light them, and put the top on the pumpkin. Place the jack-o'-lantern on a table or window sill to frighten away any spooks.

HARVEST-TIME BASKET

This autumnal arrangement of dried flowers makes an appropriate centrepiece for a Thanksgiving or Harvest Festival dinner. Begin by placing a square of florists' foam in the basket. Create a skirt-shaped outline around the basket using dried wheat ears and oats. Begin to build up the arrangement by adding some safflowers.

Fill in the shape with larger dried flowers, such as this gold-coloured yarrow. Place the yarrow deep down among the other plants to add depth to the arrangement.

Now twist lengths of florists' wire around the base of several fir cones, leaving long 'stems' of wire. Intersperse the cones throughout the arrangement, inserting the wire stalks into the florists' foam.

Using a selection of different-shaped dried flowers, such as this statice, fill in the remaining gaps to balance the arrangement.

Finish off with a few white daisies, scattering them throughout the display to provide highlights. (White flowers can often be used to lighten the effect of a flower arrangement — dried or fresh.)

FOREST FOLIAGE

The sideboard, as well as the table, needs a little dressing up at Christmas. This is bright and cheery, and the materials are quite easy to get hold of. If you don't have woodland nearby your florist should have small sections of bark for sale. Also buy a plastic candle holder. Onto the bark first put a large lump of green Plasticine (modelling clay), and on the top stick your candle holder.

Now take some plastic or silk fern and spray it gold. Break off pieces when it is dry, and stick them into the Plasticine. Also wire up strands of red paper ribbon, pine cones and red baubles and stick these in.

When the Plasticine is artistically concealed, pop a red candle in the holder, and set the arrangement on the sideboard. Put a mat under it, though, or it will scratch the surface.

CANDLE CENTREPIECE

This sort of arrangement always looks very hard to achieve, but in fact it is very simple, provided you assemble everything you need before starting. What you need is a ring of florists' foam with a plastic base, which you can get from a florist. Also buy three plastic candle holders; stick these into the foam.

You will need holly, ivy and fern, all of them either real or fake, plus a selection of dried flowers. Used here are daisy-like sunrays, yellow strawflowers or everlasting, yarrow, safflowers and sea lavender. Simply break pieces off these and stick them into the foam. Try to space the flowers evenly in between the foliage.

When you have finished, stick three candles into the holders already placed. If any of the foliage is real, make sure to keep the foam damp.

BRANCHING OUT

Spring is in the air, with a shiny silver pot plant, blossoming with pink silk flowers. You need a small plastic pot and a small, graceful tree branch. Spray them both with silver paint.

Now take a block of Plasticine (modelling clay), weighting the base with a stone if necessary. Push the silver branch into the middle and fix the Pasticine into the pot. For the 'earth' scrunch up a piece of silver foil and arrange it around the branch.

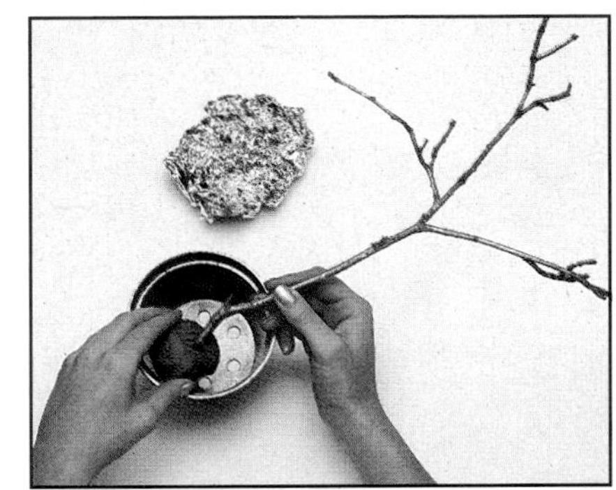

For the blossoms you need little pink silk flowers, scrunched up pink tissue, green tissue leaves and pink and green gift wrap ribbon. Glue these along the branch as shown, spacing them so as to look reasonably realistic.

A HOST OF DAFFODILS

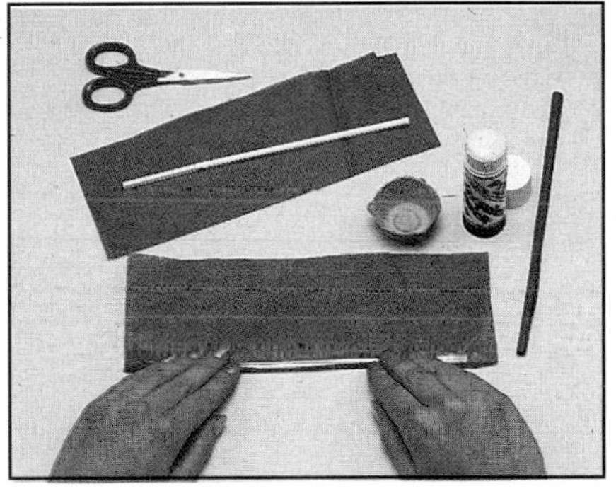

Make some spring flowers that will bloom throughout the year. For the base of each daffodil head, cut a section from an egg box and trim it down to an even edge. Use a yellow one if you can, or else paint it yellow. Next take a flexible paper or plastic straw and roll it in a strip of green tissue, gluing both long edges. Trim the ends and bend the straw without tearing the paper.

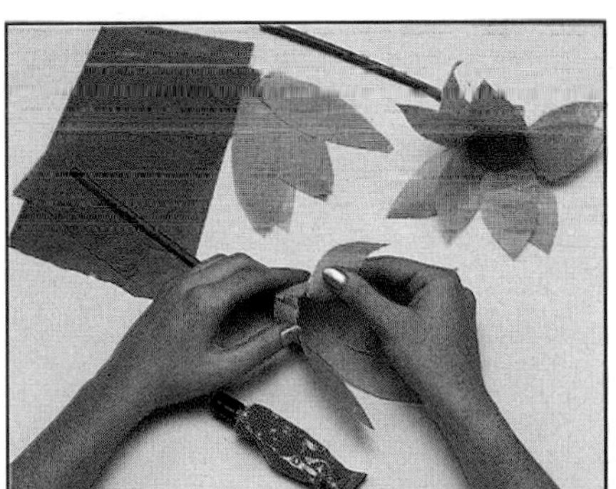

Cut out some yellow tissue petals and glue first one row, then a second, around the inside of the egg box base.

Finally, scrunch up a small piece of orange tissue paper and glue it to the centre of the flower.

MARZIPAN FRUIT PARCELS

Exquisite marzipan fruits deserve special presentation. Nestling in little tissue 'parcels' and piled into a cake stand, they make a colourful centrepiece. All you need is several different colours of tissue paper and some pinking shears. Instead of marzipan fruits, you could use chocolates or marrons glacés.

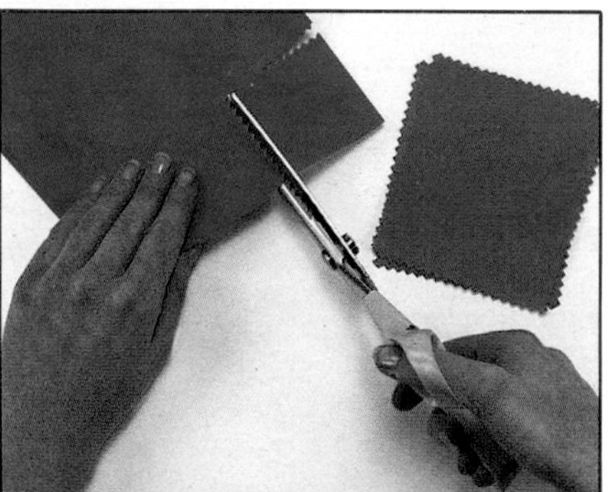

From a double layer of one colour of tissue, cut a 10cm (4in) square. Pinking shears give an attractive serrated edge. From another colour of tissue, also double, cut a smaller square, measuring about 6cm (2½in).

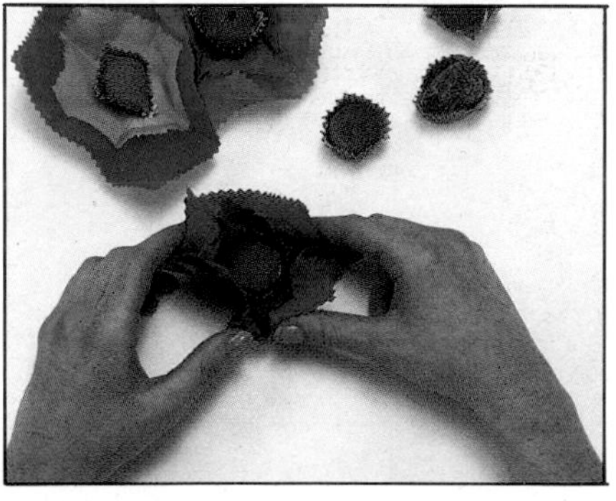

Lay the smaller square on top of the larger one. Place the marzipan fruit in the centre and gather the tissue around it. Hold it in place for a few seconds and then let go; the crumpled tissue will retain its rosette shape. Place several of the parcels on a doily-lined glass or china cake stand.

HOLIDAY CENTREPIECE

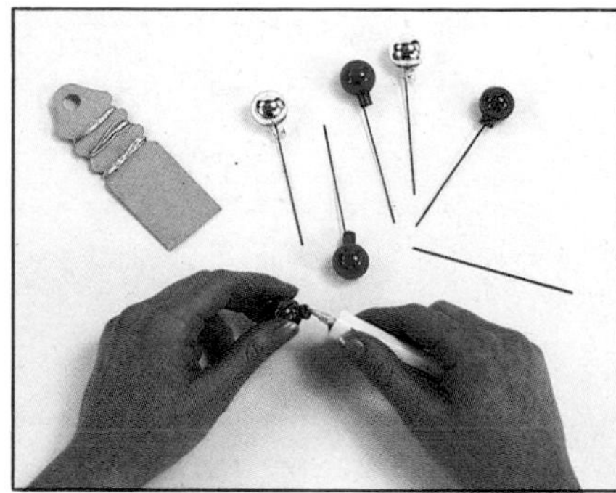

For a bright party centrepiece — ideal for Christmas or New Year's Eve — fill a glass bowl with a mixture of shiny glass baubles, foil crackers, feathers and streamers. To make clusters of small baubles, first remove the hanging string. Put a dab of glue inside the neck of each bauble and push in a short length of florist's wire. Leave them to dry.

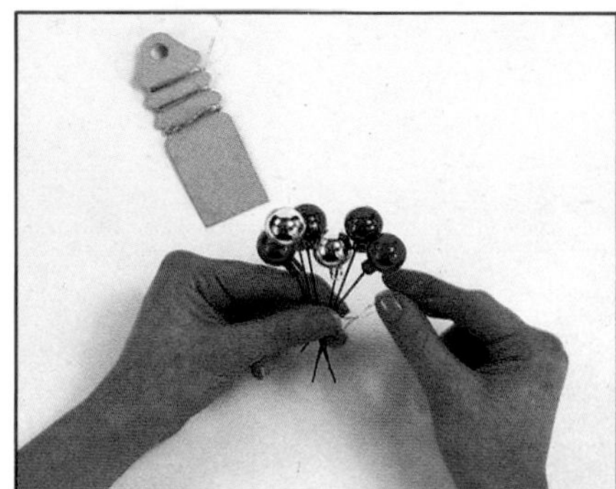

Hold the wired baubles in a cluster and wind fine fuse wire around the stems to hold them together.

Wrap a piece of shiny giftwrap ribbon around the stems and tie it into a bow. Arrange the baubles and other ornaments in the bowl as shown.

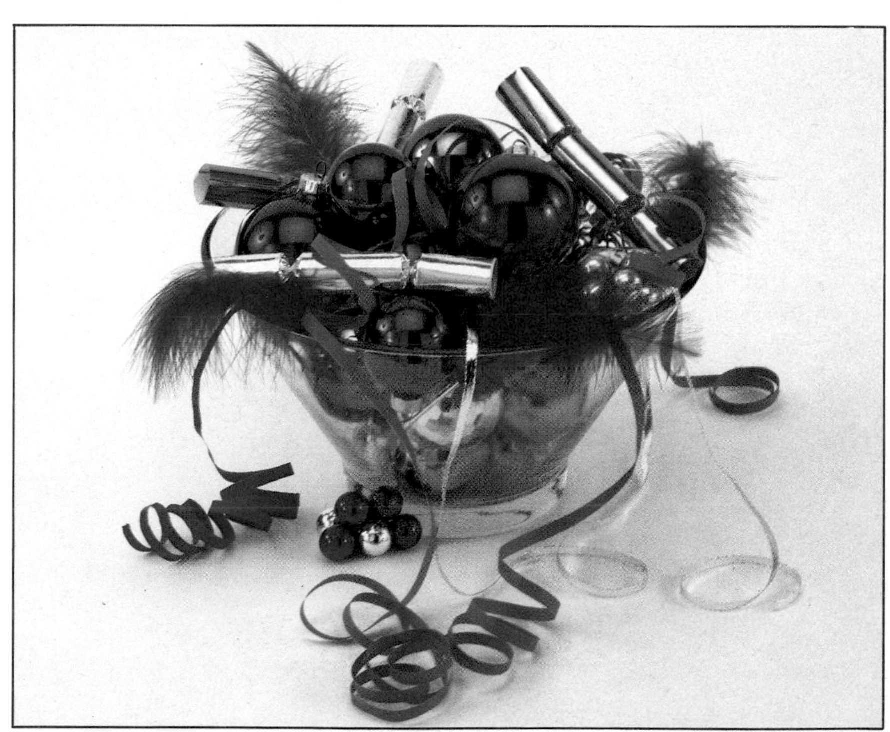

FUN FAIRY CAKES

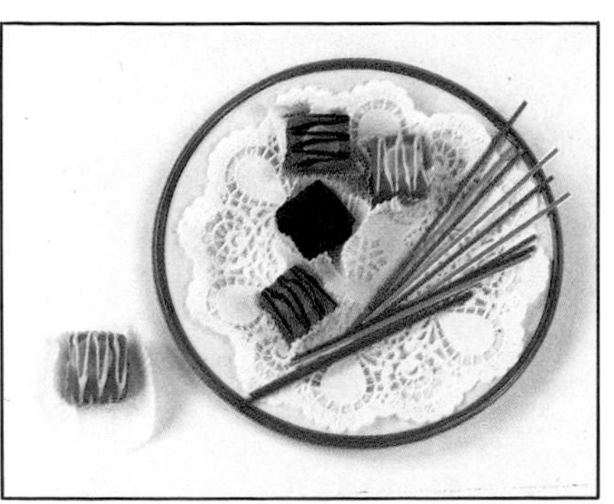

These individual cakes, each with its own candle, make an unusual alternative to a large birthday cake for a children's party and form an attractive centrepiece. Decorate each cake with a pattern, or pipe a child's name onto it.

Stick a long taper candle into each cake and arrange the cakes on a large plate. Once lit, the candles should not be allowed to burn for too long, as the hot wax will begin to drop onto the cakes.

FLOWERS AND FRILLS

This pretty centrepiece is a good wintertime alternative to a vase of real flowers. Lay a sheet of coloured tissue between two different-coloured layers of net. Place a vase in the centre of the net and tissue, and gather the three layers up around the neck of the vase.

Secure the net and tissue in place with a piece of twine or an elastic band. Tie a length of contrasting wide satin ribbon in a bow around the neck of the vase.

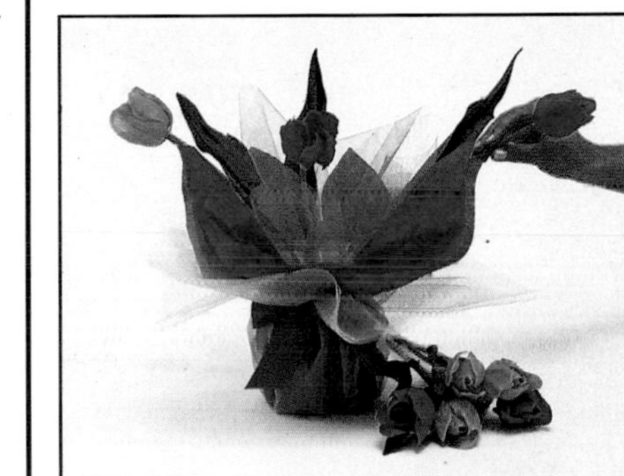

Fluff out the layers of net and tissue to create a frilled effect. Fill the vase with artificial flowers — such as the tulips shown here — or with real flowers, if you prefer.

RIBBON TREE

This small but spectacular design, placed on a table or sideboard, makes a good alternative to a proper Christmas tree. First take a medium-sized plastic flower pot, about 15cm (6in) in diameter, and fill it, up to about 2.5cm (1in) from the rim, with fast-drying cement or wood filler. When this is just setting, insert a piece of 1.5cm (½in) dowelling about 40cm (16in) long.

When the filler is dry, spray paint the pot, the dowelling and the 'earth' surface gold. Lay it down to spray it, and when one side is dry, roll it over and spray the other side. The whole thing — especially the pot — will need a couple of coats.

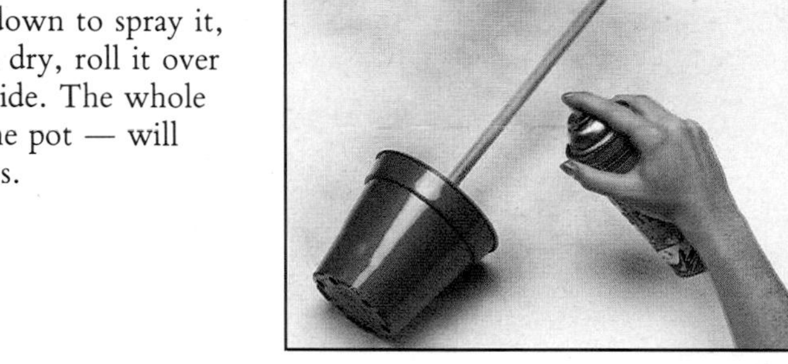

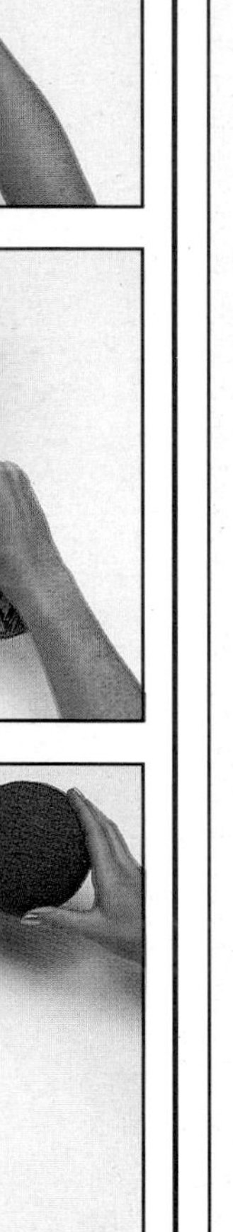

When the paint is dry, take a ball of florists' foam at least 12cm (5in) in diameter and push it on top of the dowelling.

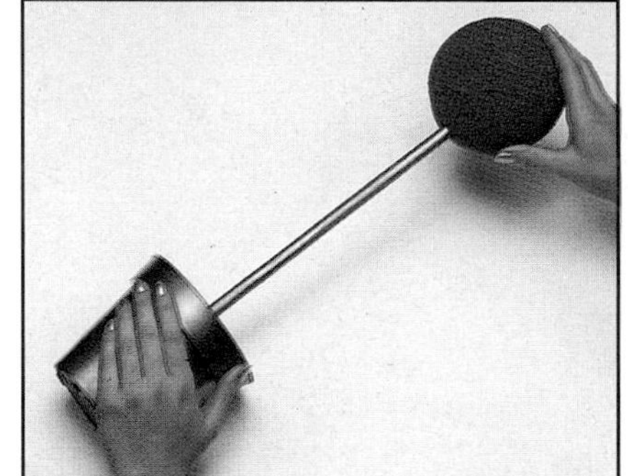

Now take short lengths of deep red and green satin ribbon, gold ribbon, shiny baubles and gold tinsel, and wire them all up, ready to push into the foam. Start with about a dozen of each; you can add to them as you go along, if necessary.

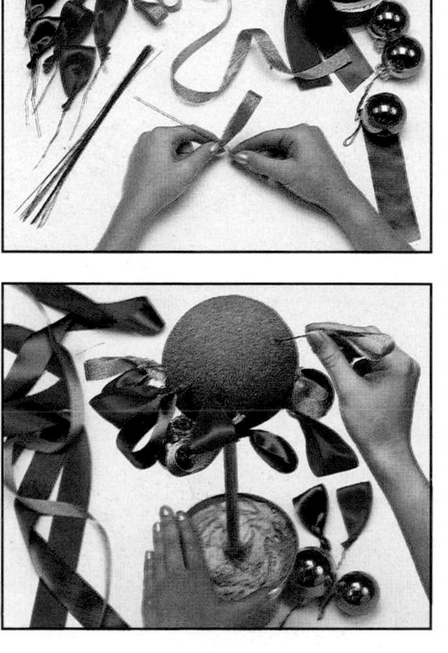

Start inserting the wires into the sphere, arranging the ribbons and baubles until it is covered, with no foam showing through. Finally wire up some curling gift wrap ribbon and insert it into the bottom of the ball. (Curl the ribbon by running the blunt edge of a pair of scissors along it.) Wind gold tinsel around the 'trunk' of the tree, and tie a large bow around the pot as a finishing touch.

GOLD AND SILVER CRACKERS

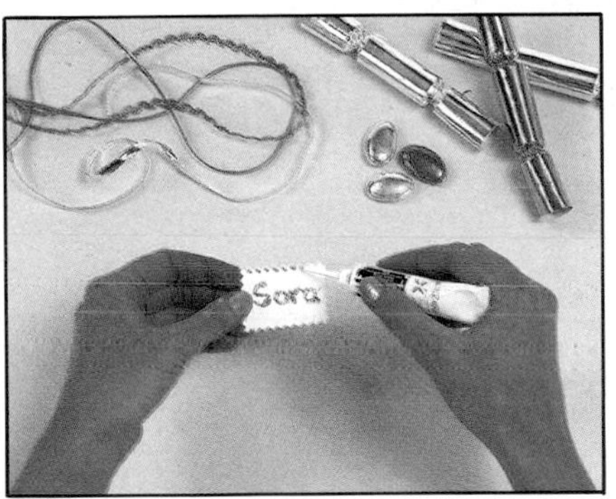

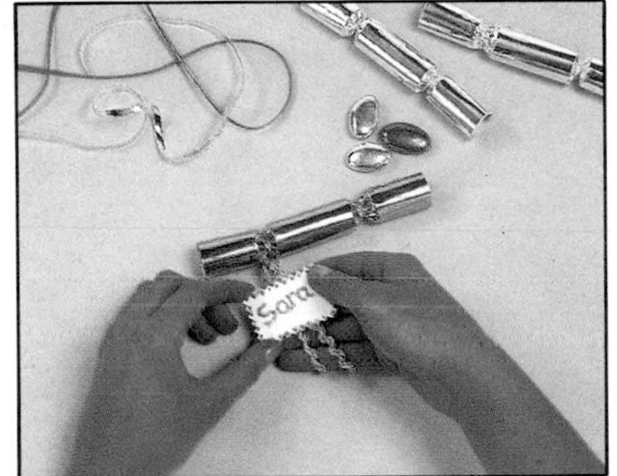

These attractive miniature crackers form an eye catching centrepiece, and the surrounding sweets make a delicious accompaniment to coffee at the end of the meal. For the name tags, cut small squares and rectangles from white cardboard. Trim the edges decoratively, then write the names and embellish the edges of the card with silver or gold paint.

Cut lengths of gold and silver ribbon or braid about 15cm (6in) long. Tie a ribbon around one end of each cracker. Dab a spot of glue on the back of each name tag and press it onto the ribbon.

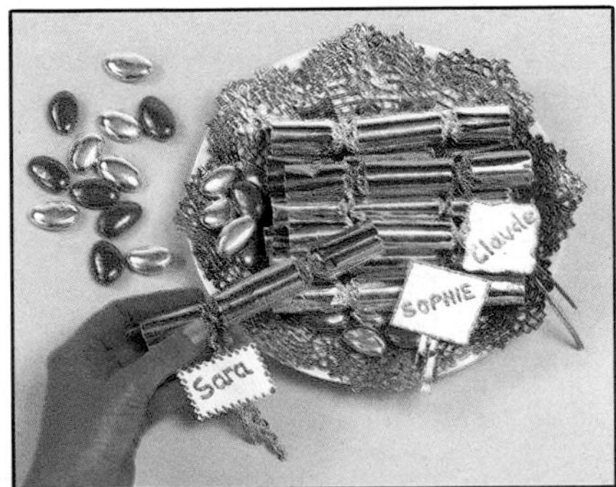

Pile the crackers onto a large plate covered with a gold doily. Place those with name cards near the top of the pile. For a finishing touch, surround the pile of crackers with gold and silver dragées.

AUTUMN GOLD

A touch of gold gives this platter of fruit and nuts extra richness. Begin by spraying ivy, clementines, bay leaves and fir cones with gold paint. (If the fruit will be eaten, make sure that the paint you are using is non-toxic.)

Place the ivy leaves around the edge of a plain oval platter. The flatter the plate, the better, for this will allow the ivy leaves to hang over the edge.

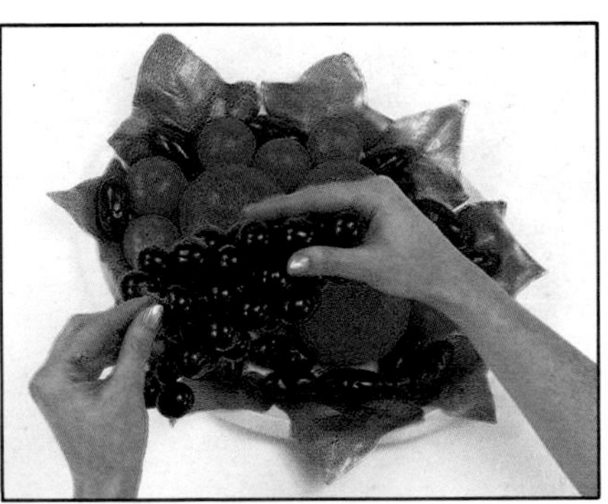

Arrange the clementines on the platter, surround them with dates and nuts, and place a bunch of shiny black grapes on top. Add the gold leaves and fir cones for a luxurious finishing touch.

 TABLECLOTHS AND NAPKINS 

In this section, you will find many different ways to give your tablecloths and napkins an individual touch. The designs on the following pages show how a combination of napkin and tablecloth works together to accentuate an overall theme. There are attractive alternatives to the traditional damask cloth using such materials as paints, ribbons and flowers. Napkins are also a necessary element of all table settings, however informal, and a variety of folds as well as craft ideas will enhance your setting. The most important requirement for folding napkins is that the napkin should be well starched and pressed.

Although designed for a Thanksgiving or Harvest Festival dinner, this setting could be used at any time of the year. The 'placemat' is really an outline printed on a plain white cloth, using a potato cut in a leaf shape; the napkin uses the same motif. Wooden-handled cutlery, hand-blown glass and dried flowers help to set the rustic theme.

ABSTRACT TABLECLOTH

Transform a plain tablecloth with this eyecatching design. Choose a brush the correct size for your design, and use a paint suitable for fabrics. (Because the paint is applied quite thickly, a paper tablecloth is not suitable.)

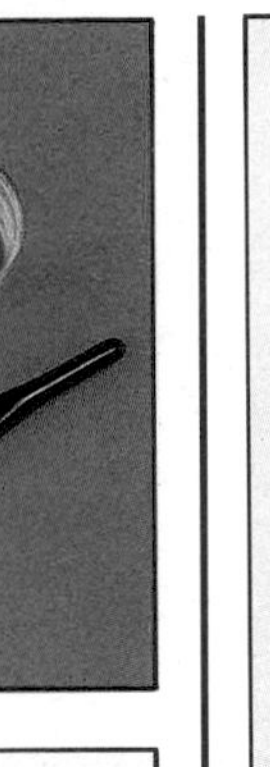

Practice first on a spare piece of cloth or paper, dipping the brush into the paint for each new stroke. Then paint the cloth, applying the lighter colour first; allow it to dry thoroughly.

Paint on the second colour in broad sweeps, allowing the paint to fade off towards the end of each brushstroke. Follow the manufacturer's instructions for fixing the fabric paint.

POTATO PRINT 'PLACEMAT'

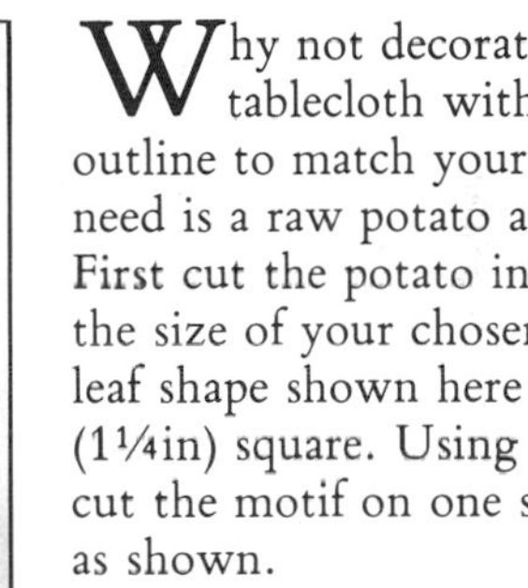

Why not decorate a plain white tablecloth with a placemat outline to match your china? All you need is a raw potato and some paint. First cut the potato into a cube about the size of your chosen motif. The leaf shape shown here is about 3cm (1¼in) square. Using a sharp knife, cut the motif on one side of the cube as shown.

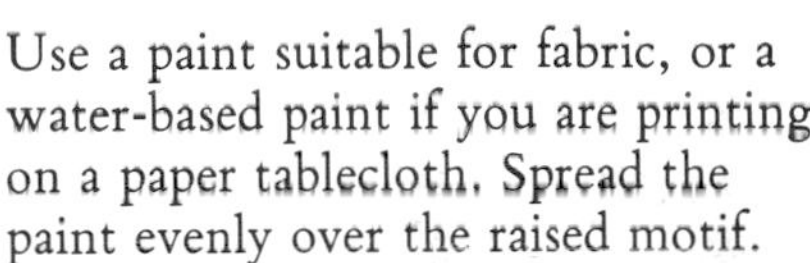

Use a paint suitable for fabric, or a water-based paint if you are printing on a paper tablecloth. Spread the paint evenly over the raised motif.

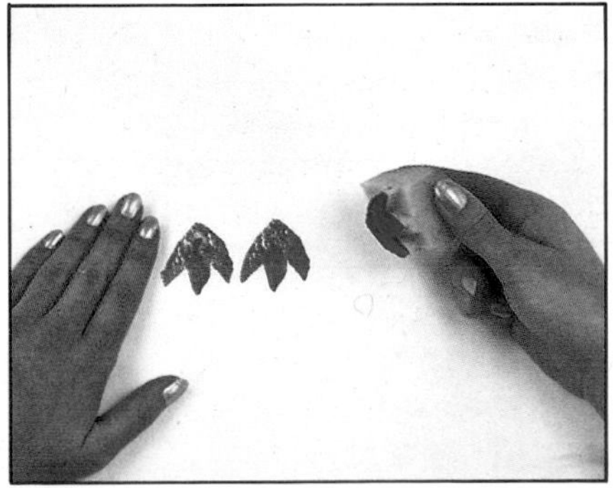

On a piece of stiff paper, draw the outline of the 'placemat' in black felt-tip pen. Place this under the cloth as a guide when printing. Press the potato down onto the cloth, taking care not to smudge it. Practice first on a spare piece of paper. The same technique can be used to print a border design around the edge of the napkin.

FLEUR-DE-LYS TABLECLOTH

Add a touch of luxury to a dinner party by decorating your own tablecloth in gold. First choose a simple image, such as the fleur-de-lys motif shown here. You can either decorate an existing cloth or buy a length of wide inexpensive cotton fabric. Draw the shape in pencil first, and then go over it in gold paint.

To echo the shape of the fleur-de-lys symbol you can dress up your table napkins as shown. A napkin with a lacy edge will look best. Fold the napkin into a square. Keeping the lacy edge nearest to you, fold the left- and right-hand corners in to overlap one another. Fold the remaining point in to meet them.

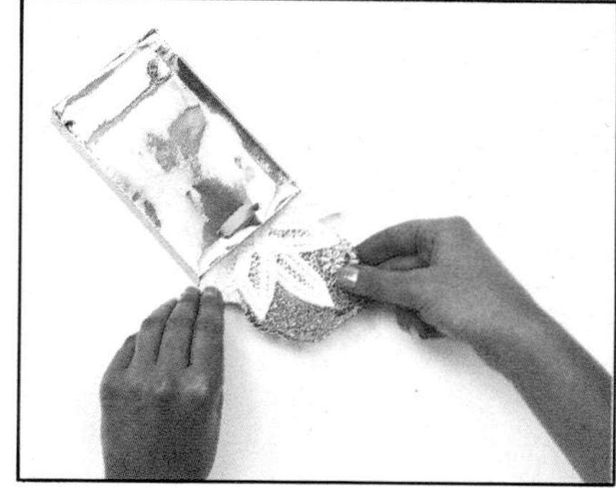

Slide the napkin, lacy edge towards you, into a shining foil gift bag. Because both napkin and china are white, a lacy gold coaster was inserted into the bag, underneath the lace detail on the napkin to give it more definition.

FLOWER-STREWN TABLECLOTH

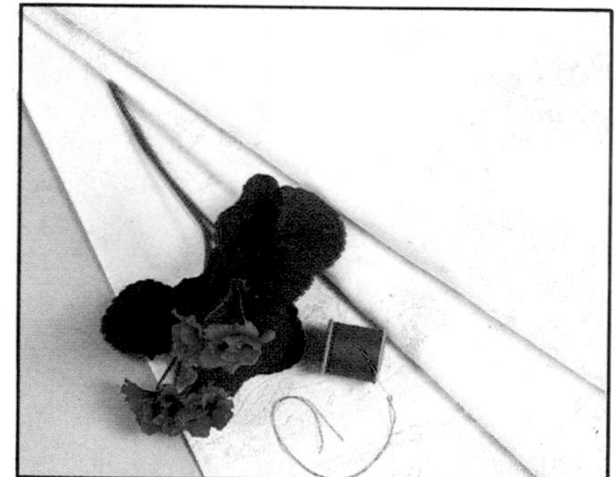

This simple idea can transform an ordinary tablecloth into something special. Choose a plain white or pastel-coloured tablecloth and artificial flowers with small blossoms. You will also need some green sewing thread and a needle.

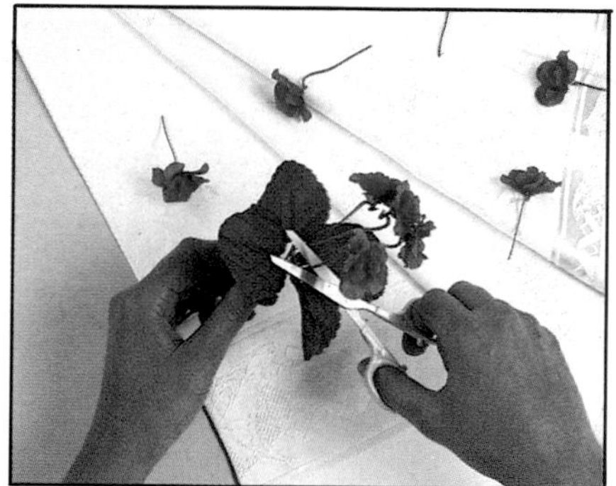

If the flowers you have chosen have several blooms to a stem, trim them into individual sprigs. Set aside the remaining leaves.

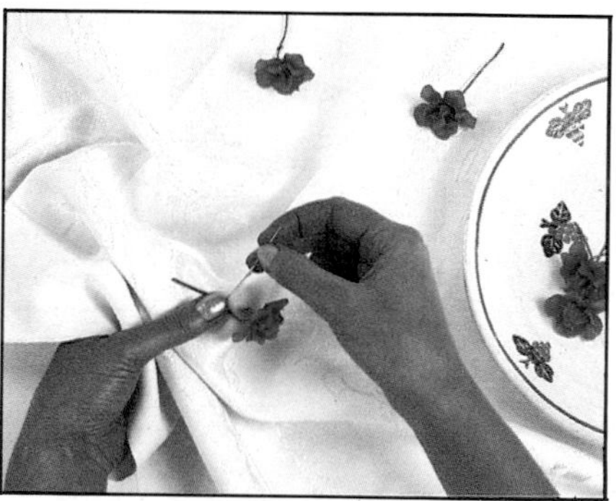

Sew the flower sprigs to the cloth. You can use as many or as few sprigs as you wish; you could sew one or two by each place setting or, for a stunning effect, cover the whole cloth with them — leaving room for place settings and serving dishes. Place the leftover leaves with a single flower sprig on each guest's plate.

RAG-ROLLED TABLECLOTH

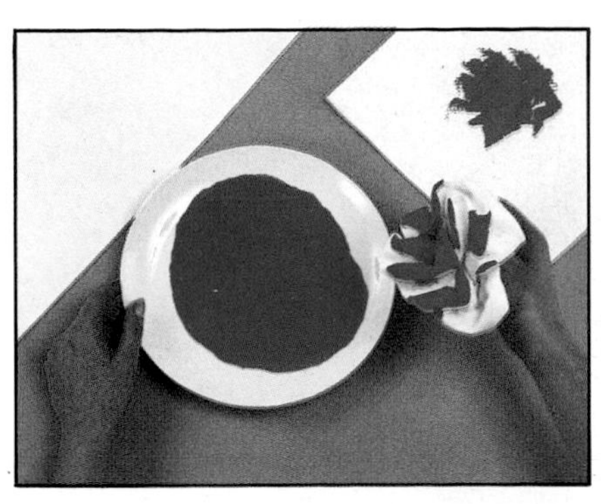

Rag-rolling, or ragging, is a quick and easy way to transform a plain fabric or paper tablecloth. Pour a water-based paint or fabric dye onto a plate, and dip a crumpled piece of cloth in it. Blot the cloth on some waste paper or fabric to remove excess paint.

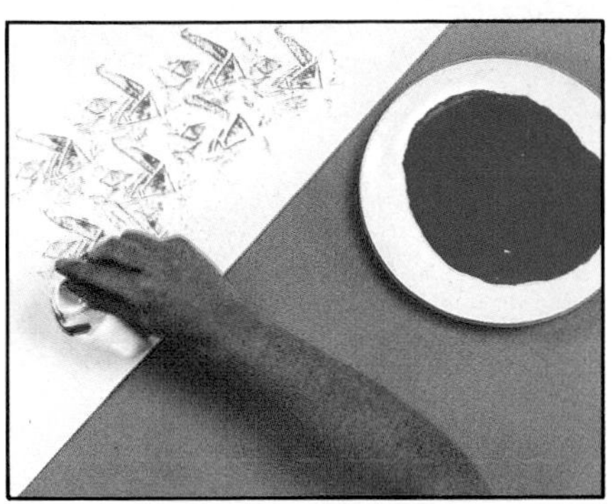

Lightly press the crumpled fabric onto a spare piece of paper or cloth to practice getting an even amount of paint over the area to be covered. Once you feel confident, rag the tablecloth, adding a second colour (once the first has dried) if desired. If using fabric dye, follow the manufacturer's instructions for fixing the colour.

RIBBON-TRIMMED TABLECLOTH

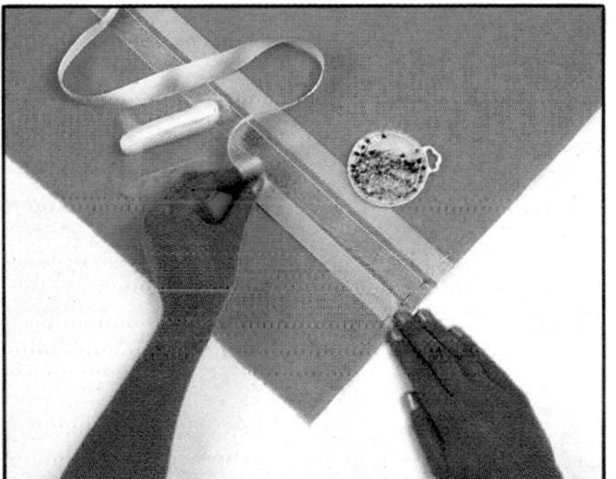

This pretty tablecloth isn't hard to make but requires a bit of patience. You can make the cloth yourself or buy one ready-made. Buy enough ribbon in each colour to run along four sides of the cloth, plus 24cm (8in) if using a ready-made cloth. Position the ribbons as shown, with fusible webbing underneath (omitting the area where they will cross), and pin them in place.

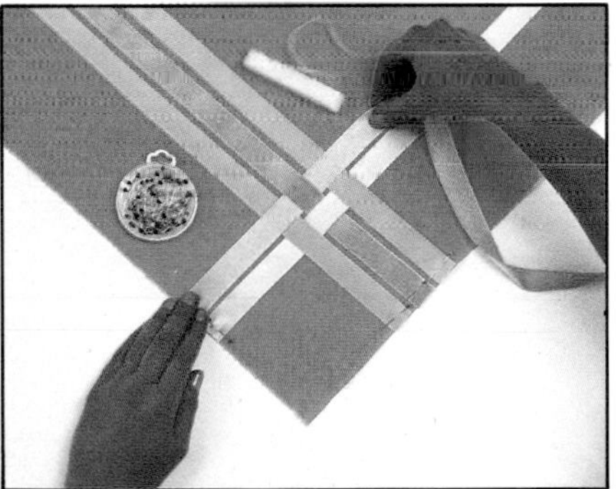

Continue to pin the ribbons in place along all the edges, making sure that you keep them straight. Thread the ribbons underneath one another to create a lattice effect, as shown. If you are using a ready-made cloth, allow the ribbons to overlap the edge by 3cm (1in); this will be folded under later.

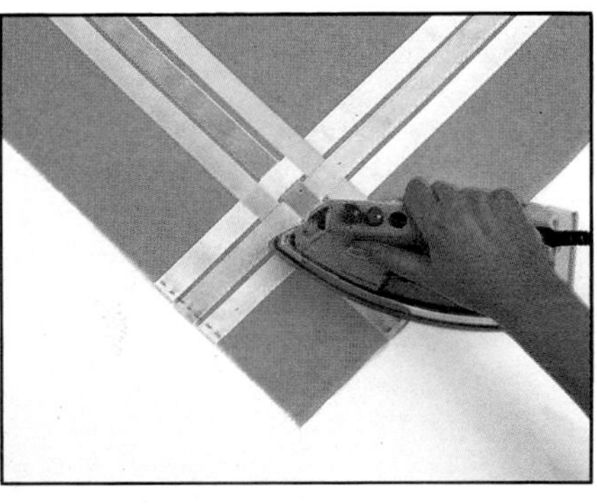

Replace the corner pins with tacking (basting) stitches, if you are working on an un-hemmed cloth; this provides extra stability. Press the ribbons in place with a warm iron, removing pins as you go and stopping just short of the tacking. Finally, hem the edges. On a ready-made cloth, sew the ribbon ends to the wrong side by hand.

PURE AND SIMPLE

This elegant napkin fold is easier to produce than it looks. First fold the napkin in half diagonally, then bring the left- and right-hand corners up to meet at the apex.

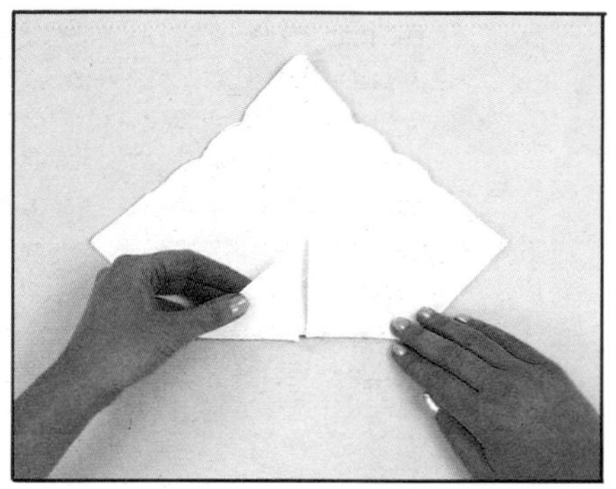

Turn the napkin over, and fold the lower corner up slightly as shown.

Fold the left- and right-hand corners underneath the napkin on a slight diagonal, pressing the folds lightly in place.

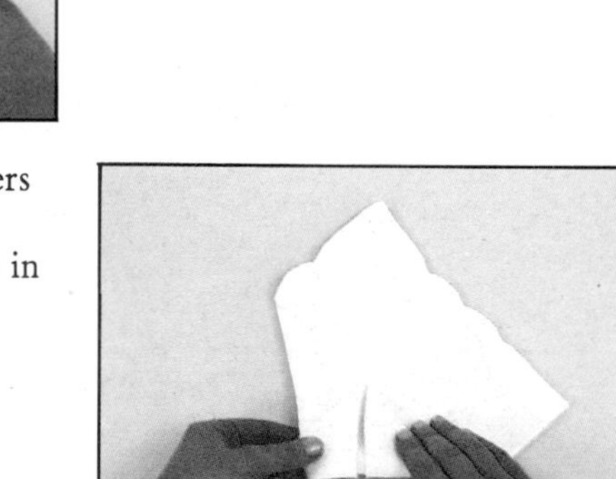

THE BISHOP'S HAT

This mitre-shaped fold can be displayed either on a flat surface (as above) or in a glass, cup or soup bowl, which allows the flaps to drape gracefully over the sides. Begin by folding the napkin diagonally to form a triangle, then pull each corner up to the apex as shown to form a square.

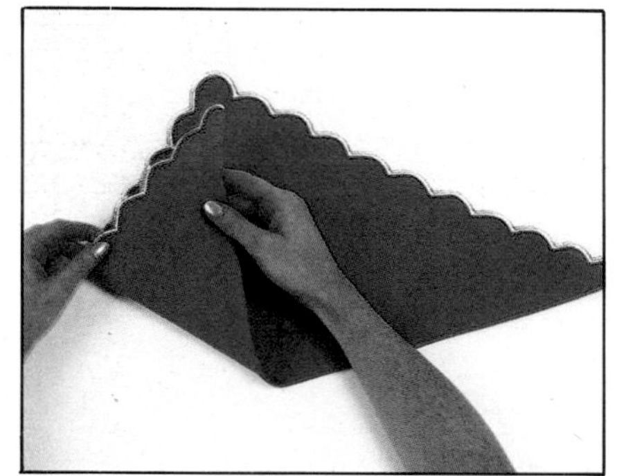

Turn the napkin over so that the free edges lie towards you. Pull the two top flaps up and away from you; then fold the remaining two flaps back in the same way to form a triangle.

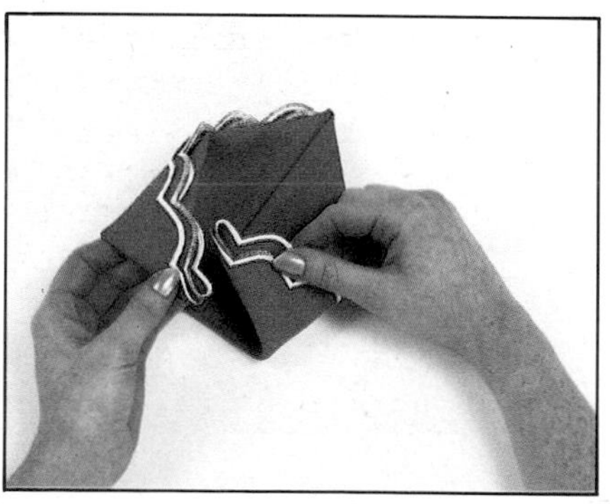

Carefully turn the napkin over once more, and pull the two outer corners together so that they overlap; tuck one flap into the folds of the other to hold them in place. Finally, turn the front of the 'hat' to face you, position the napkin upright and pull the loose flaps down as shown in the main picture.

THE BUTTERFLY

A crisply starched napkin is required for this pretty fold. Lay the napkin flat. Fold two edges to meet in the centre as shown. Then fold the half nearest you across the centre line and over on the top of the other half, to form a long, thin rectangle.

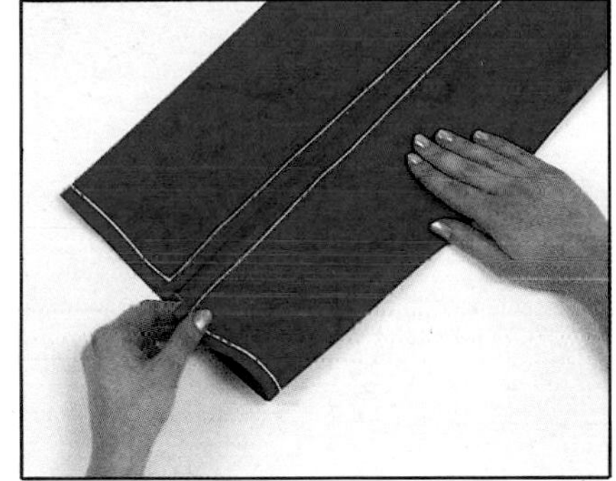

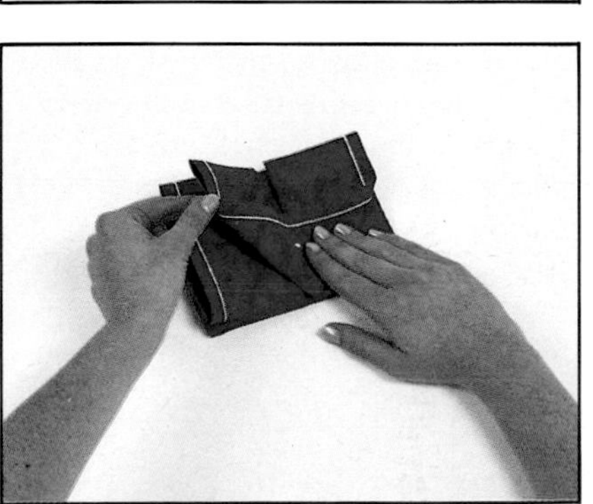

Fold the right-hand end of the rectangle in towards the centre, and with another fold double it back on itself as shown. Repeat with the left-hand side so that the double folds meet in the centre.

Pull the right-hand back corner across to the left, bringing the front edge across the centre line to form a triangle. Anchoring the right hand side of the triangle with one hand, use the other hand to fold the corner back to its original position, thus creating the 'wings' of the arrangement. Repeat the process on the left-hand side.

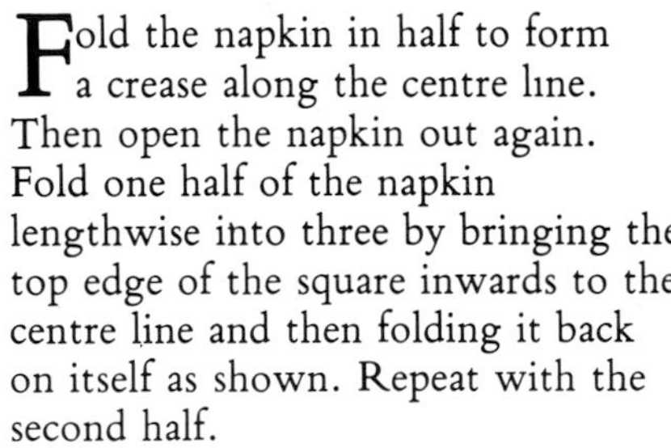

THE PRINCESS

Fold the napkin in half to form a crease along the centre line. Then open the napkin out again. Fold one half of the napkin lengthwise into three by bringing the top edge of the square inwards to the centre line and then folding it back on itself as shown. Repeat with the second half.

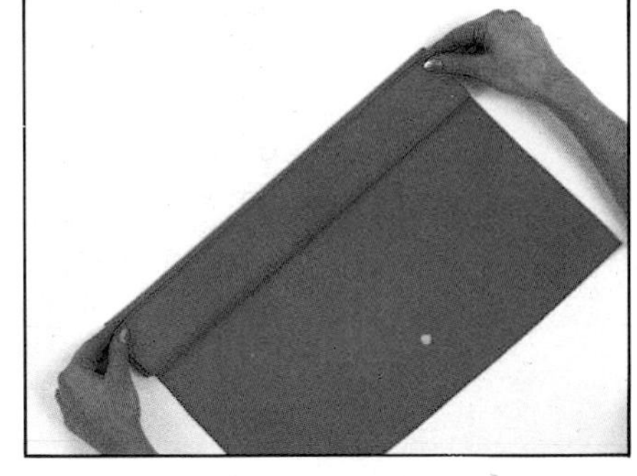

Fold the napkin in half lengthwise by tucking one half under the other along the centre line. Lay the resulting strip flat with the three folded edges facing you. Mark the centre of this strip with a finger and fold the right-hand edge in towards the centre and back on itself as shown. Repeat with the left-hand side.

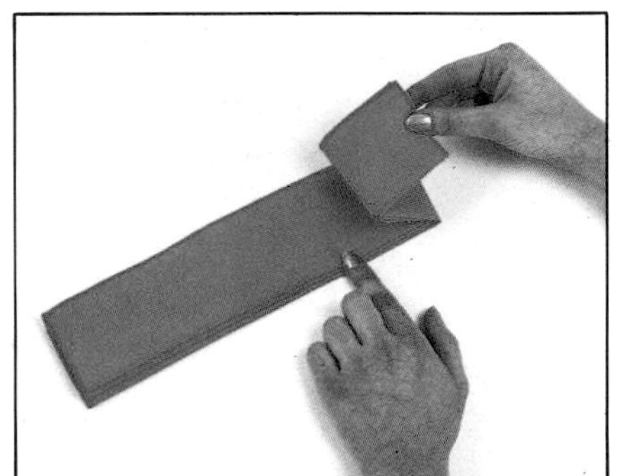

Pull the top left-hand corner across towards the top right-hand corner to create a triangle, pressing down gently along the folds to hold them in place. Repeat with the remaining left-hand folds, and then do the same with all the right-hand folds. Ease the folds open slightly and display the napkin with the centre point facing the guest.

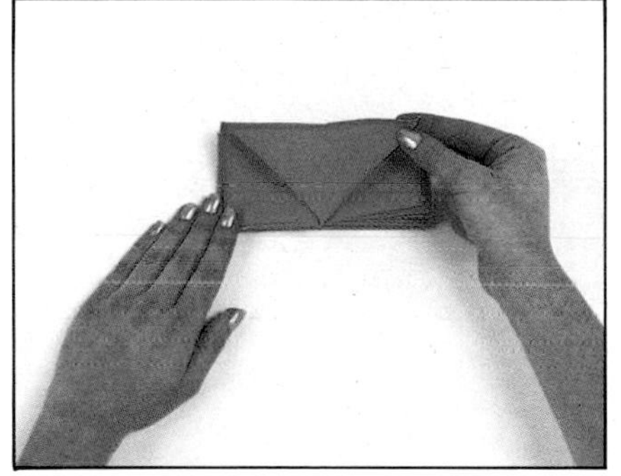

ORIENTAL FAN

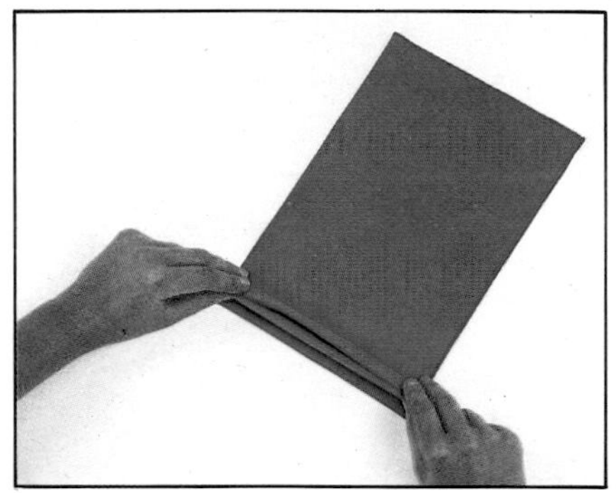

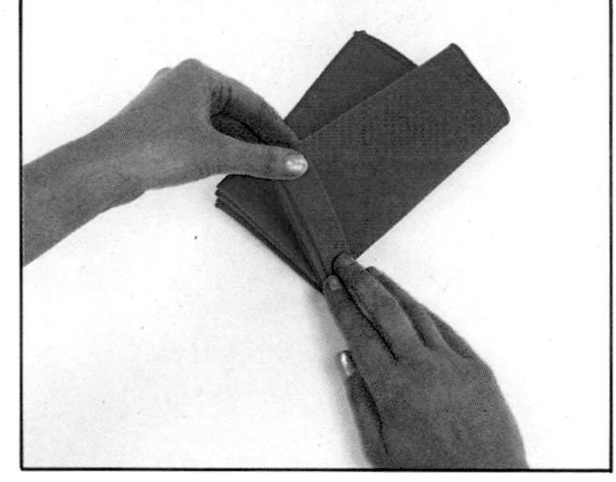

This highly effective design benefits from a well-starched napkin and is very easy to make. Begin by folding the napkin in half lengthwise and then fold one end of the oblong backwards and forwards in concertina- or accordion-style folds, until just past the halfway point.

Holding the folds firmly together, fold the napkin lengthwise down the middle to bring both ends of the 'concertina' together. Keeping the folds in position in one hand, fold the loose flap of the napkin over across the diagonal.

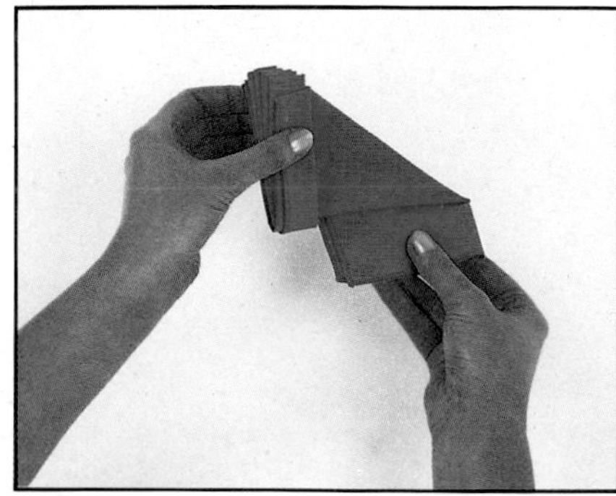

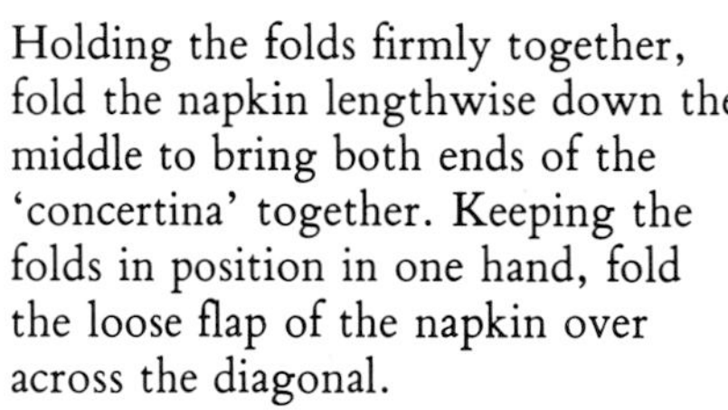

Push the flap underneath the support as shown to balance the napkin, and, letting go of the pleats, allow the fan to fall into position.

DOUBLE JABOT

Fold the napkin twice to form a square and position it with the loose corners at the top right. Fold the top corner back diagonally to meet the lower left corner, then turn it back on itself as shown. Continue to fold the corner back and forth to create a 'concertina' effect along the diagonal strip of napkin.

Lift the next layer of fabric from the top right-hand corner and repeat the process described above to create two parallel strips with zigzag edges.

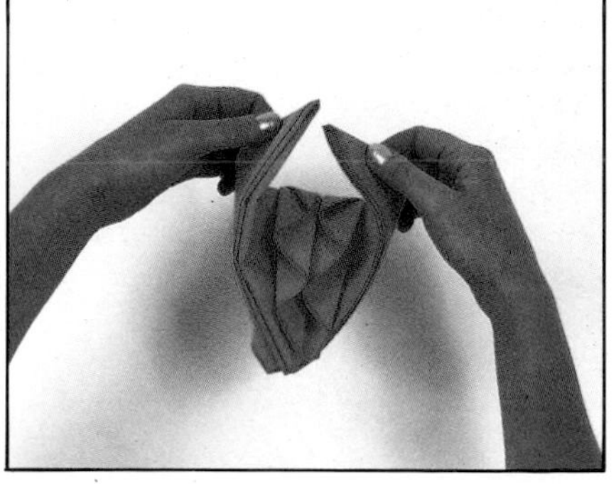

Pick the napkin up in both hands with the zigzag folds in the centre. Fold it in half diagonally to form a triangle, keeping the pleats on the outside. Take the right-hand and left-hand corners of the triangle and curl them back, tucking one into the other to secure them. Stand the napkin upright on a plate as shown.

PURE ELEGANCE

For best results use a crisply starched napkin to make this attractive fold. First fold the napkin lengthwise into three to form a long rectangle. Lay it horizontally with the free edge away from you, and fold the left- and right-hand ends in to meet in the centre.

Fold down the top right- and left-hand corners to meet in the centre, forming a point. Take the napkin in both hands and flip it over towards you so that the point is facing you and the flat side of the napkin is uppermost.

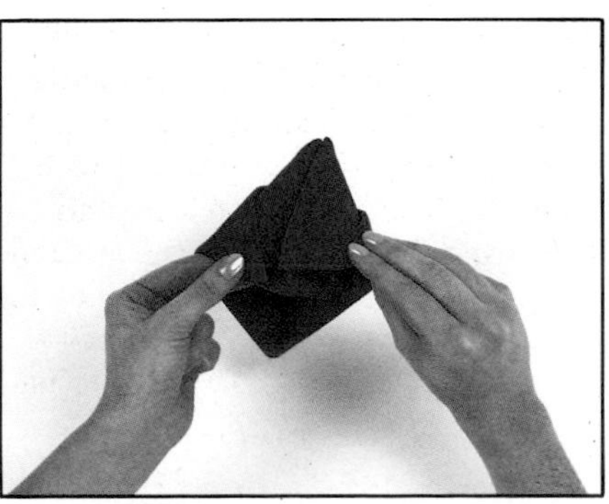

Lift the sides and pull them over towards one another to form a cone shape. Tuck the left-hand corner into the right-hand corner to secure it. Turn the napkin around and place it on a plate as shown in the main picture.

CANDLE FOLD

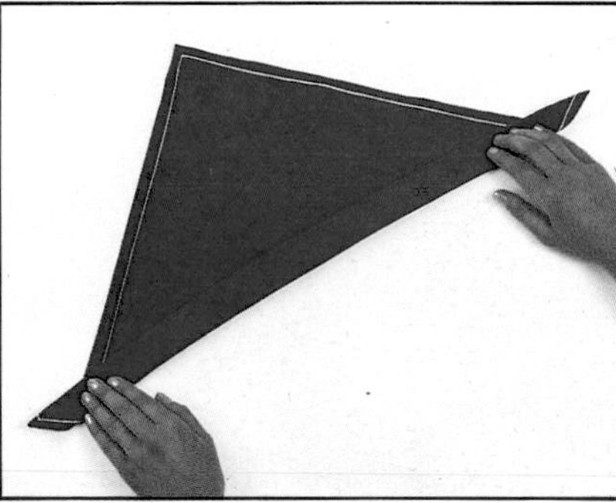

This tall candle-shade fold looks especially good if the napkin has a contrasting border. Begin by laying the napkin flat. Fold it in half diagonally to form a triangle. Turn up the folded edge about 3cm (1¼in), then turn the napkin over so that the fold is underneath.

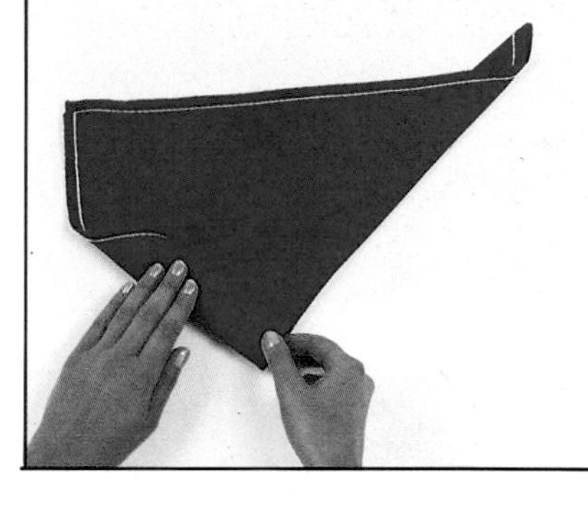

Starting at the left-hand corner, roll the napkin to form a cylindrical shape.

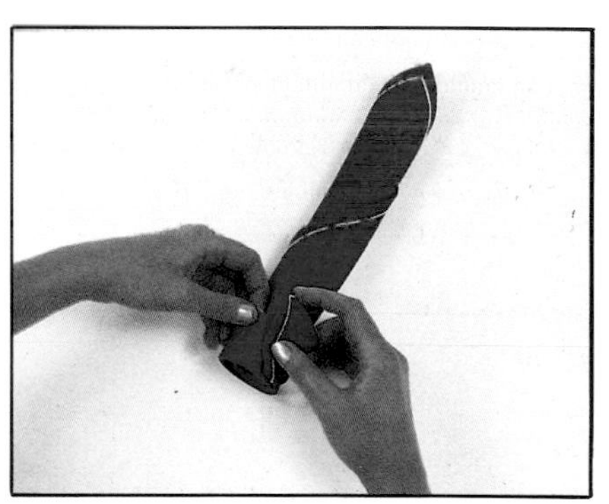

Tuck in the end to hold the roll in place. Finally, fold down the front corner at the top as shown in the main picture.

FLEUR-DE-LYS

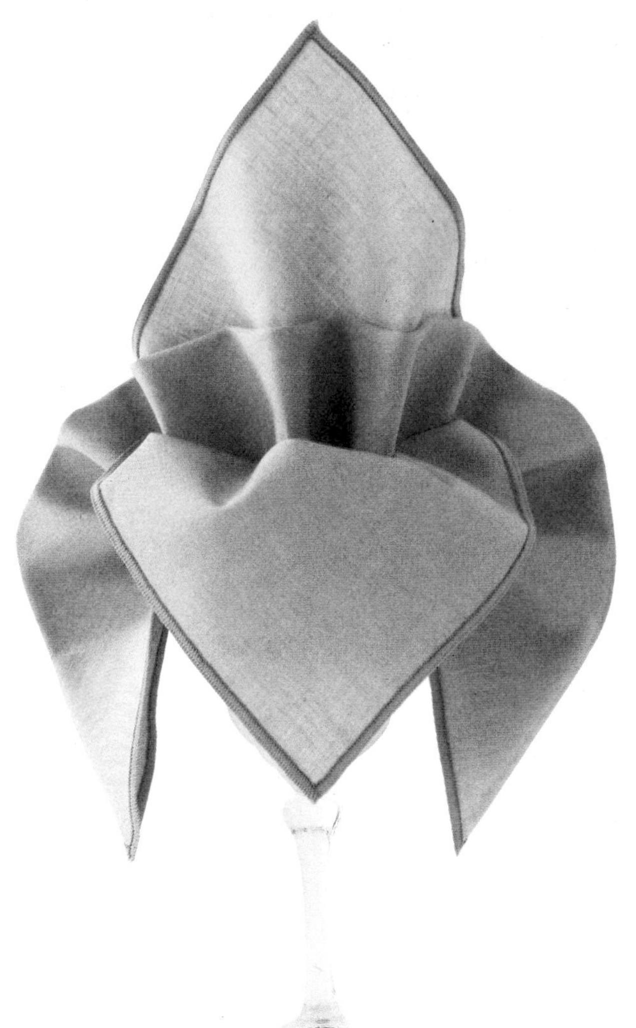

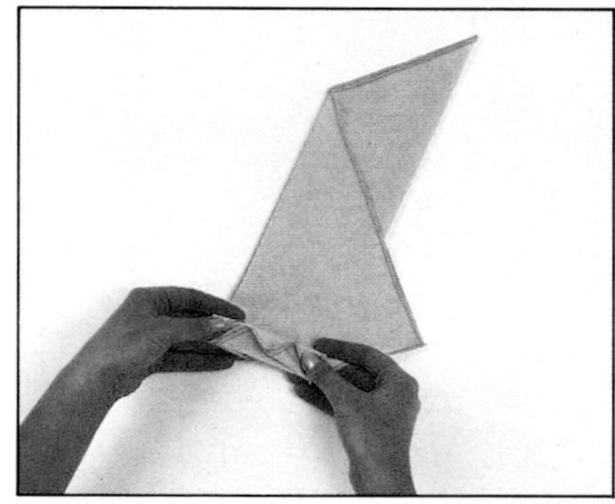

This graceful fold is easier than it looks. Lay the napkin flat and fold it in half diagonally to form a triangle. Position it with the folded edge towards you. Bring the top corner towards you, so that the point overlaps the folded edge slightly. Carefully turn the napkin over and repeat with the other corner.

Pleat the napkin evenly across from left to right, in accordion- or concertina-style, folds. Holding the straight edge of the 'concertina' firmly in position, arrange the napkin in a glass. Pull the front layer of the top point towards you, creating a pointed flap over the front of the glass.

LADY'S SLIPPER

This pretty design is ideally suited to teatime settings. Begin by folding the napkin into four — left to right, top to bottom — to form a small square. Then fold the four loose corners back across the diagonal to form a triangle.

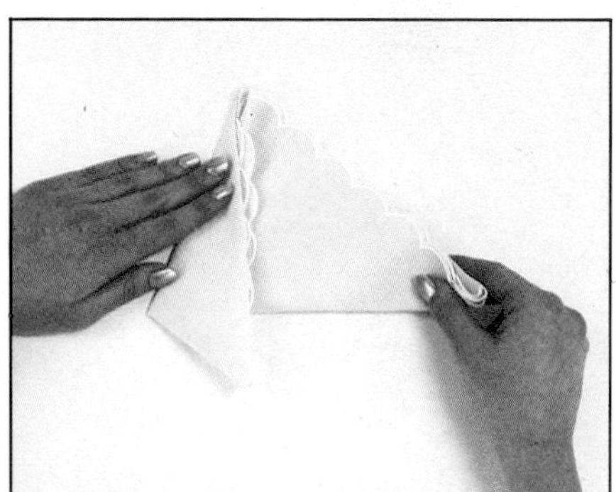

Holding the napkin firmly at the apex, fold one of the outer corners over and towards you as shown, so that it overlaps the base of the triangle. Repeat with the second corner so that the edges of both flaps meet down the centre of the napkin.

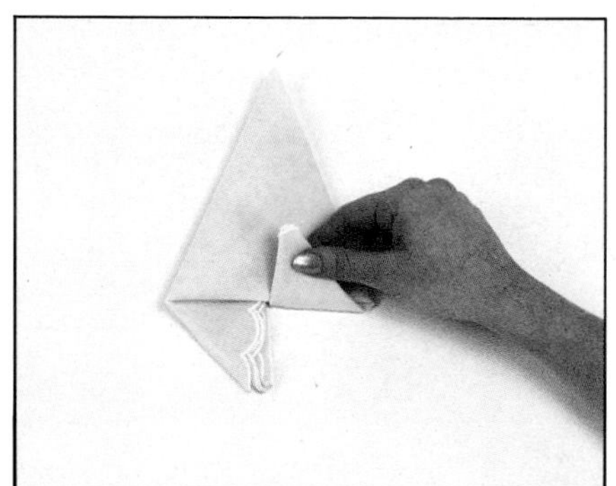

Turn the napkin over and fold the protruding flaps back over the base of the triangle. Then fold the triangle in half by pulling one of the corners over to meet the other. Finally, holding both corners firmly together, turn the napkin upright and pull the four loose corners upwards as shown in the main picture.

LOTUS BLOSSOM

This pretty design is not as difficult to create as it may appear. The technique is similar to that used in folding the origami 'fortune tellers' so popular with children. Lay the napkin flat, and begin by folding each of the four corners into the centre.

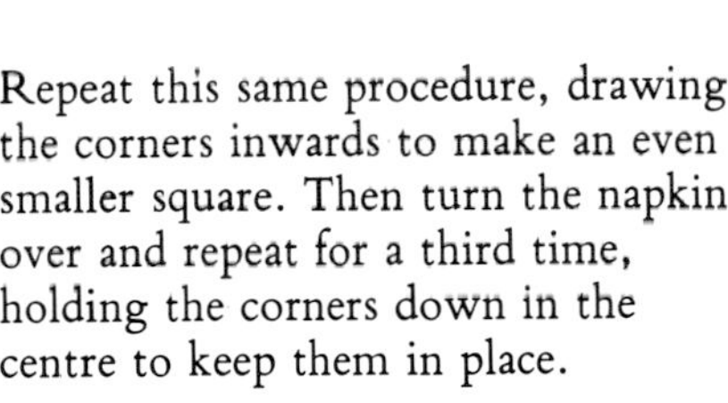

Repeat this same procedure, drawing the corners inwards to make an even smaller square. Then turn the napkin over and repeat for a third time, holding the corners down in the centre to keep them in place.

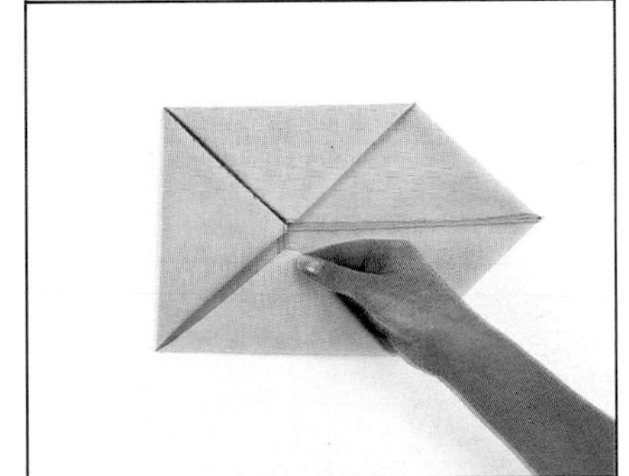

Still keeping your finger on the centre, reach behind the napkin to one of the corners tucked underneath, and draw this gently outwards as shown until it peaks out beyond the corner of the square. Repeat the process with all four flaps to form the petals. Finally, reaching underneath again, pull out the four single flaps to make the sepals.

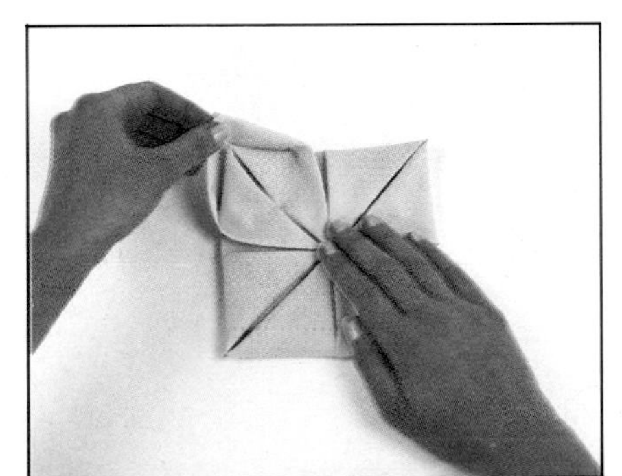

FOUR FEATHERS

This simple fold looks elegant placed in a wineglass. Open the napkin flat. Fold it in half diagonally to form a triangle, and place the folded edge towards you. Place your index finger on the centre of this edge. Using the top layer of fabric only, bring the apex down to meet the left-hand corner.

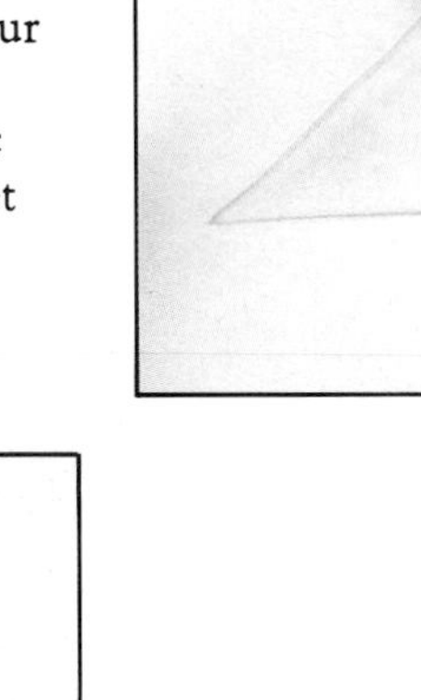

Again working with the top layer only, bring the far corner down and across to the bottom left-hand corner.

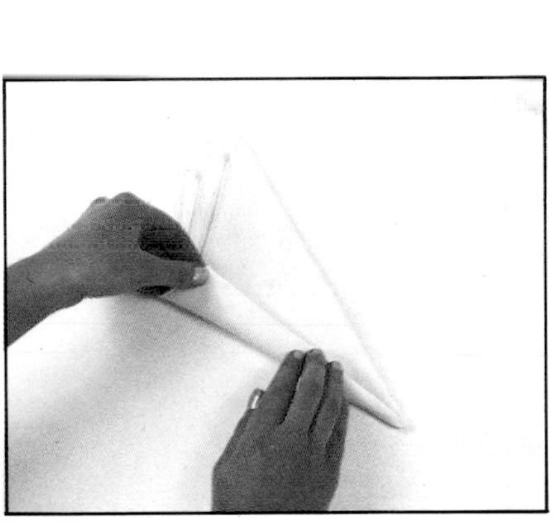

Bring the remaining top corner down and across to the lower left corner as before, forming a triangle once more. Splay the folds slightly, then turn the napkin over so that the folds are underneath. Lift the edge and roll the napkin into a loose cone shape as shown, stopping about halfway across. Fold up the bottom point and insert the napkin in the glass.

LACY NAPKIN FOLDER

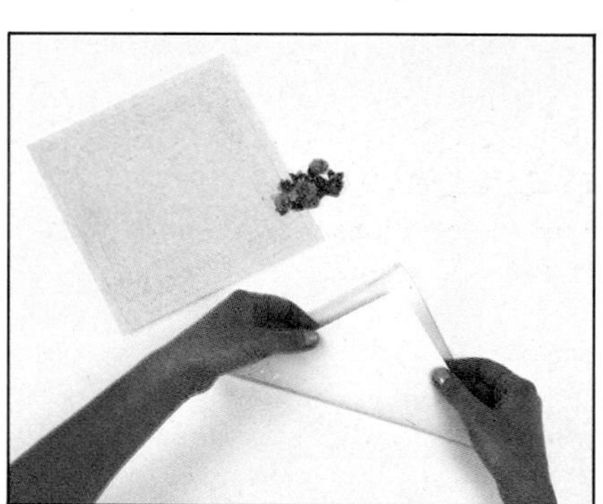

Here's a quick and simple way to dress up a plain napkin for afternoon tea. All you need is a square paper doily, preferably in a colour contrasting with the napkin, and a floral motif. Begin by folding the napkin into a triangle.

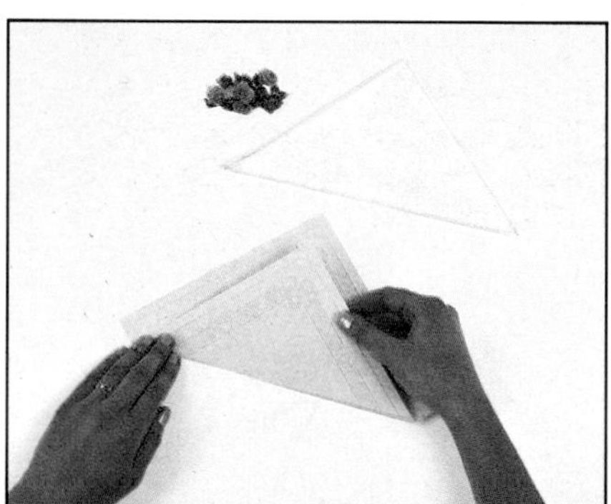

Fold the doily diagonally. To create a 'spine' to allow for the thickness of the napkin, unfold the doily and make another crease about 1cm (3/8in) from the first fold.

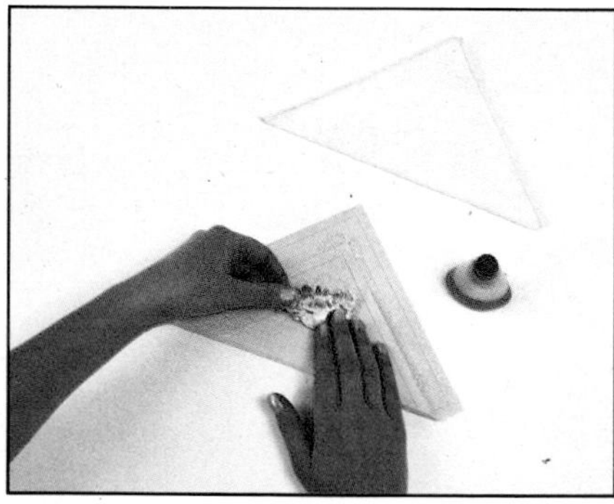

Cut out a Victorian scrap or other floral motif and glue it to the centre of the smaller (top) side of the doily. Insert the napkin.

PASTEL NAPKIN BOX

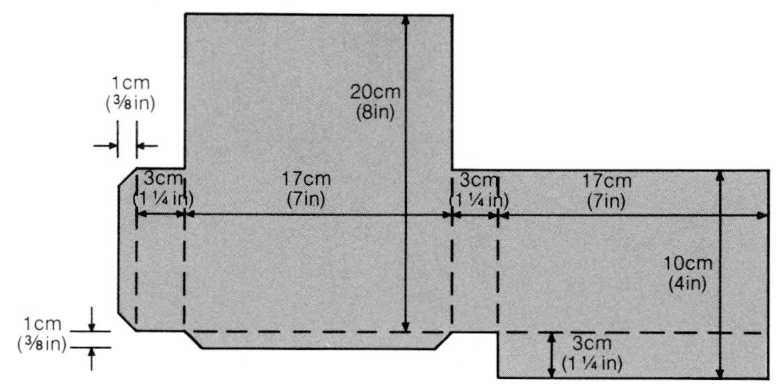

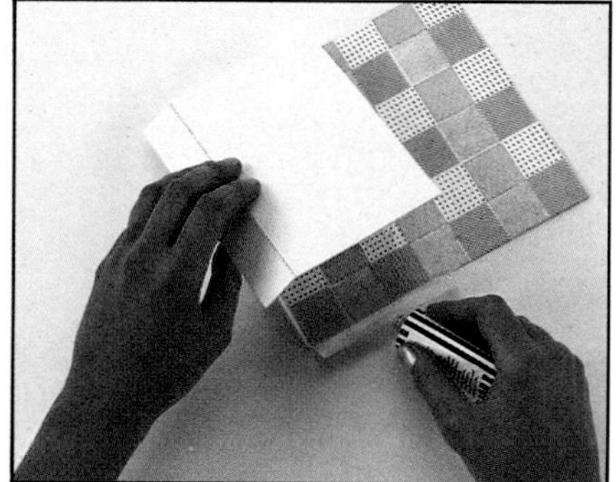

To make this attractive napkin box, draw the above diagram to the measurements indicated. Cut it out with a sharp knife and score the folds marked with a dotted line. Cut out a piece of water-resistant paper or PVC, approximately 21 by 19cm (8½ by 7½in). Stick it down onto the front inside area of the box, and fold overlapping paper to the back of the card; glue it in place.

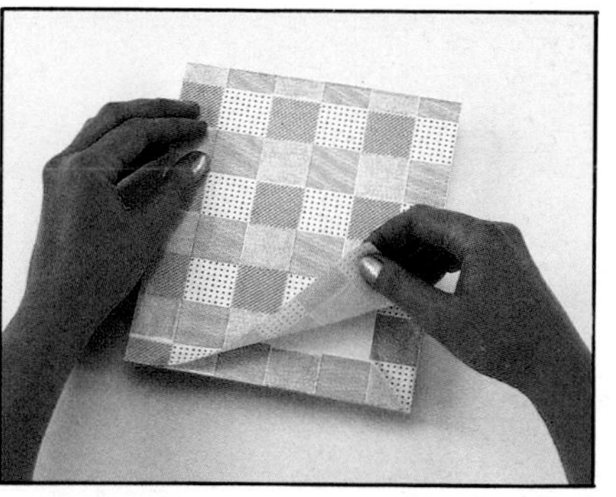

Apply glue to the sides and base of the box and stick the box together. Cut out a second piece of paper 26 by 12.5cm (10½ by 5in) and glue it onto the outside front and sides of the box, snipping the corners to enable you to tuck the free edges in. Finally, cut a third piece of paper 20 by 17cm (8 by 7in) to glue to the back of the box and cover all the untidy edges.

BUFFET ENVELOPE

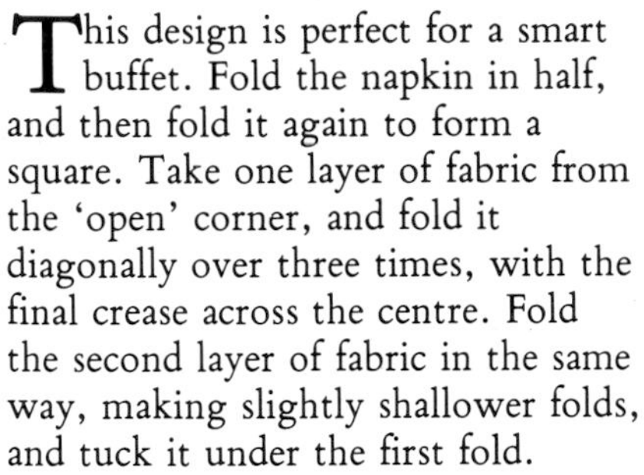

This design is perfect for a smart buffet. Fold the napkin in half, and then fold it again to form a square. Take one layer of fabric from the 'open' corner, and fold it diagonally over three times, with the final crease across the centre. Fold the second layer of fabric in the same way, making slightly shallower folds, and tuck it under the first fold.

Fold the left- and right-hand sides to the underside, leaving a central panel in which to place the cutlery. Or use the napkin as it is (without the cutlery inside) for a sit-down meal.

POCKET NAPKIN

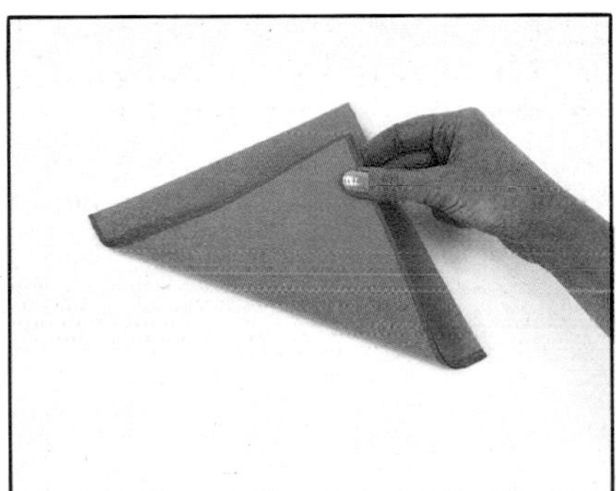

This simple napkin fold is embellished with a few artificial flowers tucked into the pocket. Fold the napkin in half and then in half again to form a square; then fold it across the diagonal to form a triangle.

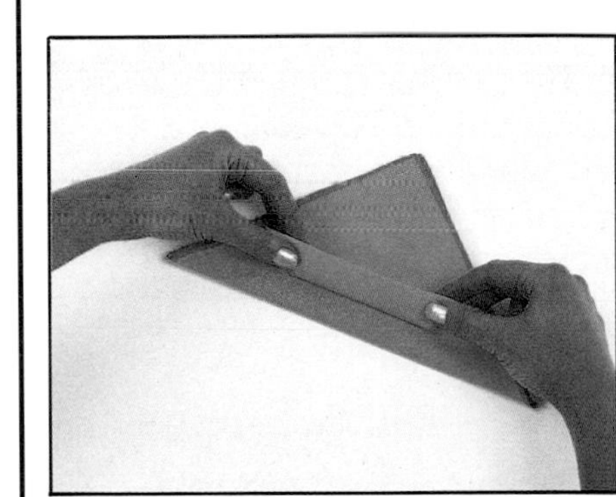

Position the napkin as shown with the four loose corners uppermost. Working with the top layer only, fold it down several times to make a cuff at the bottom.

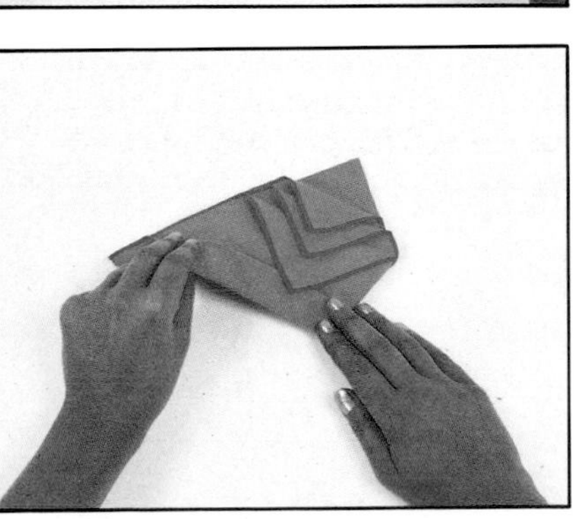

Fold the next (single) corner over so that the tip touches the top edge of the cuff. Fold the next two corners over to form three tiers. Finally, turn the right and left corners of the triangle to the underside and overlap them. Position the napkin as shown in the main picture and insert the flowers.

NET NAPKIN RING

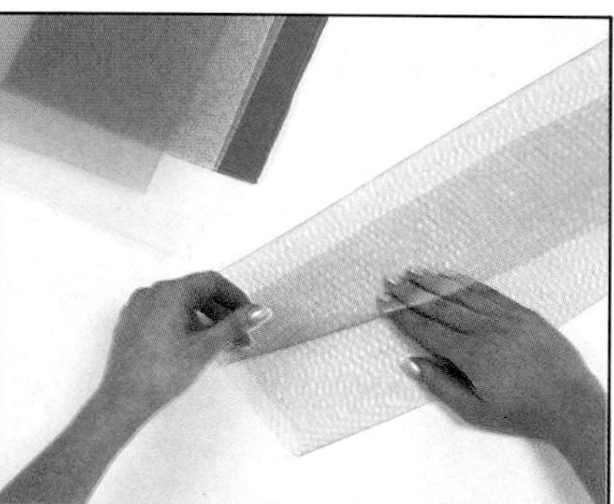

For a touch of frivolity, tie your table napkins in several shades of net. For each napkin cut three different-coloured rectangles of net, 45 by 35cm (18in by 13in). Fold each piece crosswise into three equal sections.

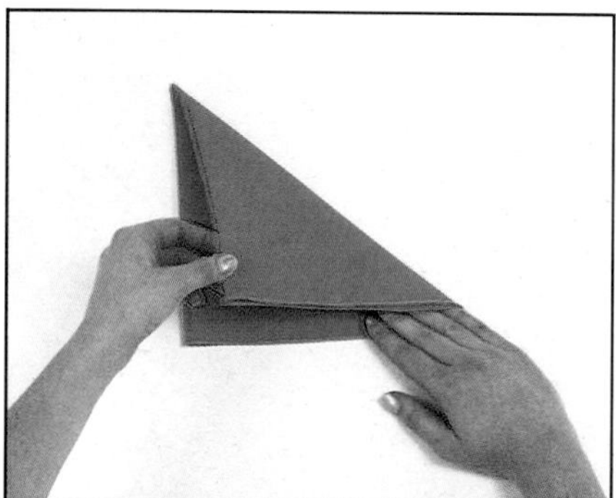

Fold the napkin twice to form a square, and then fold it diagonally to form a triangle. Now roll it lengthwise.

Place the lengths of net on top of each other; tie them around the napkin and fan out the ends.

CIRCULAR NAPKIN

This original napkin fold makes a pretty circular shape and is embellished with a bead and ribbon trimming. Paint a plain 25mm (1in) wooden bead with a water-based paint to match your napkin. Then paint on a pattern with a harmonizing or contrasting colour. Allow the paint to dry between coats.

Fold the napkin in half once along its length, and then pleat it accordion-fashion along its length, making sure the folds are the same size.

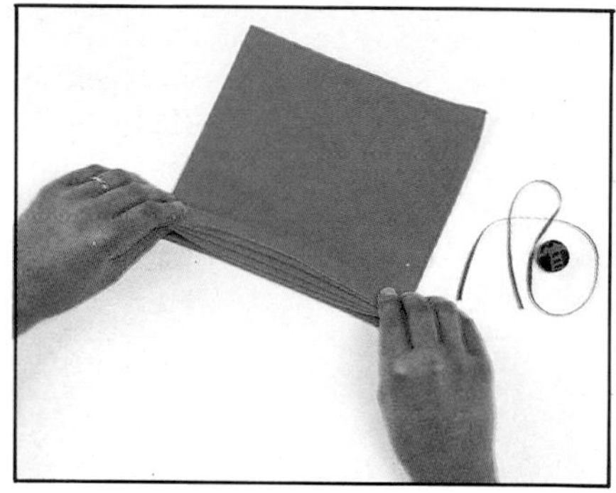

Thread a length of thin ribbon through the bead and tie it to hold the bead in place. Wrap the ribbon around the centre of the napkin, and tie it in a neat bow just below the bead. Fan the napkin out so that it forms a full circle.

STENCILLED SHELL NAPKIN

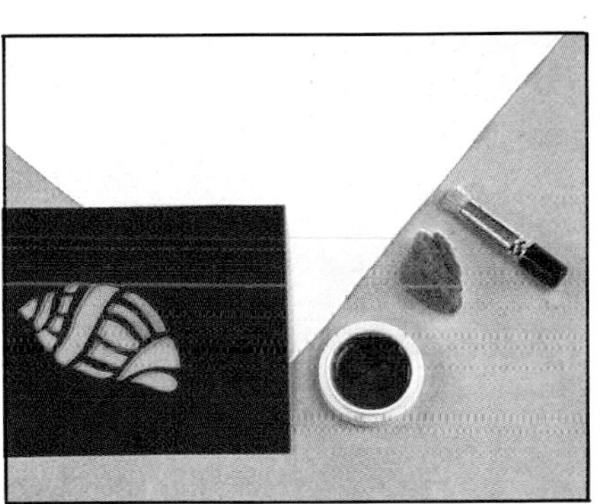

If you can't find a ready-made napkin to complement your china or decorative scheme, you can easily decorate your own with a stencil design. All you need is a plain napkin or a hemmed square of fabric, a stencil motif — either bought (quilters' suppliers have them) or original, a natural sponge and some fabric paint.

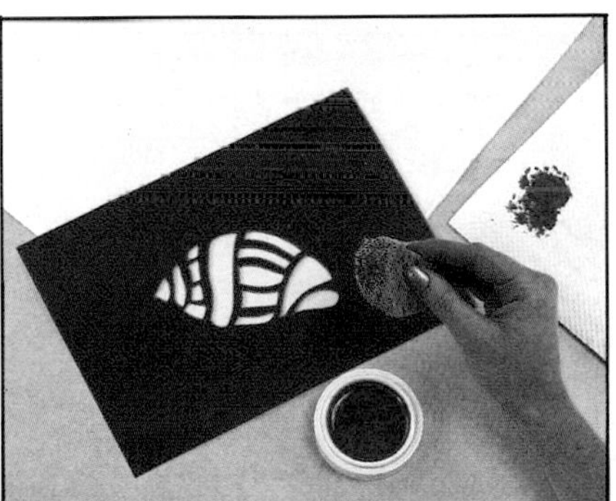

Position the stencil on the napkin. Mix the paint in a saucer or palette. Dip the sponge into the paint and dab it on a piece of scrap paper to remove the excess. As an alternative to a sponge you can use a stencil brush, which will give a slightly different effect. It is worthwhile trying both to see which best suits your design.

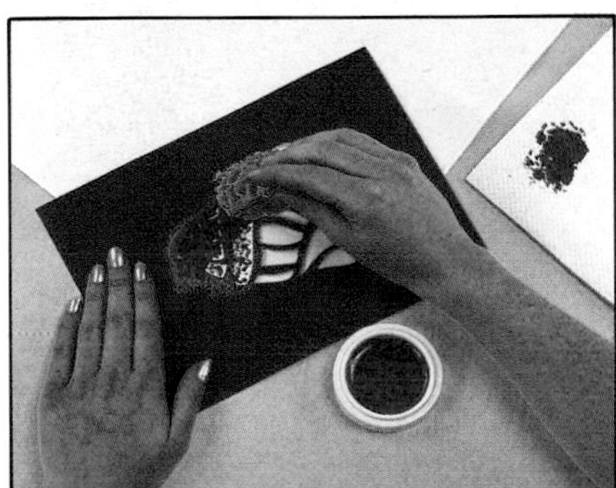

You can either hold the stencil in place with your fingers or fasten it with tape. Dab paint through the stencil onto the fabric, taking care that it doesn't seep under the edges. When the paint is dry, fix it following the manufacturer's instructions.

TASSEL NAPKIN RING

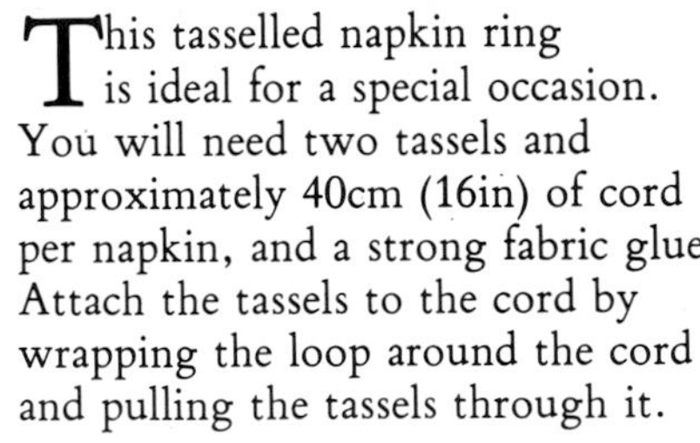

This tasselled napkin ring is ideal for a special occasion. You will need two tassels and approximately 40cm (16in) of cord per napkin, and a strong fabric glue. Attach the tassels to the cord by wrapping the loop around the cord and pulling the tassels through it.

Make the ring by feeding the cord through both loops of the tassels twice more. Make sure that the ring is large enough to slip easily over the napkin.

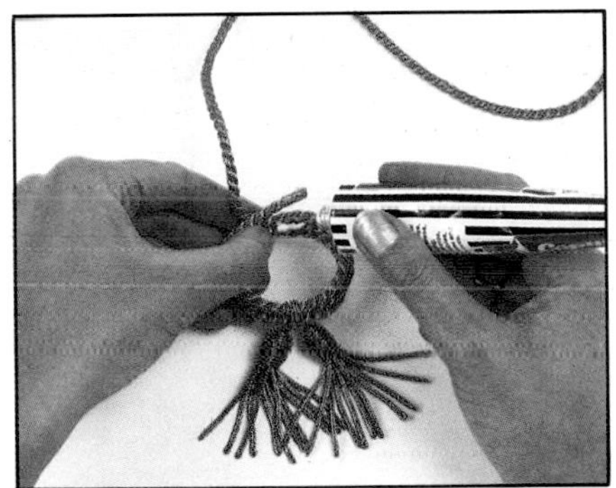

Using a strong glue, secure the ends of the cord to the back of the ring. Lay one end along the back and trim it. Having applied the glue to the inside of the ring as shown, wrap the remaining end over the cords, covering the trimmed end. Cut the remaining piece of cord on the inside, and clamp it in position until it is dry.

LACY NAPKIN BOW

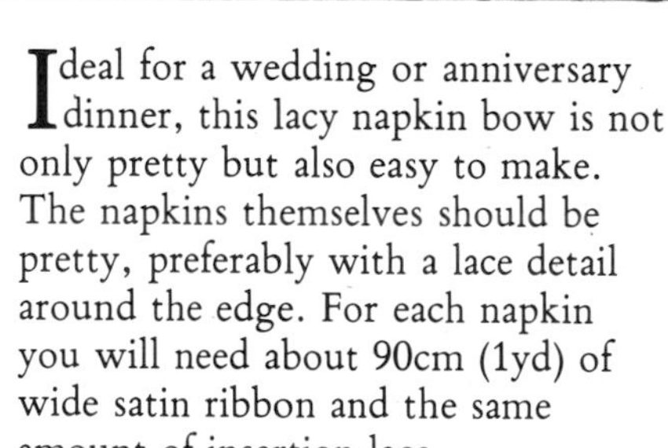

Ideal for a wedding or anniversary dinner, this lacy napkin bow is not only pretty but also easy to make. The napkins themselves should be pretty, preferably with a lace detail around the edge. For each napkin you will need about 90cm (1yd) of wide satin ribbon and the same amount of insertion lace.

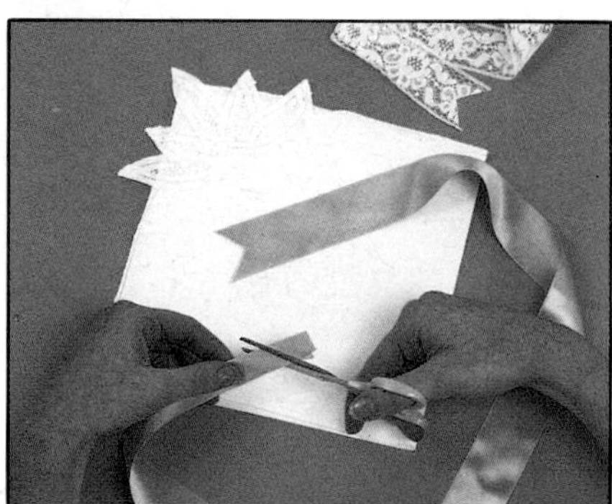

For best results, the napkin should be starched and well ironed and folded into quarters. To cut decorative points for the ribbons and lace, fold the ends as shown and cut them diagonally.

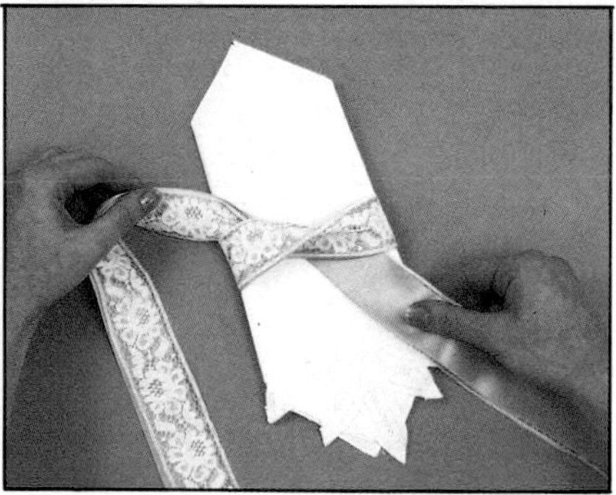

Fold under two corners of the napkin to overlap in the centre, forming the shape shown here. Iron the folds flat. Lay the ribbon and lace flat, wrong side up, with the ribbon on top. Place the napkin on top and tie the ribbon and lace around it in a bow.

THANKSGIVING NAPKIN

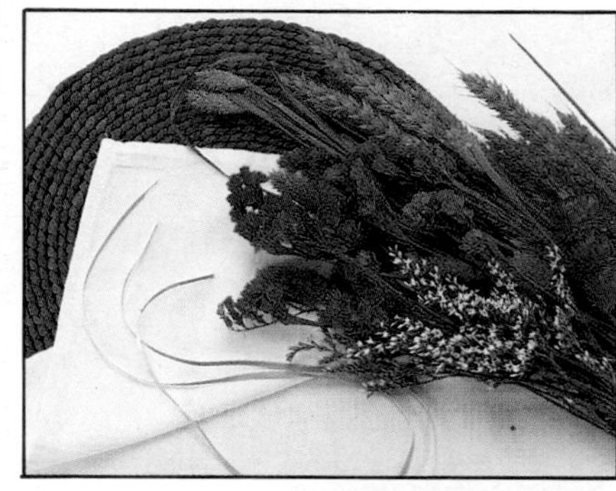

This simple place setting is perfect for a Thanksgiving or Harvest Festival dinner. Use a sisal or straw placemat and a plain white napkin. For the decoration you will need a selection of dried flowers and grasses and three lengths of beige or wheat-coloured ribbon, each about 50cm (20in) long.

Tie the lengths of ribbon together at one end. Plait them until the plait is long enough to tie around the napkin twice with a little left over.

Group the bunch of dried flowers and grasses together, securing them with thread or twine. Fold the napkin in half twice to form a long, thin rectangle. Lay the flowers on top of the napkin. Wind the plaited ribbon around the napkin and flowers twice and tie the ends under the napkin.

DECORATED NAPKINS

Here are a couple of ideas for jazzing up ordinary paper napkins. For the blue napkin, cut a star shape from a piece of cardboard — the cardboard must be slightly wider than the folded napkin. Hold the cardboard firmly in place over the napkin and spray silver or gold paint over the area. Let the paint dry for several minutes before you allow anything else to touch it.

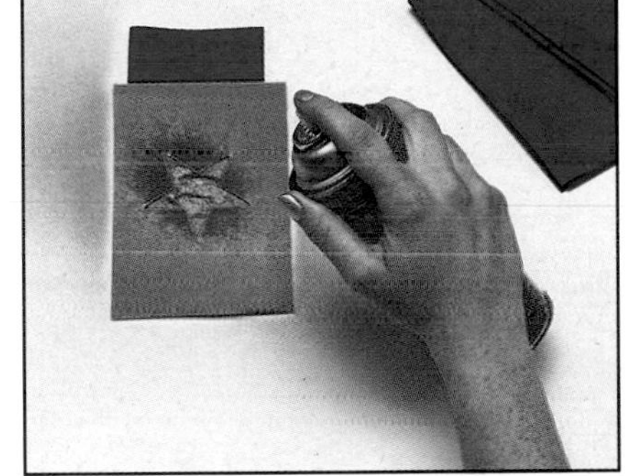

The white napkins have a design stencilled on them with oil-based stencil crayons. You can buy these separately or in packs, with ready-cut stencils. Choose your design, then place it over the area you want to stencil — in this case the corner of the napkin. Rub the crayon over a spare area of stencil, then take the colour up onto the brush and paint it over the stencil, in a circular motion.

Use the brush only over the parts you wish to show up in that colour. Now switch to the next colour. It is best to use a different brush for each colour if you want clear colour definition.

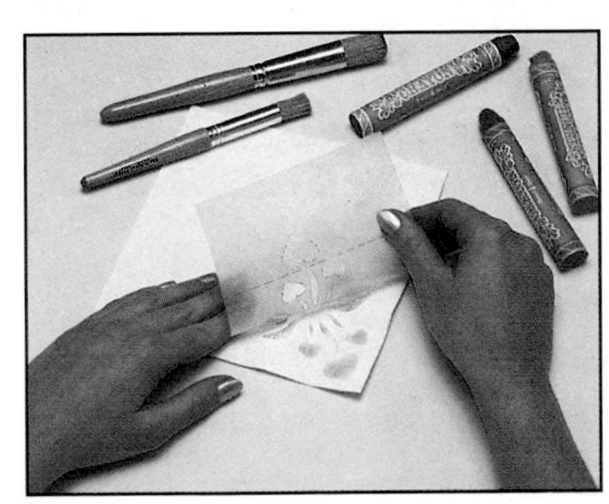

FLORAL NAPKIN RING

This charming flower-trimmed napkin ring adds a touch of elegance to a table setting and is very easy to make. Bend a short length of florists' wire into a circle; twist the ends together to secure them.

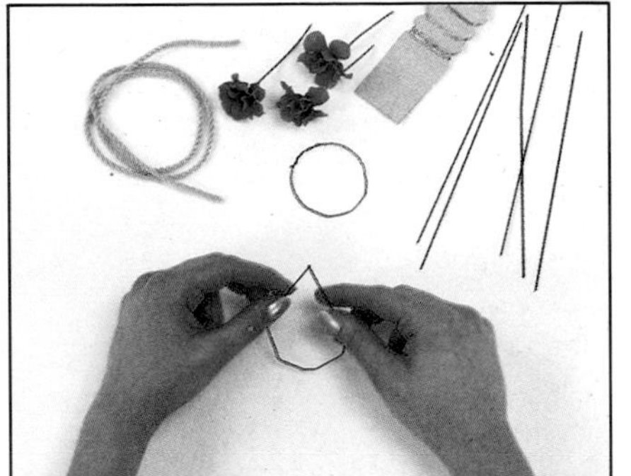

Wind some fine fuse wire around one or two small silk flowers — chosen to co-ordinate with your china and table linen. Then twist the ends of the fuse wire around the circle of florist's wire to hold the flowers in place.

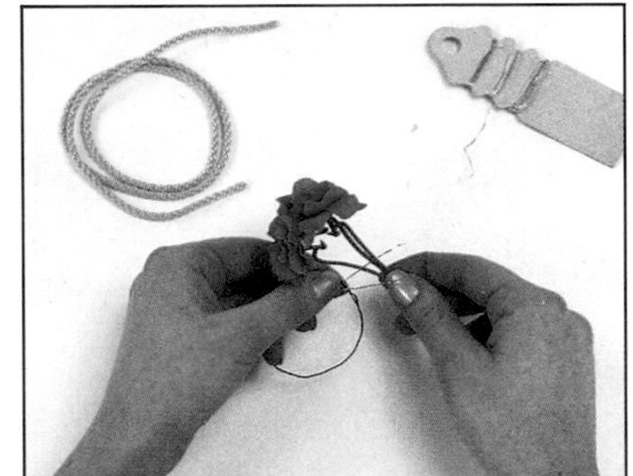

For covering the ring choose a fine ribbon or decorative braid. Hold one end in place with one hand, and use the other hand to twist the braid around the circle to cover it completely, beginning and ending underneath the flowers. Secure the ends with glue. Insert the napkin and add a fresh flower for the finishing touch.

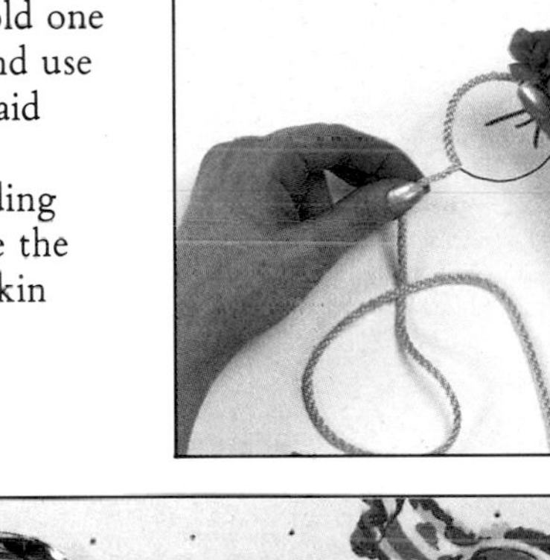

 *PLACE CARDS AND PLACEMATS* 

Place cards have traditionally been used to organize the seating at large banquets. But instead of only thinking of them as formal and ceremonious, we should see them as adding an element of fun and individuality to a table. The novel designs on the following pages range from comic and colourful to pretty and elegant, so they can be used in either formal or casual settings.

Placemats are simple to make and they can be matched to any party theme. They are the perfect alternative to a tablecloth, and those that are easy to clean are particularly suitable for children's parties.

A harlequin theme prevails in this striking table setting — perfect for a fancy-dress party. The chequered square place card sits in a black-stemmed cocktail glass, with a pink streamer tumbling gracefully over the edge. You can also make papier-mâché *harlequin masks for each guest; or you can just make two and place them back to back to form a centrepiece.*

HARLEQUIN PLACE CARD

FREE-STYLE PLACE CARD

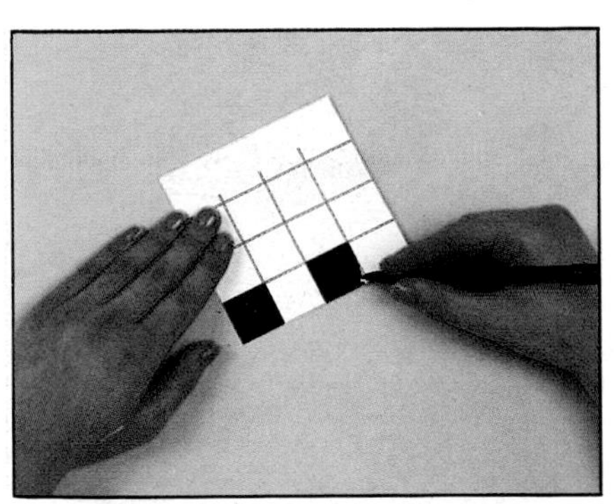

Make cocktail glasses look extra smart with this chequered place card. It matches the black and white setting on page 60. First cut a 7.5cm (3in) square from a piece of stiff white cardboard. Use a pencil and ruler to mark off 2.5cm (1in) divisions and join these up to form a grid. Colour in alternate squares with a black felt pen to give a chequer-board pattern.

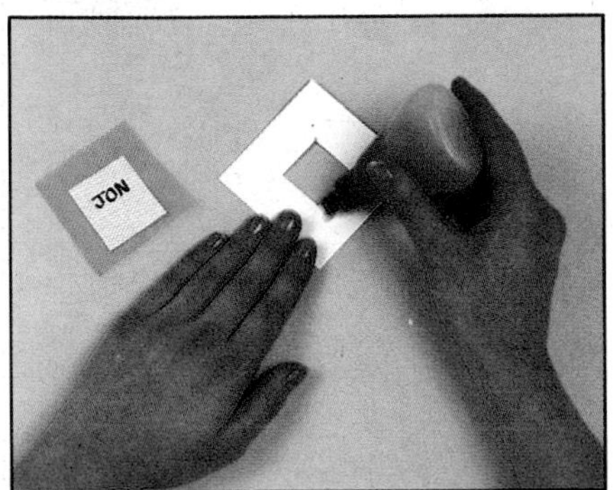

On a 5cm (2in) square of cardboard write the name. Cut out a 6cm-(2½in)-square piece of pink net fabric; set it aside. Using a sharp craft knife, cut out the centre of the chequered card to leave a hole 2.5cm (1in) square. Turn the card over and apply some glue around the edges of the hole.

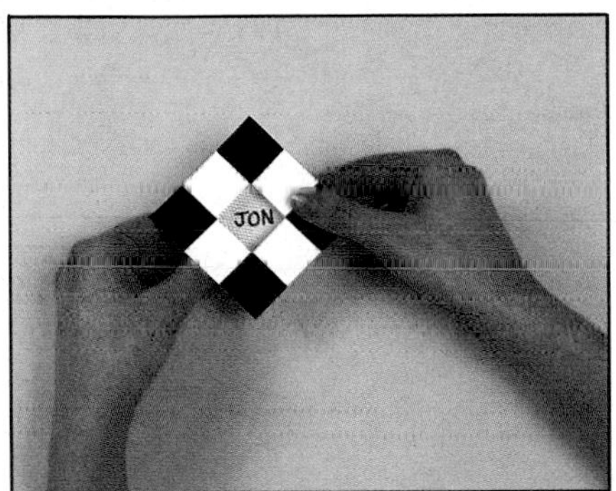

Place the piece of net over the card with the name, and hold them together in one hand while positioning the chequered card diagonally over the top. Press firmly to apply the glue to all three surfaces. Leave the card to dry for a few minutes.

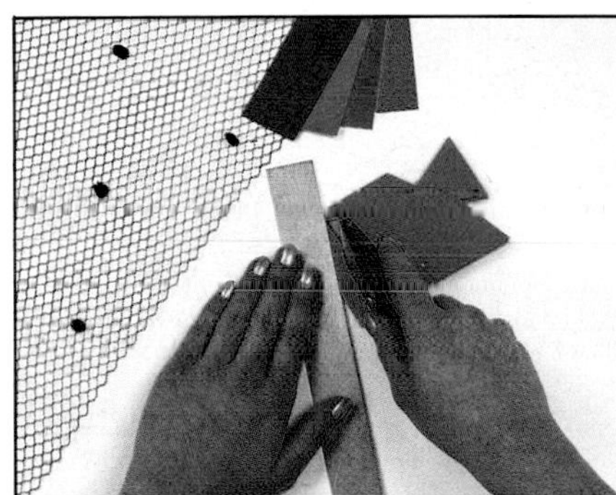

This original place card is simple to make using different colours of stiff paper and scraps of net. First cut a rectangle out of lightweight cardboard, twice the depth of the finished card; fold it in half. Using a craft knife and a steel ruler, cut sections of the card away to create an irregular edge. The cards can be any shape; in fact, it is more fun if they all look a little different.

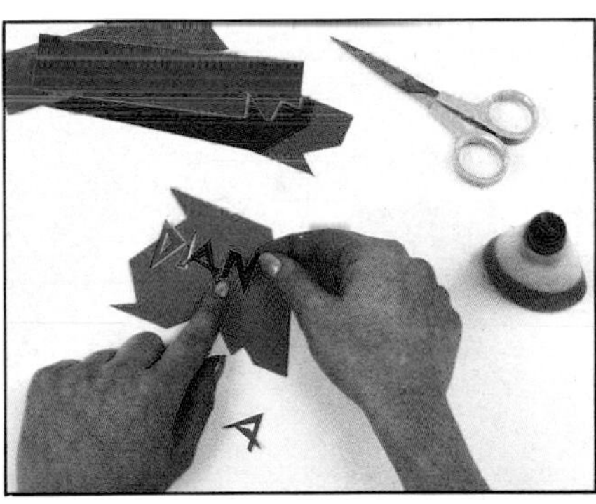

From the coloured paper cut the letters to spell each guest's name. Don't try to cut rounded shapes, as this is more difficult. It may be easier to make some letters from two pieces. For a letter A, for example, cut a V shape, turn it upside down, and add a separate strip for the crossbar. Glue the letters in place.

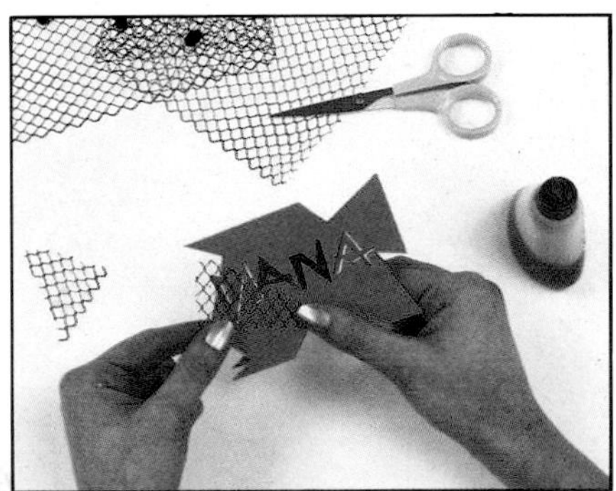

Cut irregular pieces from a scrap of net, and lightly glue these in place over the name. Place each card on a plate on top of a folded napkin, as shown.

FLORAL PLACE CARD

This charming place card looks especially good on floral china. Cut the posies from Victorian floral transfers, or from magazines, seed catalogues or greeting cards.

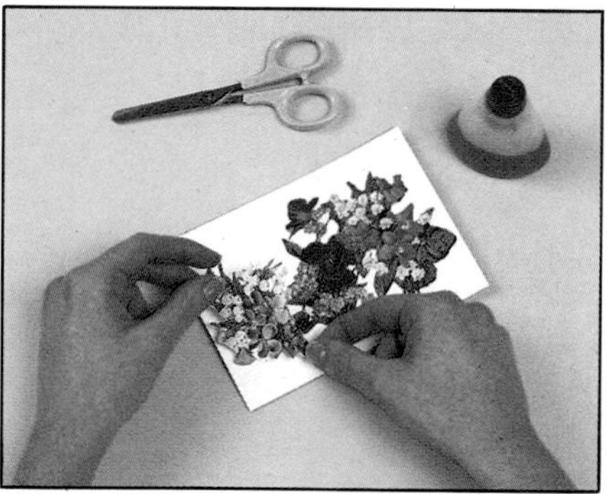

Cut a piece of thin white cardboard about 10 by 8cm (4 by 3in). Group the flower shapes on the card as shown. Once you have created a pleasing arrangement, glue the shapes in place on the card. Set it aside to dry.

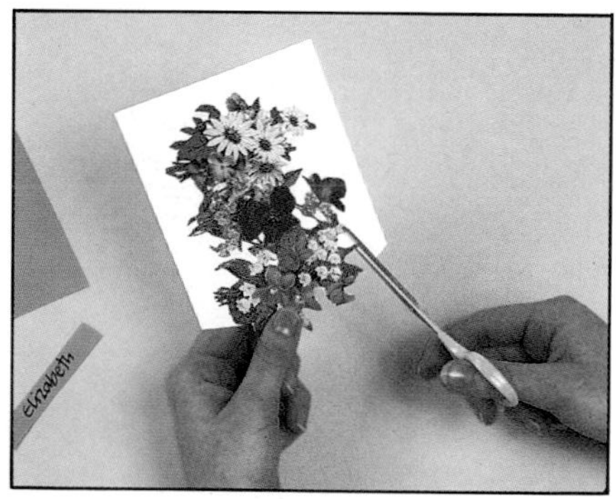

Cut a strip of pastel-coloured stiff paper, and write the name on it. Set it aside. Cut around the flower shapes, leaving a 1cm (½in) strip of white cardboard along the bottom. Fold this backwards to form a stand for the place card. A tiny posy of dried lavender can be placed on each plate alongside the card.

RICEPAPER FANS PLACE CARD

Tiny pleated fans decorate these pastel place cards. From pale pastel stiff paper cut a rectangle about 9 by 12cm (3½ by 5in). From darker paper cut a rectangle about 5mm (¼in) shorter and narrower. Cut several thin strips from a sheet of ricepaper, and fold them concertina-style as shown.

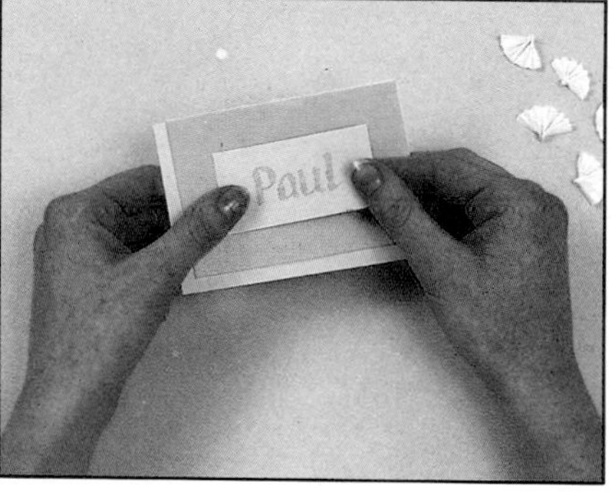

Allowing 10 or 12 folds per fan, snip the folded strips into several pieces. Pinch them at one end to form tiny fans. Fold the two rectangles in half, and place the darker one over the other. Lightly glue them in place. Cut a small rectangle from the paler paper for the name; glue it onto the front of the card.

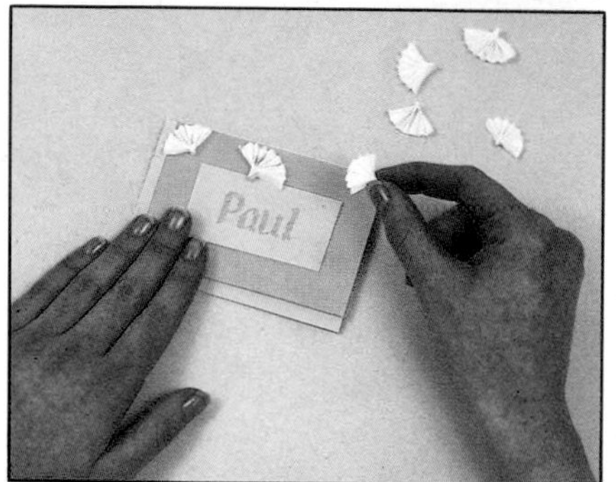

Put several dabs of glue on the card and glue the fans in place as shown.

COLOURFUL CUPCAKES

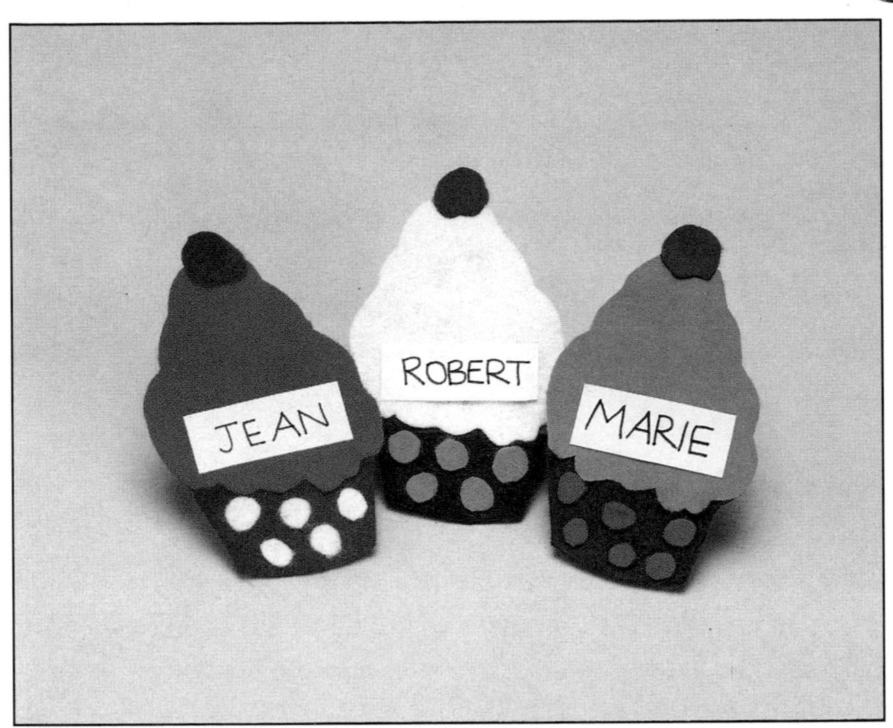

To break the ice at a kids' party — iced cupcake name badges. The template for the pieces is on page 91. Cut each cake shape from thin cardboard as a base for the felt. Then cut out the top and bottom pieces, again in cardboard.

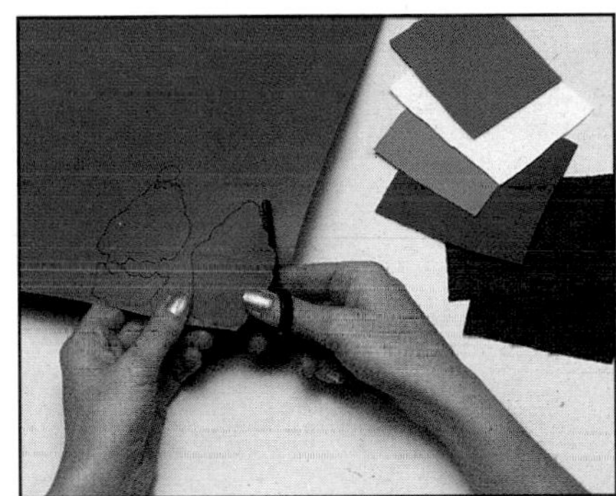

Glue the latter pieces to different colours of felt and cut around them. Now glue these separate pieces to the base card.

Finish off by sticking a name label to the front of the bun and a little double-sided tape to the back. When the little guests arrive simply tear off the backing from the tape and label them!

COLLAGE PLACE CARD

This collage place card can be made from wrapping paper and scraps of plain stiff paper. Select a gift-wrapping paper with a design that is appropriate to the theme of your party and plain paper in a harmonizing colour. Cut a rectangle of the plain paper about 14 by 9cm (5½ by 3½in) and fold it in half as shown.

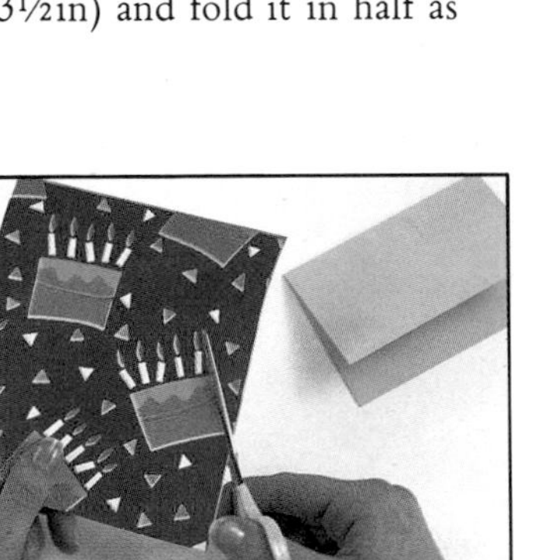

Cut around the shape you have decided to use and stick this to the card with double-sided tape or glue.

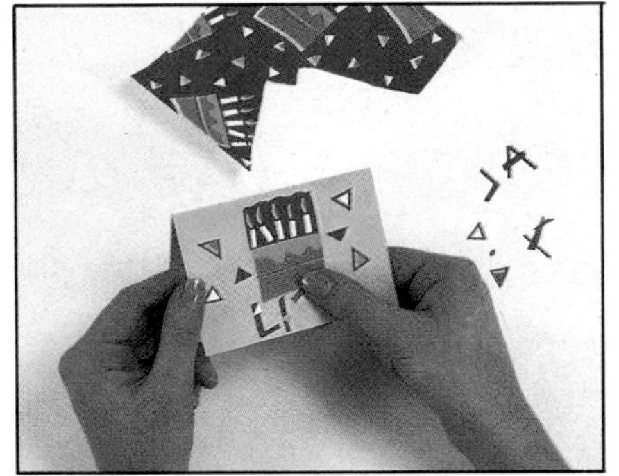

Stick additional shapes onto the card as desired. Put double-sided tape onto the back of a small area of the wrapping paper, and cut thin strips with which to make up the names. Peel off the backing and attach the strips to the card to form the letters.

KITE PLACE CARDS

These colourful place cards are perfect for a children's party. For each kite you will need stiff paper in two colours. From each colour cut two rectangles, each 10 by 15cm (4 by 6in). Draw a line down the centre, then another line at right angles across it, 5cm (2in) from one end. Join up the points, then cut off the four corners; set them aside.

Use two of the corners of the red card to decorate the yellow kite, glueing them in place as shown. Similarly, use two of the leftover pieces of the yellow card to decorate the red kite. Write the name on each kite.

Cut out squares of coloured tissue, allowing three for each kite. On the back of each kite, glue a 40cm (16in) strip of thin ribbon. Pinch the squares of tissue together in the centre and tie the ribbon around them. Cut a small strip of cardboard, fold it in two and glue it to the back of the kite; use this hook to attach the kite to a glass.

TEDDY BEARS' PICNIC

Teddy not only tells the little ones where to sit, but can be taken home afterwards as a little party gift. Draw a teddy shape using your favourite bear as inspiration and folding the paper at the top to produce a double shape as shown. Cut the shape from a spongy textured paper or from felt. Now glue this to some brown cardboard and carefully cut around it.

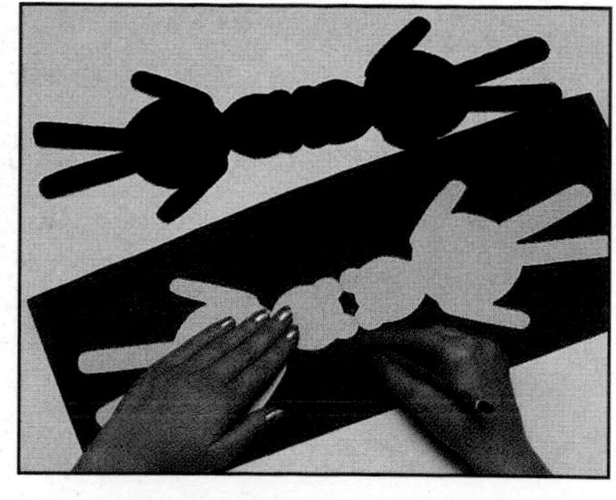

Now cut out two yellow circular tummies, some pink ears and paws — the forepaws slightly smaller than the back ones — black and white eyes and black noses, all from felt. The mouth is a tiny piece of black yarn. Glue all these in place.

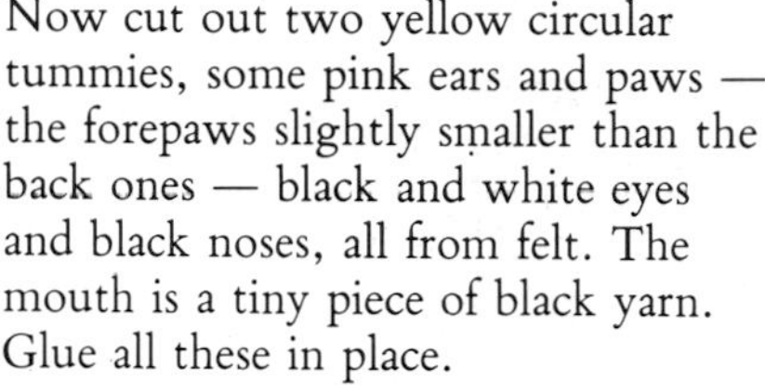

Fold the teddies in half across the ears, and stick a label on each tummy with the child's name written on it.

EASTER PLACE MARKER

This unusual place marker is perfect for an Easter table. Pierce the top of an egg with a pin and the bottom with a darning needle, plunging the needle well in to break the yolk. Hold the egg over a cup and blow through the smaller hole, forcing the contents out through the bottom. Rinse the shell under a tap. Pencil on the name and design.

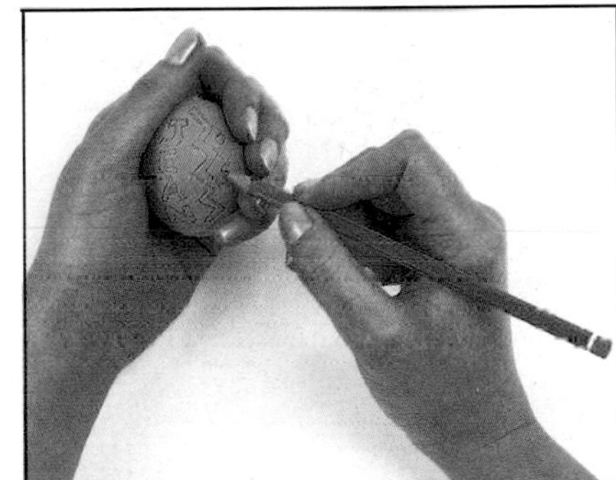

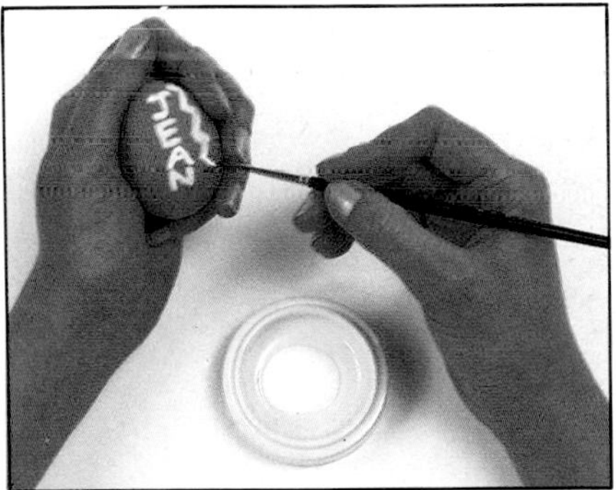

Using a white water-based paint, fill in all the areas that will be painted in light colours. This will help to ensure that the colours are true.

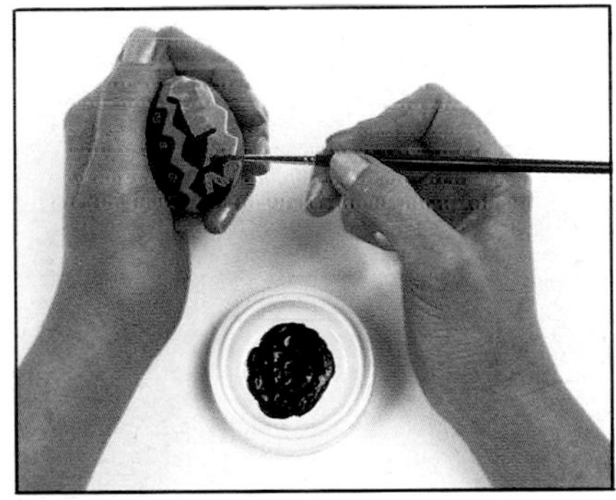

Use your chosen colours to paint over the white areas. There's no need to worry if the outline is untidy, since the darker background will cover all the edges. Finally, paint the background in a dark colour.

CUTOUT PLACE CARD

Bold cutout letters complement a modern table setting. Use white cardboard against coloured napkins, or vice versa. On a sheet of tracing paper, draw two guidelines about 8cm (3in) apart. This will be the height of the letters. Use a ruler to help you draw the name, making sure that each letter is linked to the next.

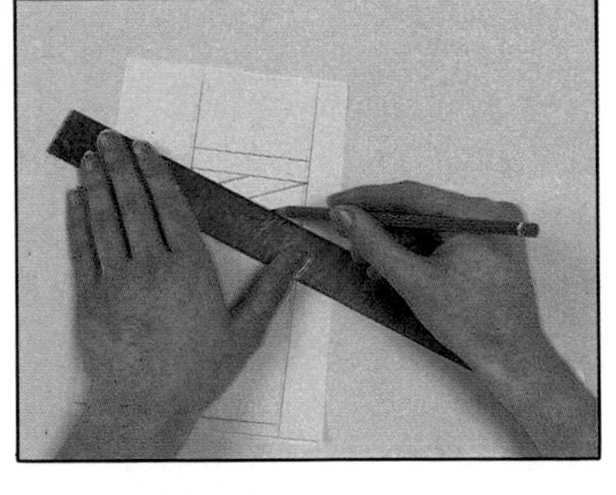

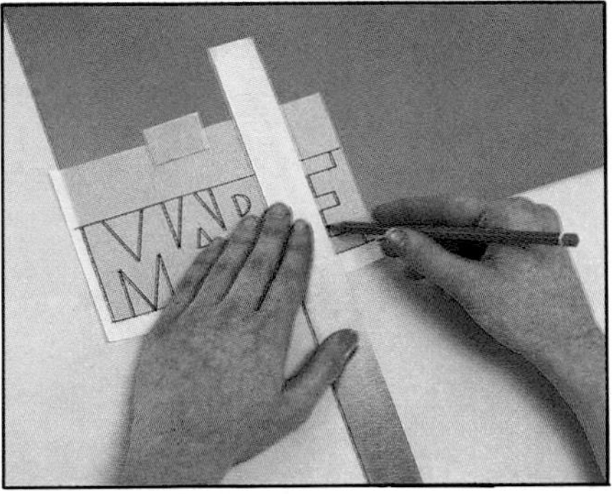

Lay the traced name on a sheet of thin cardboard, and secure it in place with masking tape. Draw over all the letters again, using a hard lead pencil or ball-point pen to make an imprint on the cardboard.

Remove the tracing paper. Cut the name out of the cardboard, using a ruler and a sharp craft knife. Take care to follow the imprinted lines exactly, for an incorrect cut might result in the letters becoming detached from each other.

VALENTINE PLACE CARD

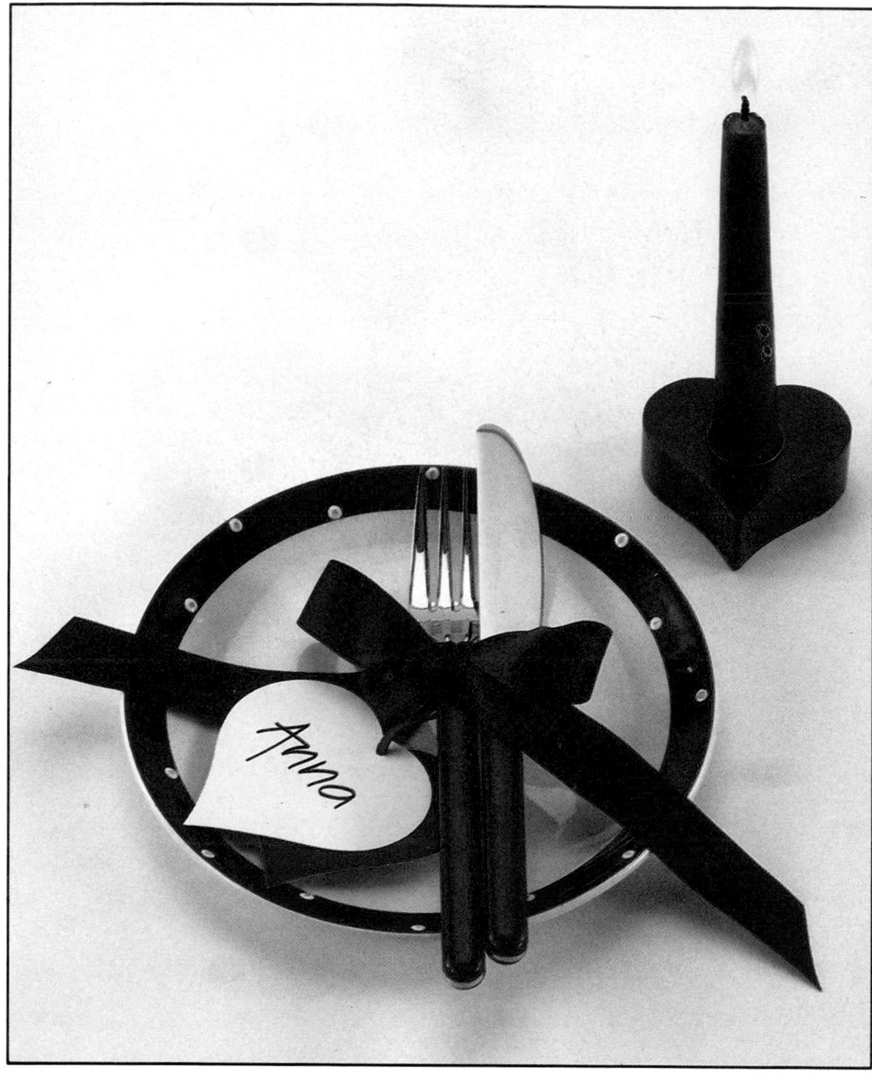

Heart-shaped place cards are perfect for a romantic dinner or Valentine's Day supper. Using the template provided, trace heart shapes onto shiny red and plain white lightweight cardboard, and carefully cut them out.

Write the person's name on the white heart. Punch or cut a hole at the top of each heart, and thread a thin red ribbon through the hole. To add the finishing touches, tie the cutlery together with a wider ribbon, making a pretty bow. Then loosely tie the place cards to the bow, securing the cutlery as shown above.

GINGERBREAD MAN ENVELOPE

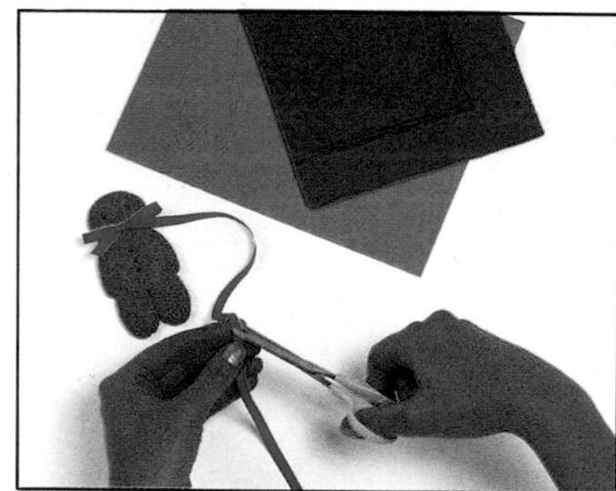

Sure to be a hit with children, each little gingerbread man is tucked into a napkin and has his own place card 'shadow'. Copy the shape of the gingerbread man onto stiff coloured paper; set it aside. Using a length of thin satin ribbon, tie a bow around the neck of the gingerbread man, leaving an end about 15cm (6in) long.

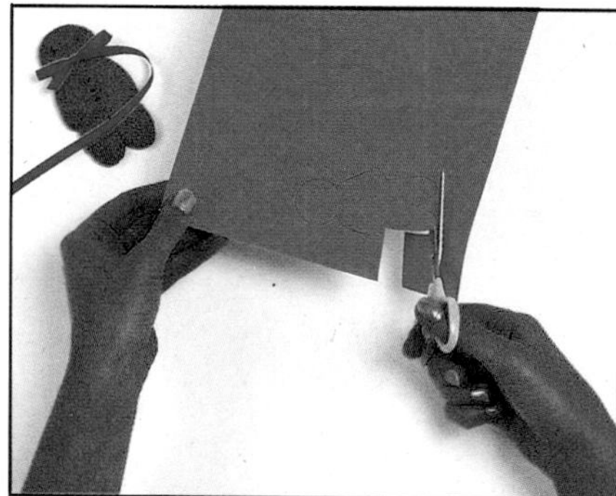

Cut the ends of the ribbon into points by folding them double and cutting a diagonal across the fold. Cut the drawn shape from the coloured paper.

Write the child's name on the shape. Apply a dab of glue and stick the card shape onto the ribbon. Fold back one corner of a bright-coloured paper napkin to make an envelope for the gingerbread man.

TARTAN PLACE CARD

For a traditional Hogmanay or Burns Night celebration, make tartan place cards for your guests. Use plaid ribbon and either white or coloured lightweight cardboard, and add a kilt pin for the finishing touch.

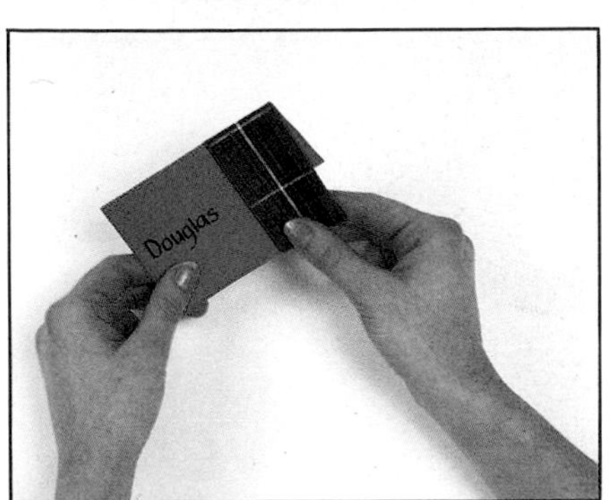

Cut a rectangle of cardboard about 10 by 12cm (4 by 5in), or a size to fit the plate. Fold it in half, and write the name on the left-hand side. Cut a piece of ribbon to edge the card front and back, allowing a little extra to turn under the edges.

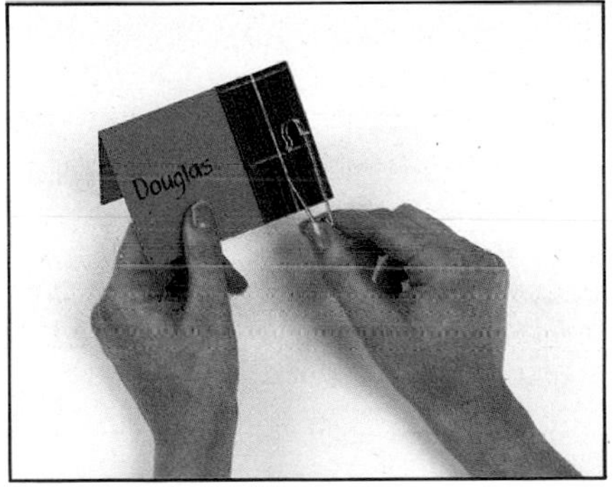

Stick ribbon onto the card with fabric glue, folding the excess underneath as shown. Pin the kilt pin through the ribbon and card to complete the authentically Scottish look.

TEDDY PLACE MARKER

For a children's party at Christmas or any time of the year, this ingenious place marker is sure to be a winner. First, cut two boot shapes from bright-coloured felt, making sure that they are large enough to enclose a chocolate teddy or other favour. Stick the shapes together with fabric glue, leaving the top open.

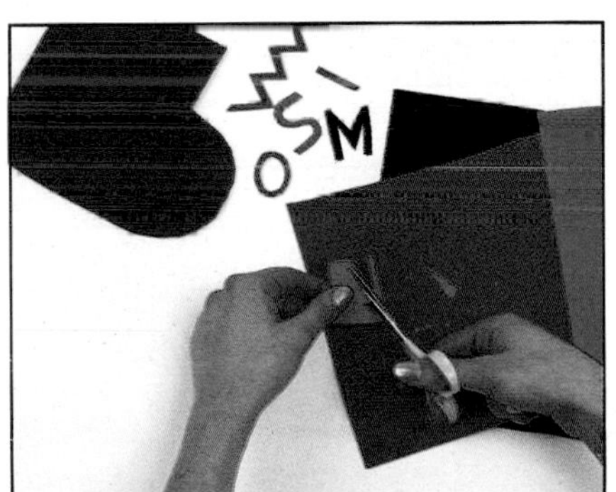

From contrasting felt, cut a zigzag strip for the upper edge and some letters to make the name.

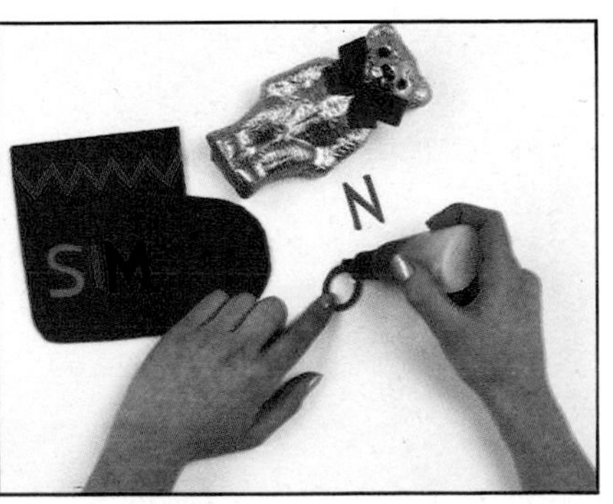

Glue the strip and the letters to the boot as shown. Finally, insert the chocolate teddy into the boot.

PRETTY PVC PLACEMAT

Attractive and simple to make these PVC (vinyl) placemats will also readily wipe clean. Cut a 30cm (12in) square from a sheet of thick cardboard. Take the diagonal measurement of the square — 42.5cm (17in) for this size mat — and mark a square of that size on the wrong side of the PVC; cut it out.

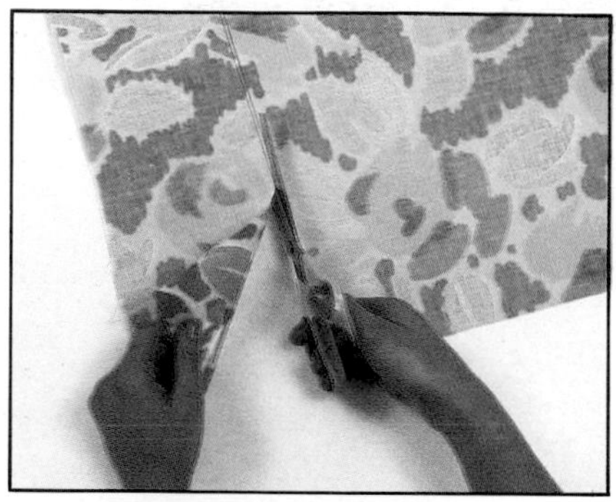

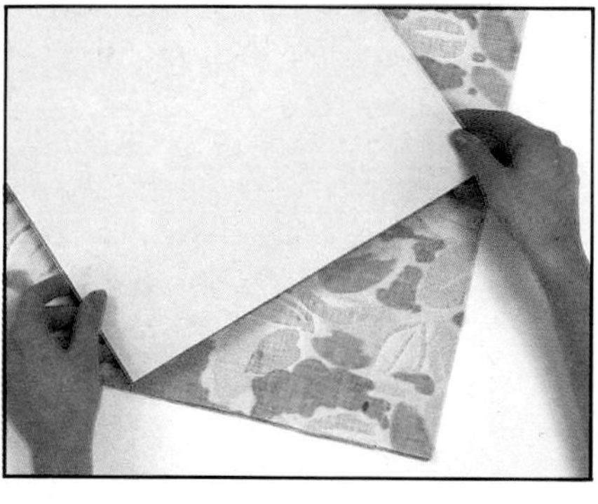

Place the cardboard square diagonally on the larger square of PVC. Spread a strong glue all over the cardboard and also on the exposed triangles of PVC. Allow them to dry until tacky.

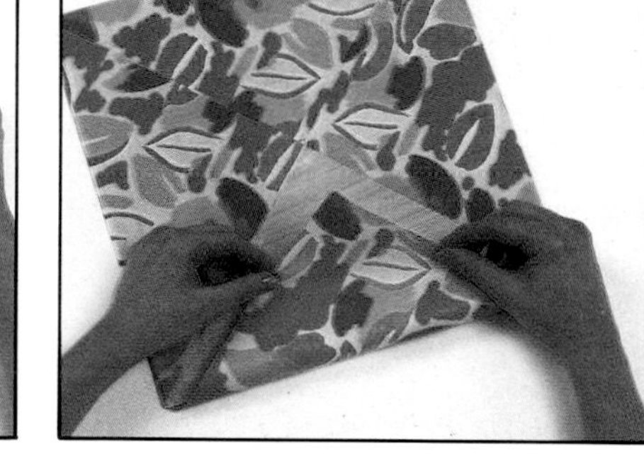

Fold each triangle of PVC into the centre of the cardboard square so that they all meet. Press them firmly in place on the surface with a soft cloth to ensure that there are no air bubbles.

LACE-TRIMMED PLACEMAT

Delicate lace edging and pastel ribbon give a pretty, feminine look to a place setting. Use a plain white handkerchief, or hem a piece of fabric about 30cm (12in) square. Cut a length of lace trimming approximately 130cm (50in) long, and sew it around the edge of the fabric, gathering it at each corner and joining the ends neatly.

Cut four lengths of 1cm- (3/8in-) wide ribbon and stick them down along the join with double-sided tape. (See page 70 for instructions on mitring corners.)

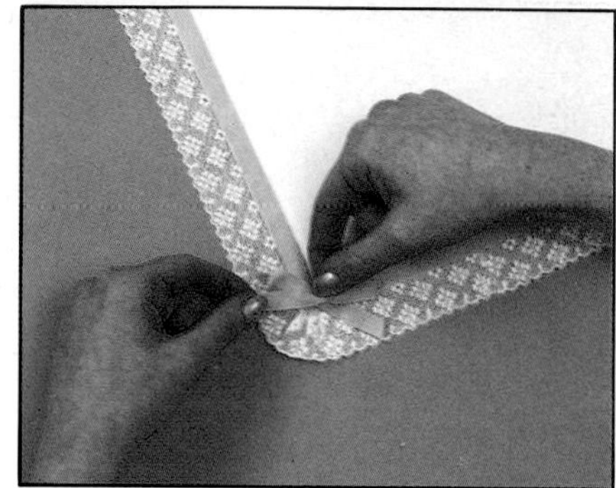

Cut a 20cm (8in) length of ribbon and tie it in a bow; trim the ends neatly. Attach it to the corner of the mat with double-sided tape, or sew it on with a few stitches. The ribbon can easily be removed when the mat needs washing.

GO FOR GOLD

Give a touch of luxury to plain white china by using a larger gold plate underneath each dinner plate. You will need some old white china plates, about 1.5 to 2.5cm (½ to 1in) wider all around than your dinner plates, a few ivy leaves (at Christmas use holly and mistletoe as well), gold spray paint and a few gold or silver dragées.

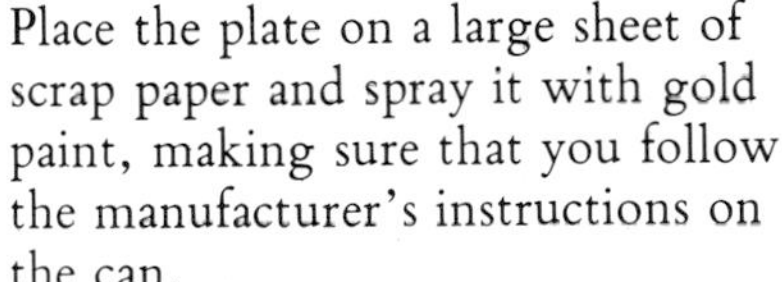

Place the plate on a large sheet of scrap paper and spray it with gold paint, making sure that you follow the manufacturer's instructions on the can.

Lay the holly and ivy leaves on a sheet of scrap paper and coat them with gold paint. Leave them to dry for 10 to 15 minutes, and then arrange the painted leaves on the smaller white plate with an unsprayed sprig of mistletoe for contrast. Add a few silver dragées for the finishing touch.

GLITTER TREE PLACEMAT

This sparkling placemat is an obvious winner for Christmas. First draw a Christmas tree on the reverse (matt) side of a piece of shiny green cardboard. The length should be about 10cm (4in) longer than the diameter of your dinner plate and the width about 20cm (8in) wider. Cut out the mat using a craft knife and a steel ruler.

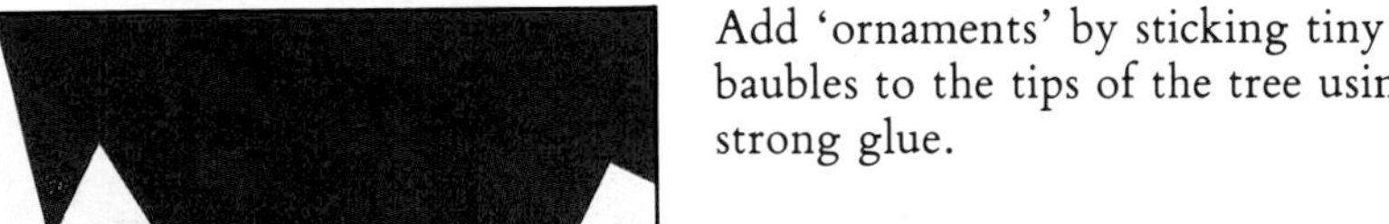

Add 'ornaments' by sticking tiny baubles to the tips of the tree using strong glue.

Cut out or buy a star shape to put at the top of the tree. Finally, stick small silver stars over the mat. Or, if you prefer, just scatter the stars freely over the mat, first positioning each mat on the table.

COLOUR-FLECKED PLACEMAT

The perfect solution if you can't find tablemats in the right colour — paint your own, using plain cork tablemats and two colours of water-based paint. For applying the paint you will need an artist's paintbrush and a natural sponge.

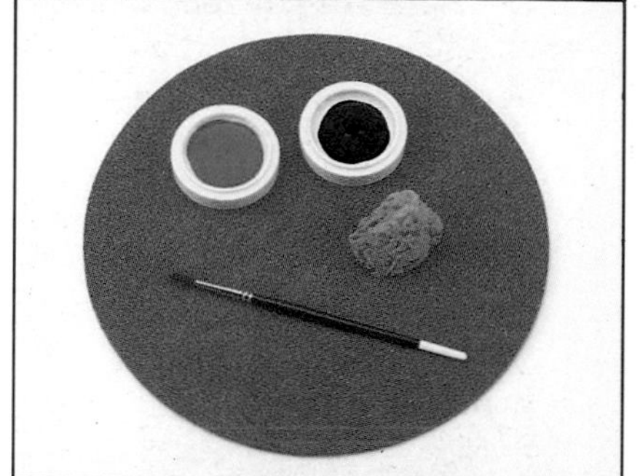

Paint the cork mat all over with the lighter-coloured paint. Allow it to dry. If the colour is very pale you may need to apply a second coat.

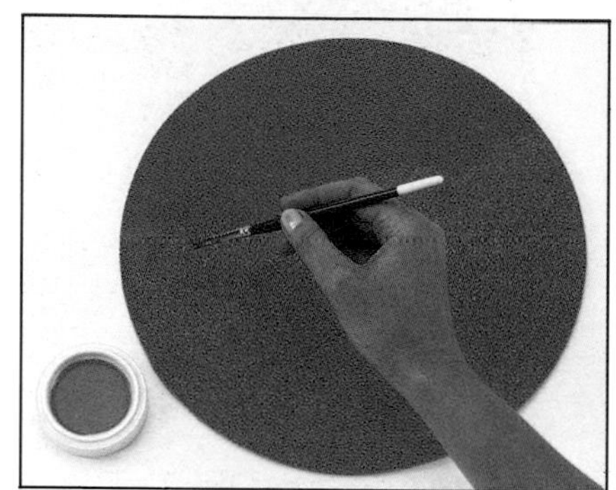

Dip the sponge into a saucer containing the colour; dab it a few times on a piece of scrap paper to remove any excess paint. Sponge the mat all over, allowing the first paint colour to show through. When the paint is dry apply a coat of clear polyurethane varnish for protection.

INSTANT PLACEMAT

Jolly up a plastic or paper tablecloth for a children's party by using colourful strips of ribbon to mark out individual place settings. All you need, besides the tablecloth, is 1.3m (50in) of patterned ribbon for each setting and some double-sided tape.

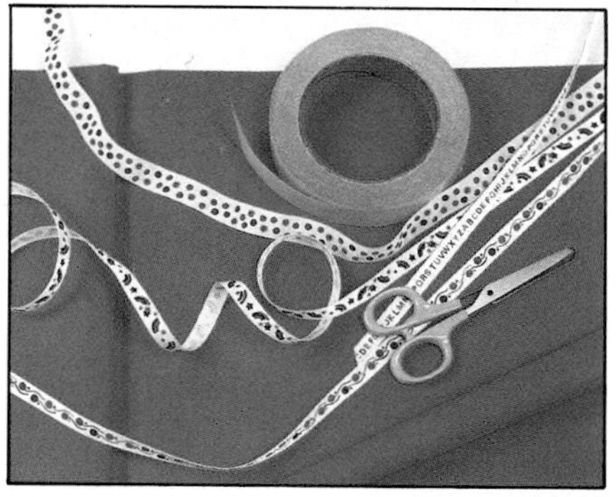

For each setting draw a 30cm (12in) square on the tablecloth. Use a ruler and set square (right-angled triangle) for accuracy. Cut the ribbon into four equal lengths. Stick tape onto the back of each ribbon and remove the backing. Stick the ribbon onto the cloth, overlapping it at the corners as shown and smoothing it just enough to hold it in place.

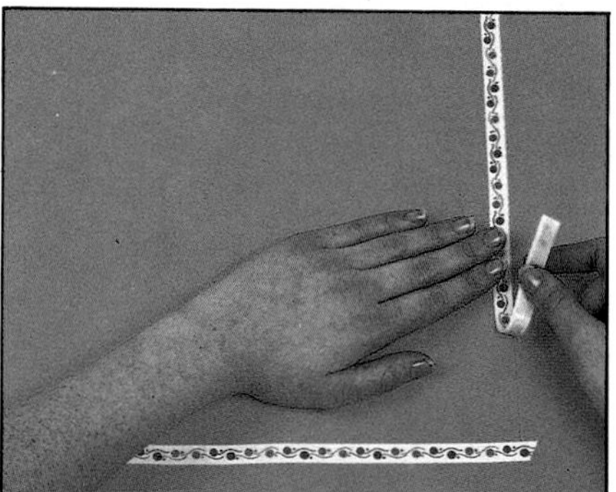

Where the ribbons overlap, at the corners, lift them gently and cut diagonally across them to give a neatly mitred corner. When you have trimmed each corner, run a finger along the ribbons, sticking them firmly in place.

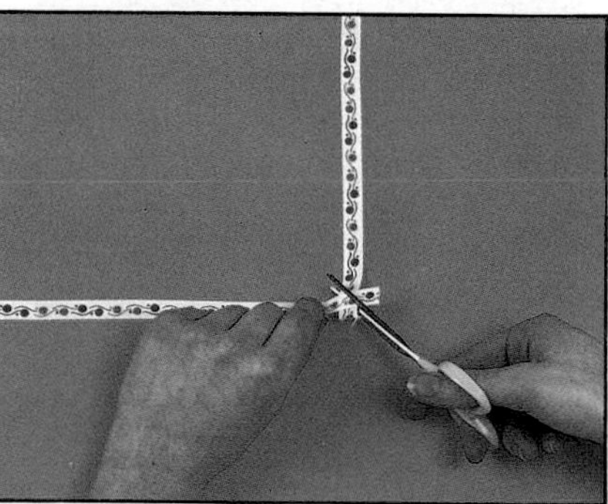

PICNIC TRÈS CHIC

HARLEQUIN PLACEMAT

Convenient and stylish, too, this placemat roll wraps up each person's cutlery and napkin until needed. For each roll you will need a quilted cotton placemat and matching napkin and three co-ordinating ribbons, about 55cm (22in) long.

Lay the placemat flat, wrong side up. Lay the napkin and cutlery on top, then roll them up together as shown.

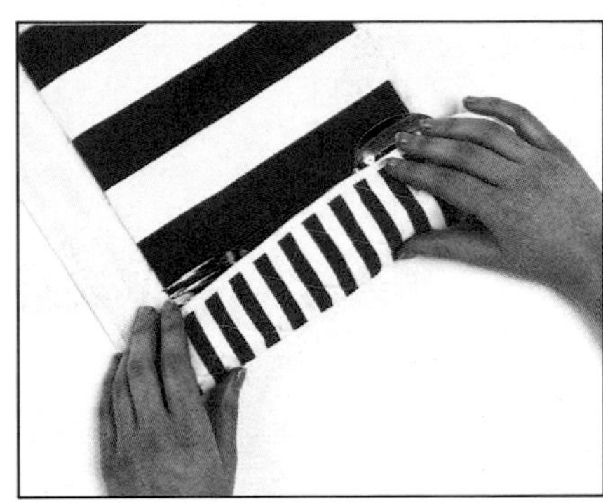

Trim the ends of the ribbons diagonally. Lay the roll on top of the ribbons and tie them around it into a bow.

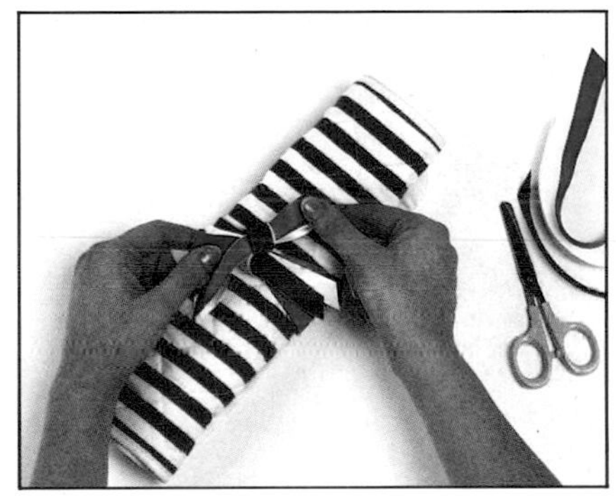

This unusual placemat is easily made from cardboard and a wallpaper border. A black and white border has been chosen to co-ordinate with the table setting on page 60. Cut a 30cm (12in) square from a sheet of thick cardboard, using a steel rule and craft knife to ensure precision.

Cut the border into four strips, allowing a little extra on each strip for trimming. Apply double-sided tape to the back of each strip, but do not peel off the protective backing yet. Lay two adjacent strips in place; where they meet at the corners, try to match the pattern repeat. Holding one strip on top of the other, cut diagonally across the corner.

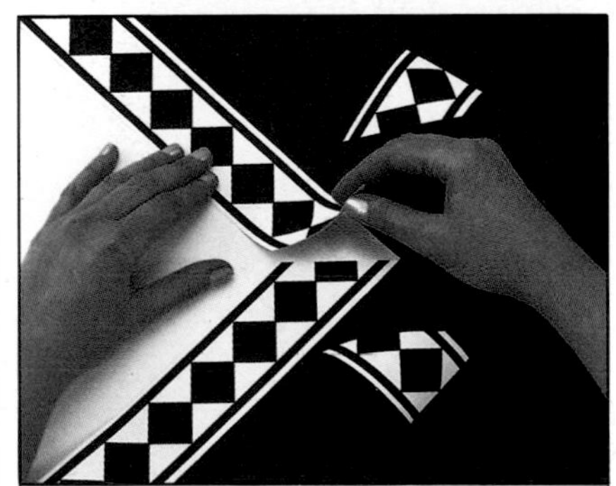

Holding each strip in place along its inner edge, begin to peel back the protective paper from the double-sided tape, as shown. Rub a soft cloth along the border as you peel to stick it in place.

HATS AND MASKS

Hats are great fun to wear and to make, and the basic techniques are very useful to know, for with them you can make the headgear to go with practically any fancy dress costume. This section includes basic shapes and more complicated papier-mâché designs. Masks add the finishing touch to any costume and can also serve as a disguise. A useful fact about making masks is that the measurement from pupil to pupil is virtually the same for everyone: 6.5cm (2½in).

JOKEY JESTER

To make this jaunty jester's cap, first draw a graph paper pattern, using the template on page 91. The inner marked line is to be used for wadding (batting). Cut the red satin in two and place both pieces together, satin side upwards. Overlay the pattern and cut the satin double thickness, allowing a 1cm (3/8in) seam allowance along the straight, centre edge.

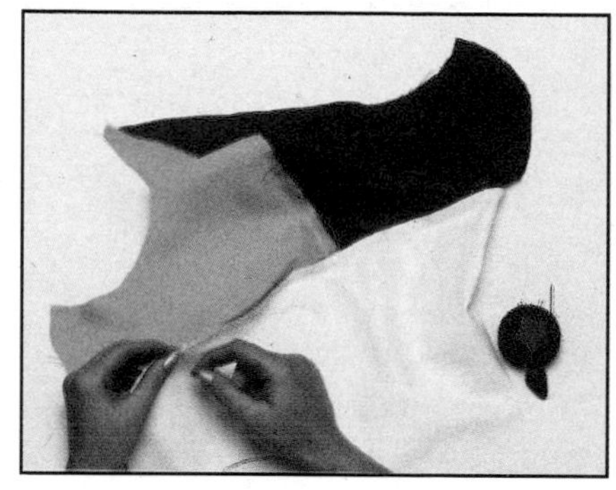

Repeat for the yellow satin. Use the main pattern against a fold to cut out two pieces of white lining fabric, and then use the smaller, inner pattern to cut two pieces of lightweight wadding (batting). Sew red and yellow sections together, then join them to the lining along the lower edge as shown. Fold the lining over the satin along the seam line, placing wrong sides together.

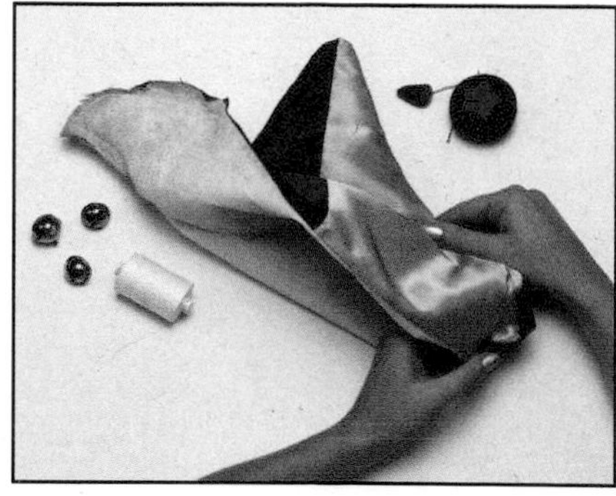

Slip each piece of wadding between the lining and satin, and pin all of the pieces together, with the satin on the inside. Sew them together, 1cm (3/8in) from the raw edges. Turn the cap right side out, pushing out the points. Finish it by sewing a jingle bell to each point.

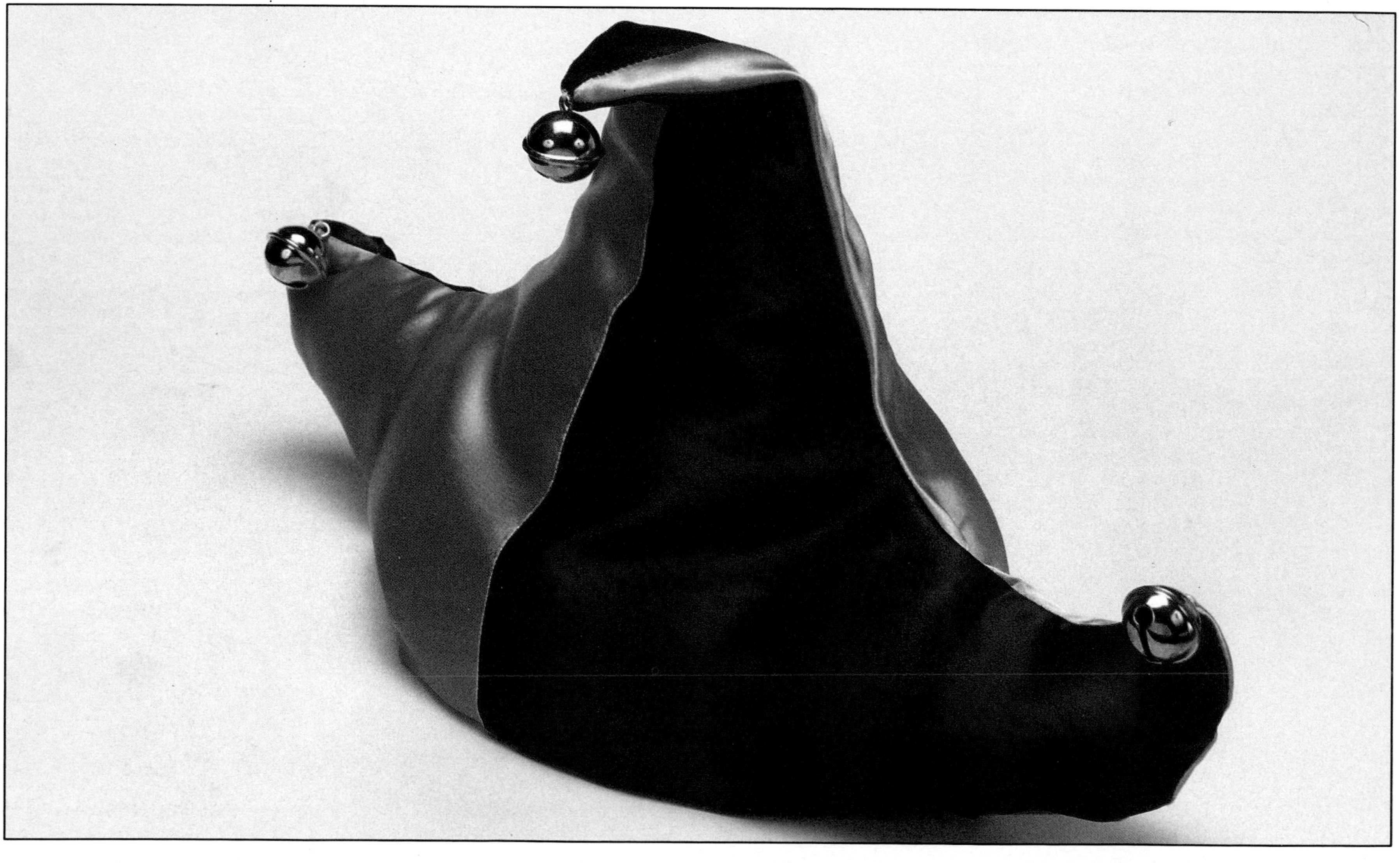

CLOWNING AROUND

Feel free to act the clown in this colourful hat. First of all, make a papier-mâché mould using a pudding basin (small mixing bowl) or plastic microwave dish. (See page 94 for instructions for making paper-mâché). When it is fully dry, remove the mould and paint it with white emulsion (water-based) paint. Sand down any rough edges and give it a second coat of paint.

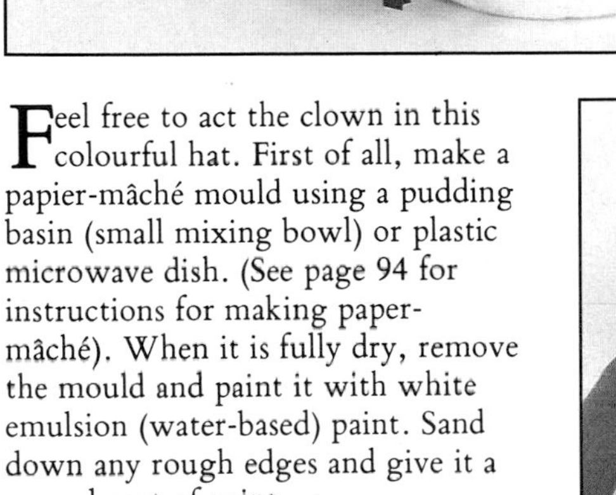

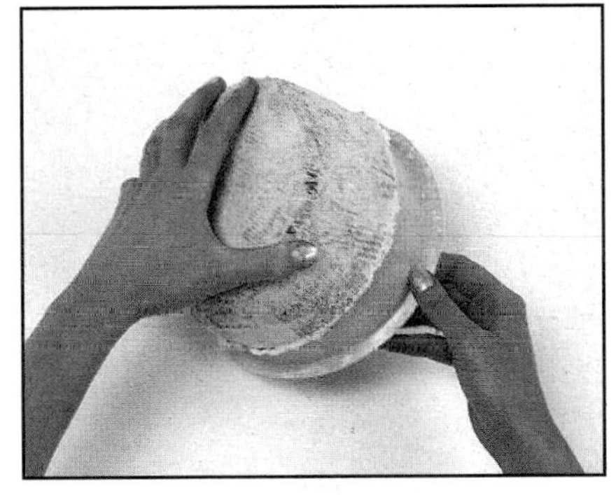

Make the 'hair' from red crepe paper — you will need about six layers of paper, stapled together along the top. Cut the paper into even strips, stopping about 2.5cm (1in) from the stapled edge.

Cut out a brim from light cardboard, allowing about 5cm (2in) for the brim itself and an extra 2.5cm (1in) on the inside for attaching the brim to the crown. Make triangular cuts around the inside of the brim, fold the triangles up and glue them to the inside of the hat. Decorate with a crepe paper band and large coloured spots. Finally, glue the hair to the inside of the hat.

CROWNING GLORY

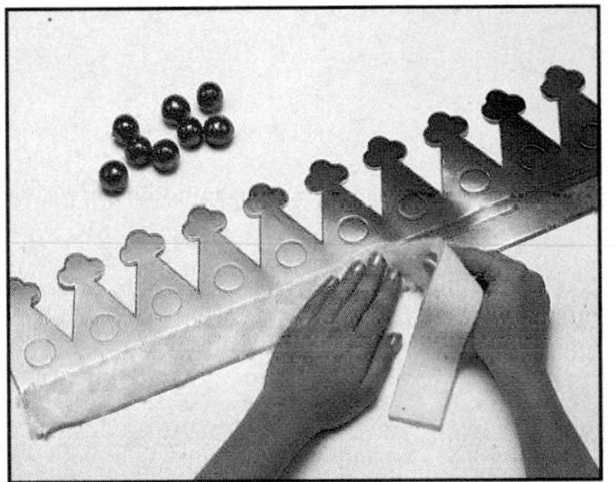

To make the crowns illustrated, we cheated a little by buying a pack of crown strips, which are available at some craft shops. In case you can't get them, there is a choice of templates on page 91. Cut out the crown in gold cardboard, first measuring the person's head for the length. Cut a strip of white fake fur 4cm (1½in) wide, and fix this to the crown with double-sided tape.

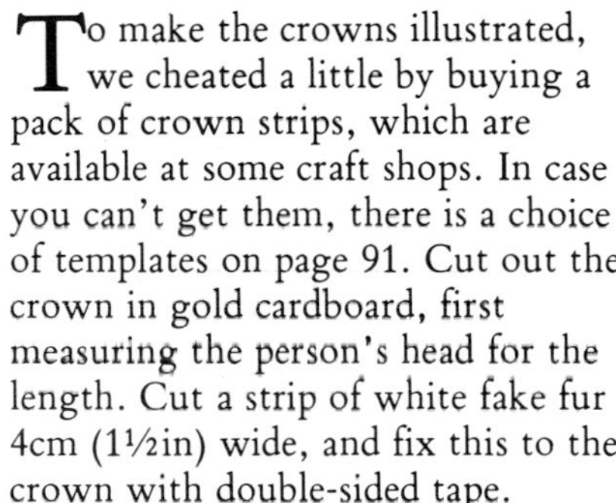

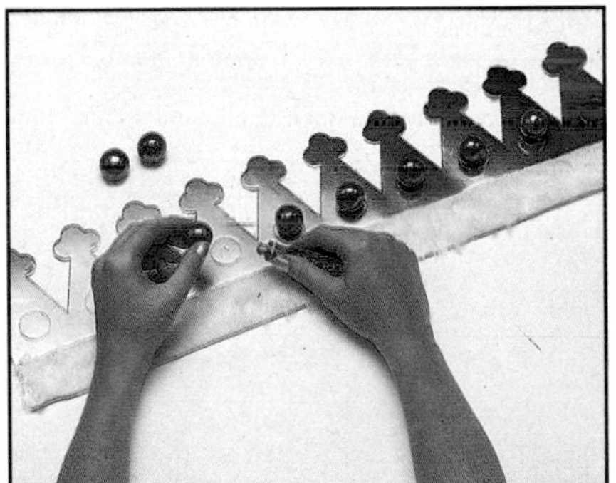

Above the fur glue fake jewels such as these painted wooden beads; if you can't get hold of any, large red sticky-backed spots will do. Now stick the two ends of the crown together with tape on the inside.

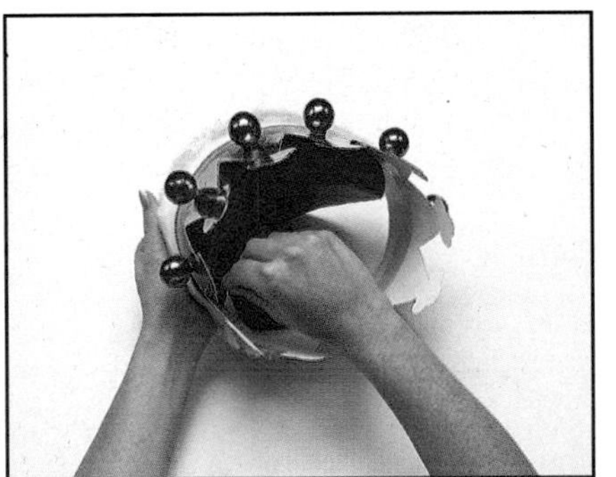

Finally, cut out a circle of red satin (draw around a large dinner plate). Put a strip of double-sided tape on the inside of the crown, and carefully pleat the satin onto it, shiny side up.

WICKED WITCH

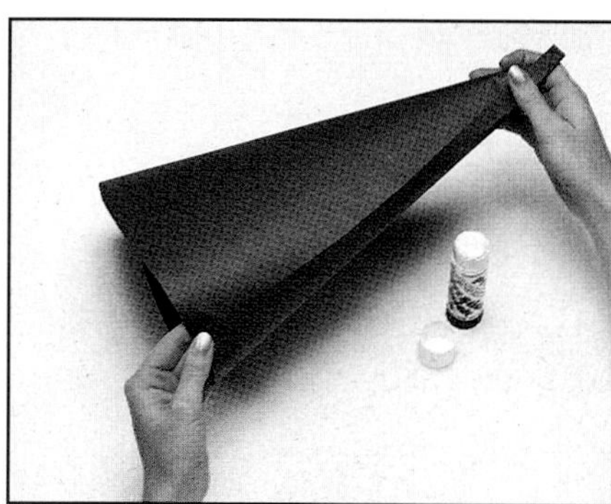

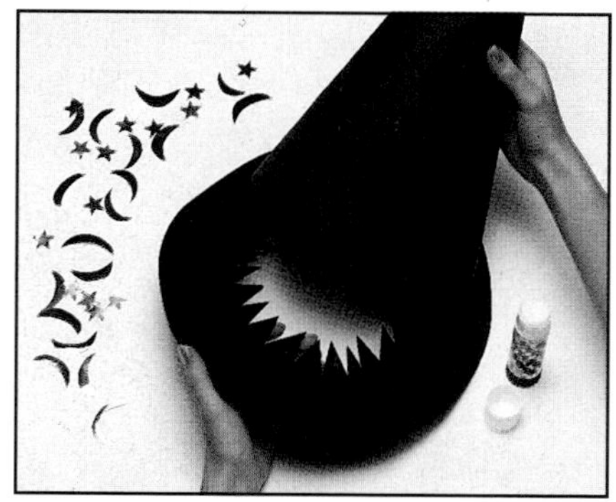

For this you need a large piece of black art paper, 38 by 39.5cm (15 by 15½in). Mark a 1.5cm (½in) border at one end of the longer side so that you have a 38cm (15in) square. Take a compass, string and a white pencil and mark an arc between two corners (see Pierrot Hat for details). Cut along the arc, spread glue on the border, and use this to join the edges of the cone together.

Use the cone to mark a circle on some black cardboard. Draw another line around the first, about 5cm (2in) from it, then another just 2.5cm (1in) inside the first line. Cut along the inner and outer lines, then make triangular cuts on the inside of the brim. Fold them up and glue them to the inside of the cone. Decorate the hat with gold stars and moons cut from sticky-backed plastic.

PIERROT HAT

Cut out a 38cm (15in) square of craft paper and mark a diagonal line between two corners. Then, using a pencil, string and compass, or drawing pin (thumbtack), draw an arc between the other two corners as shown. Cut along the arc. Fold the piece along the diagonal and use it to mark out two pieces of sticky-backed plastic. Add a 1.5cm (½in) border to one straight edge of black plastic.

Cut out the pieces. Peel off the backing and stick the white plastic into position on the paper. Do the same with the black, leaving the backing only on the border. Form a cone, remove the border backing and stick the edges of the cone together. Make two holes along the front join and insert red pom-poms (see page 93). Secure ends on inside with tape.

FASCINATING FEZ

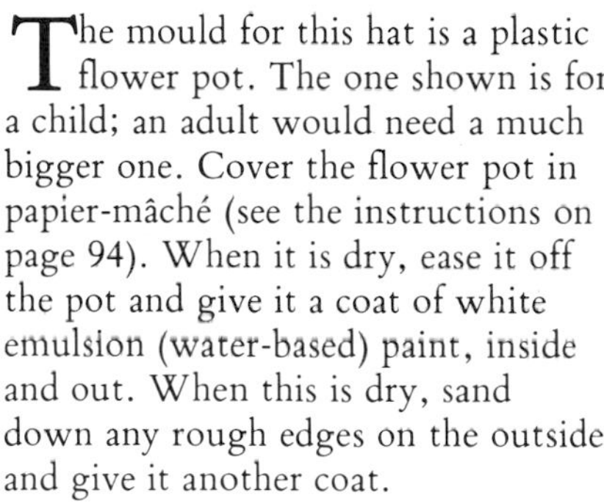

The mould for this hat is a plastic flower pot. The one shown is for a child; an adult would need a much bigger one. Cover the flower pot in papier-mâché (see the instructions on page 94). When it is dry, ease it off the pot and give it a coat of white emulsion (water-based) paint, inside and out. When this is dry, sand down any rough edges on the outside and give it another coat.

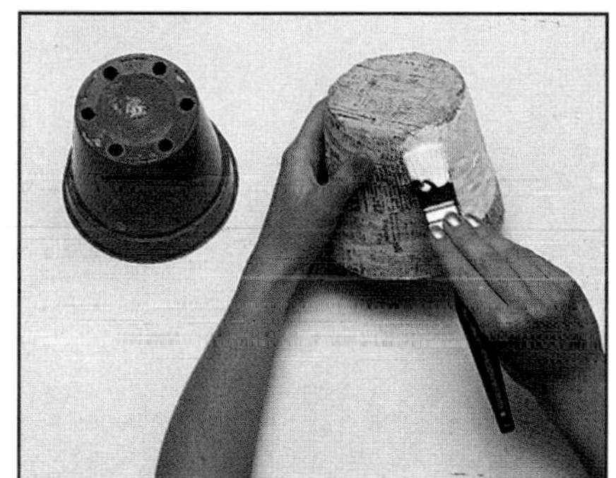

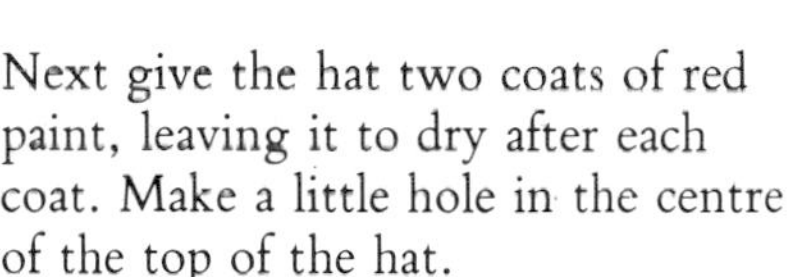

Next give the hat two coats of red paint, leaving it to dry after each coat. Make a little hole in the centre of the top of the hat.

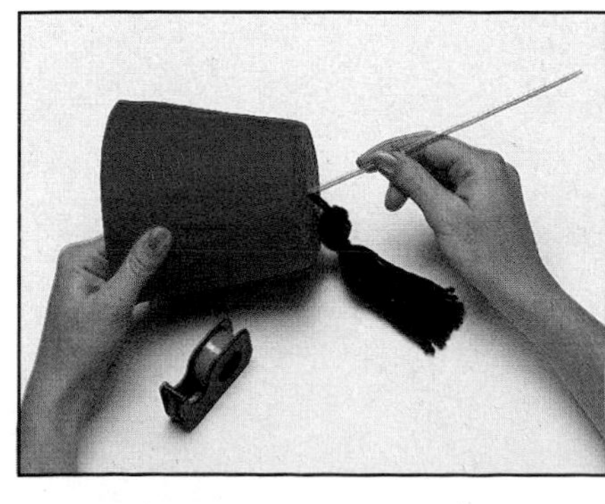

Now make a tassel of black yarn (see the instructions on page 93), and thread it through the top of the hat, fastening it on the inside with a little sticky tape.

JOLLY ROGER

Every would-be pirate should have one of these for dressing up! The template for the hat is on page 92. First cut out two shapes in black art paper or construction paper, and glue them together around the edges. Remember to leave the bottom edges open so that the hat can be put on!

The pattern for the skull and crossbones is superimposed on the hat template. Cut this out in silver paper and glue it to the front of the hat.

Finish the hat with a trimming of silver ribbon on the bottom of each side. For a more permanent hat, you could use felt or fabric stiffened with iron-on interfacing and sew the pieces together.

VICTORIAN BONNET

The pattern pieces for this fetching bonnet are on page 92. From a remnant of summery fabric cut out one back crown piece, one main crown piece and two brim pieces. Also cut out the crown pieces in a plain lining fabric. Make up two crowns, one in each fabric, gathering the main pieces onto the backs. Slip the lining section into the patterned one, wrong sides together.

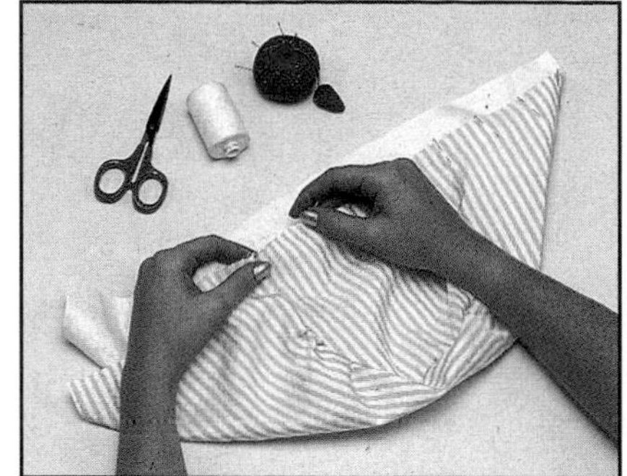

Cut out a paper brim, 1cm (½in) smaller than the fabric pieces all round. Glue one fabric piece to the paper brim along the outer curved edge, folding the edge of the fabric over the paper and sticking it down. Turn in and press the long edge of the other piece of fabric, and glue it on top as shown, leaving the inner edge open.

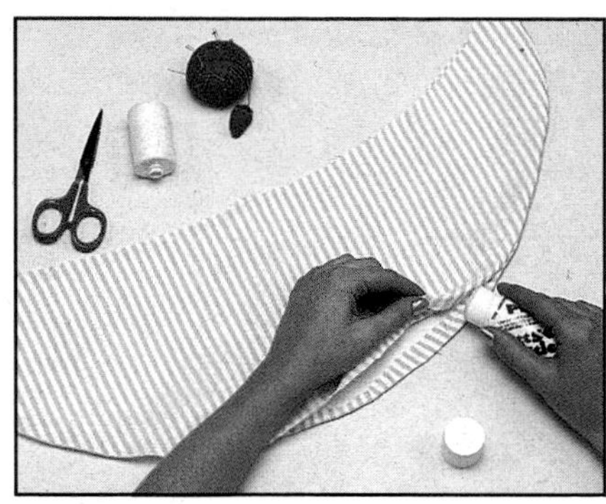

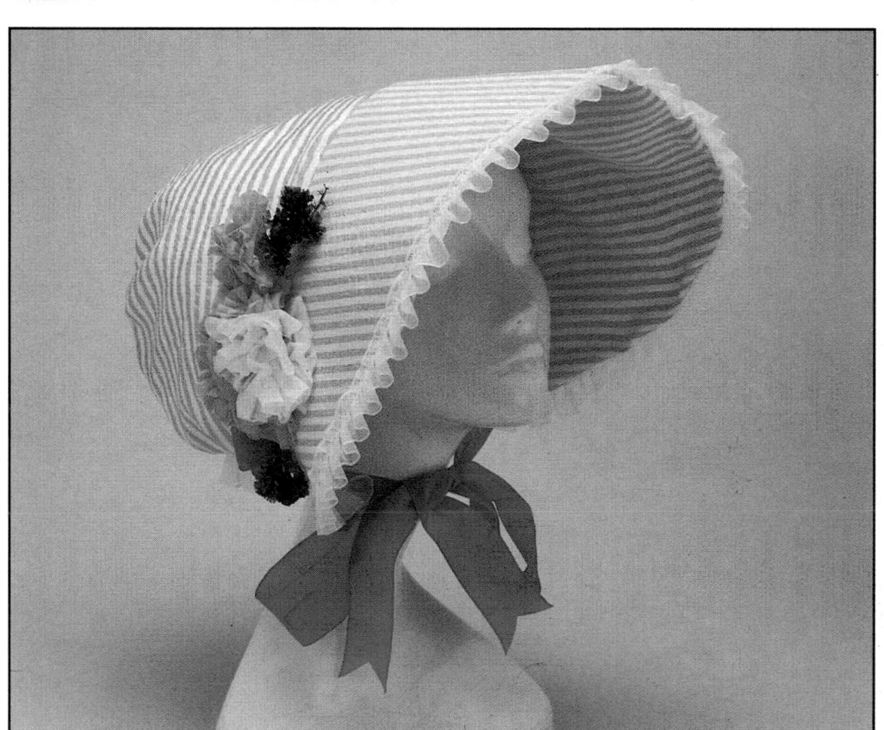

Turn in and press the inner edges of the fabric brim, clipping them as required, and press. Slip the crown inside, and slipstitch the upper brim over it. On the underside, slipstitch the lining over the brim. To finish, sew a lacy edging around the brim and sew ribbons and paper flowers on either side. (Instructions for paper flowers are on page 94.)

MEDIEVAL LADY

This glittery version of the medieval lady's hat, with its net veil, is sure to attract a knight errant. Cut out a 38cm (15in) square of black craft paper. Using a white pencil, string and compass, draw an arc from one corner to another. Cut along the arc.

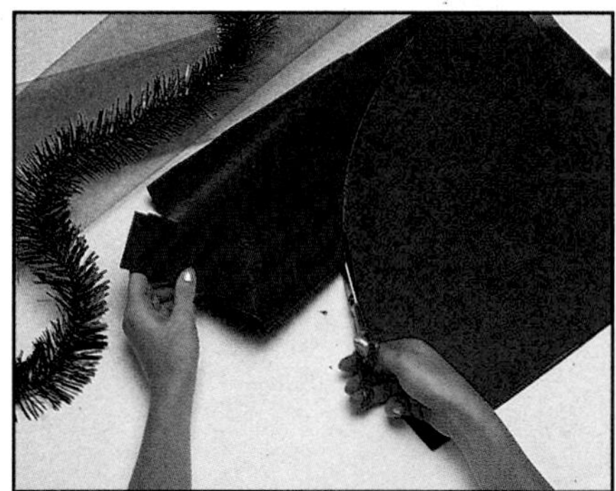

Peel the back off some sticky-backed plastic and stick the black paper down onto it. Cut out the shape, leaving a 1.5cm (½in) border on one straight edge. Use this to stick the hat together.

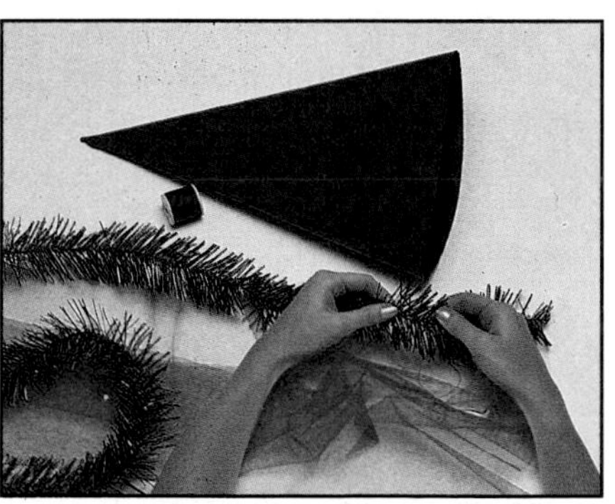

Sew tinsel around the edge of a square of net, then attach this, with a little sticky tape, to the top of the hat. Make sure that the seam in the plastic is at the back. Finally decorate the hat with a few stick-on silver stars.

HARLEQUIN MASKS

For a stunning party mask, buy a ready-moulded mask from a stationer's or toy shop. The half-mask shown here is coloured with oil stencil pencils. Start with the pink; apply a little to a piece of waxed paper, then pick it up on the stencil brush. Using a circular motion, cover about half the mask. Repeat with the blue, filling in the gaps and giving the eyes a semblance of eyeliner.

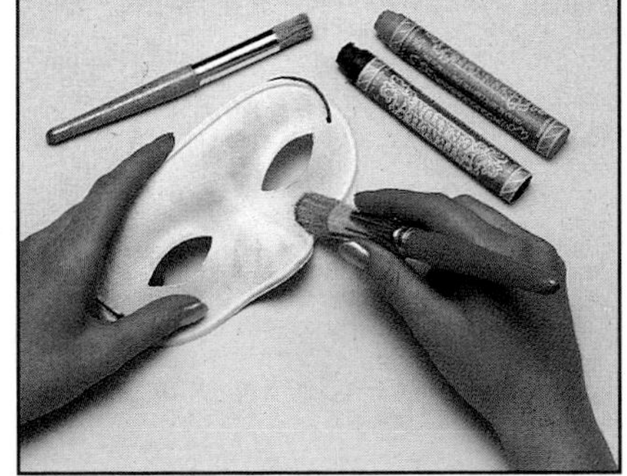

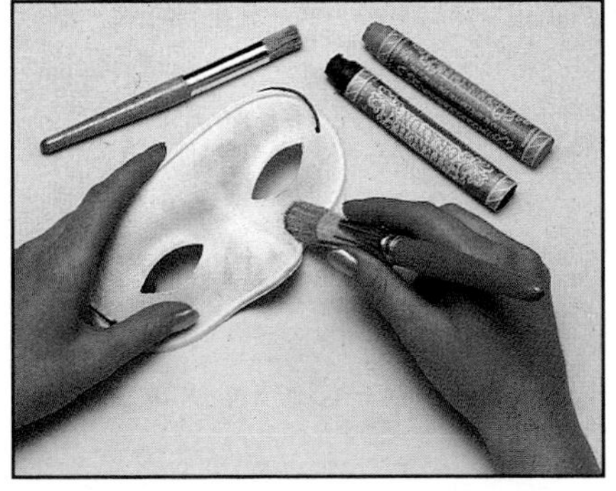

Next take a short length of lace and glue it to the back of the top half of the mask, down to where the elastic is attached. Glue some strands of curling gift wrap ribbon on either side. (Curl the ribbon by running the blunt edge of a pair of scissor along it.) Lastly, glue some large sequins over the tops of the ribbons to hide the ends, and glue another one in the centre of the forehead.

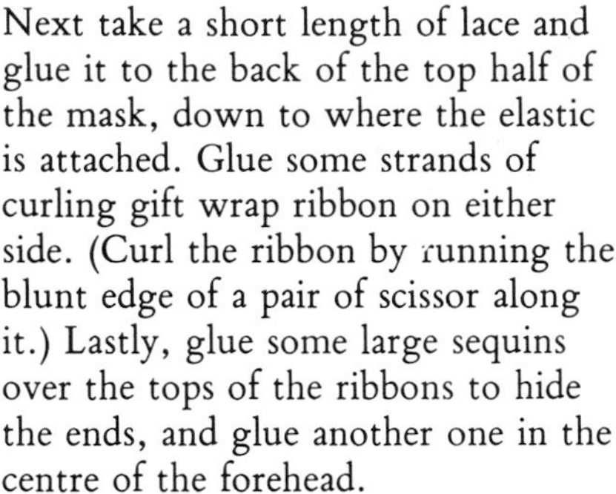

For the black mask, first sew some silver tinsel wire around the edge and around the eyes. Sew on some pearl beads either side, then sew two or three grey or white feathers under the edges for an owlish look.

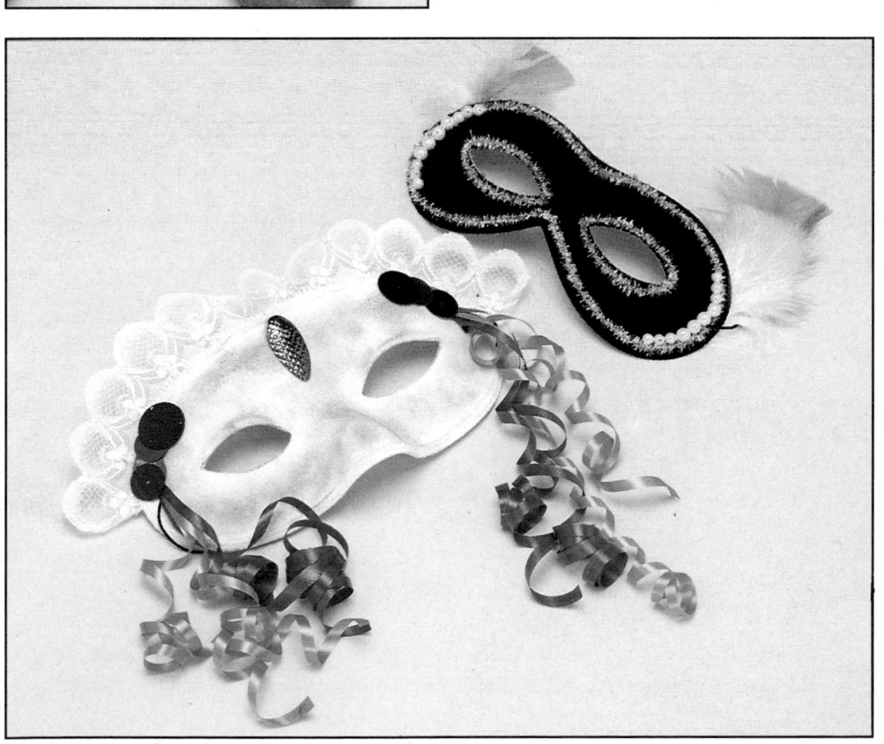

MASQUE BALL

This glamorous mask is perfect for a summer ball or fancy dress party. Cut the basic shape from thin cardboard, using the template on page 92. Cover it with a fluorescent fabric, cut 1cm (½in) larger all round, clipping the edges as shown and also clipping through the eyeholes. Fold the borders over and stick them down on the reverse side.

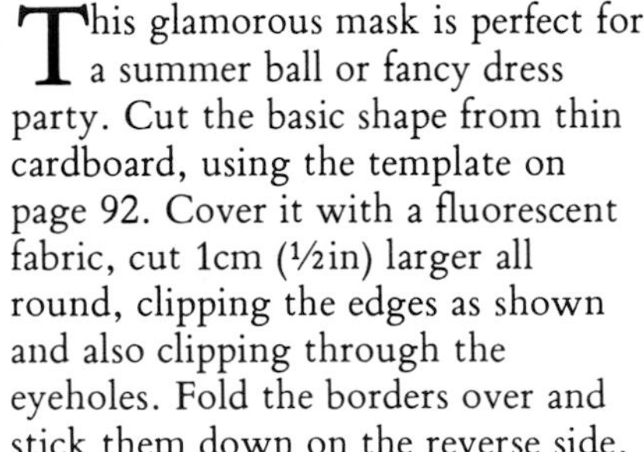

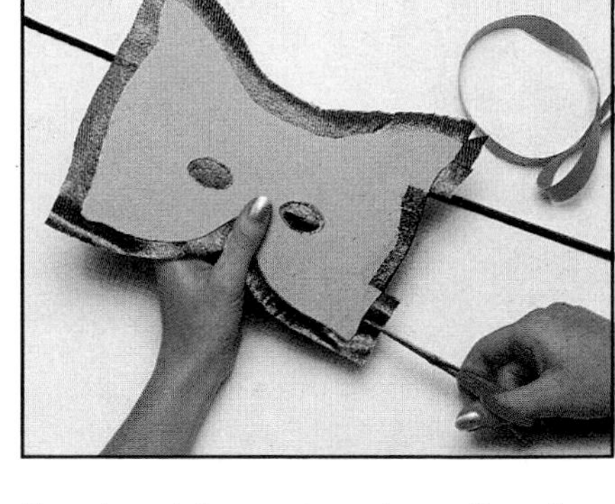

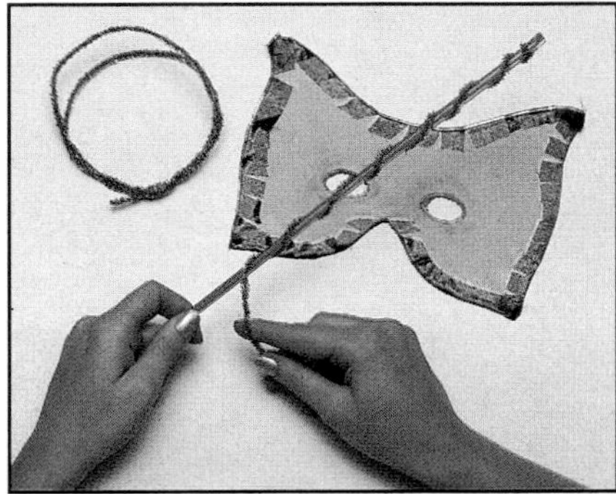

For the stick, cover a piece of garden cane with a strip of ribbon, and glue it in place. Wind fine tinsel or gold thread around it, and glue the ends down.

Cut a piece of gold foil paper to fit the back of the mask. Glue it down, first attaching the stick on one side. Decorate the front of the mask with sequins, feathers and pieces cut from a gold doily. If you can find only white ones in your local stores, spray a white one with gold paint.

CHARLIE CLOWN

Although a bit more complicated to make than a cardboard mask, this mask will last much longer. The face is made from papier-mâché (see page 94 for instructions); the mould is a balloon. Blow the balloon up as big as you can without bursting it, and build up the papier-mâché over at least one half. When it is dry, gently let the air out of the balloon by piercing the knotted end.

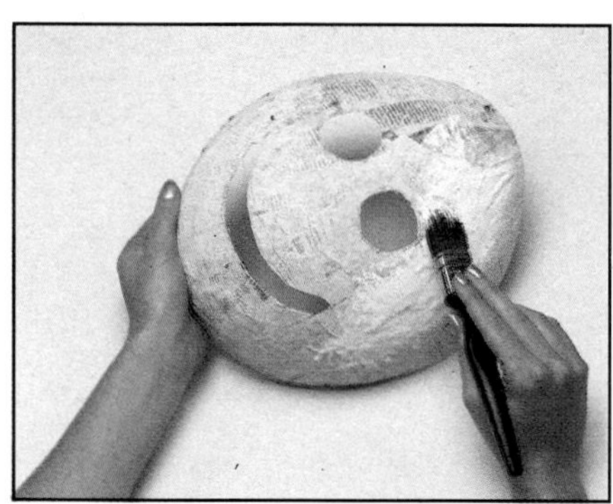

Trim the mask down, cutting the pointed end into a forehead. Cut out circular eyes and a curved mouth. Now give the mould a coat of white emulsion (water-based paint), sand it down and give it another two coats to make it as smooth a surface as possible.

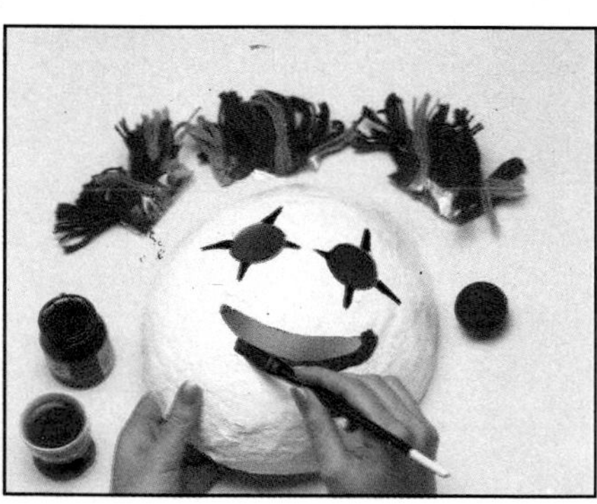

Around each eye paint four slightly triangular stripes. Also paint large red lips and cheeks on either side. For the nose, paint a ping pong ball red and glue it in place. For the hair, cut short lengths of yarn and attach them to strips of sticky tape; stick these to the back of the mask. Finally, take a piece of elastic, staple it to either side, and paint over the staples with a touch more emulsion.

TOTAL DISGUISE

With this on, you are sure not to be recognized! First make the glasses shape from garden wire, then wind narrow ribbon all the way around them. Glue the ends in place to make sure it doesn't come undone.

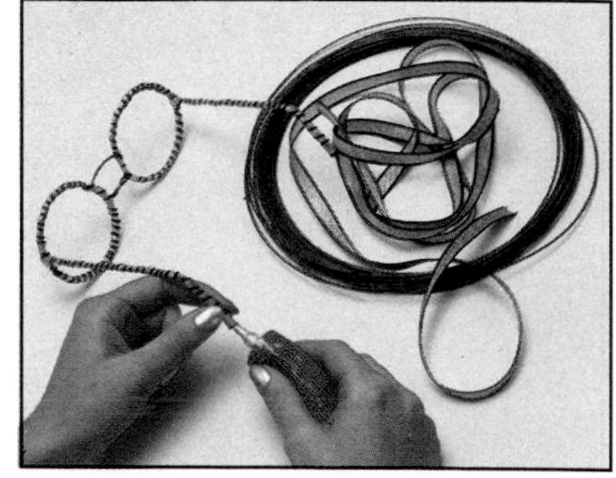

The nose is made from paper with a spongy finish. Cut a piece 9 by 10cm (3¾ by 4in). On the back, along one of the shorter sides, mark two lines, 3cm (1¼in) long and 3cm (1¼in) apart. Cut along these lines, so that you have three equal sections. Fold the two sides in and glue them on top of each other. Now glue the middle section over the others. Glue the edge of the nose to the glasses.

Finally, make the beard from a piece of white fake fur, cutting a hole for the mouth. Attach a narrow strip of paper to the inside of the nose and staple either end to the back of the beard. Finish off by sticking a silver star to the glasses, just over the nose.

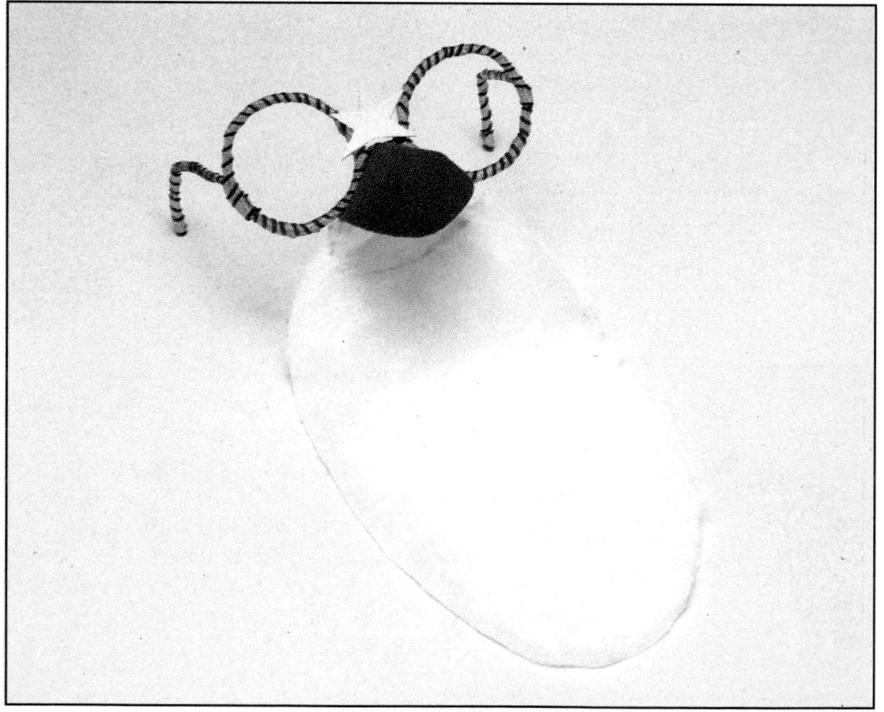

CURIOUS CAT

MISCHIEVOUS MOUSE

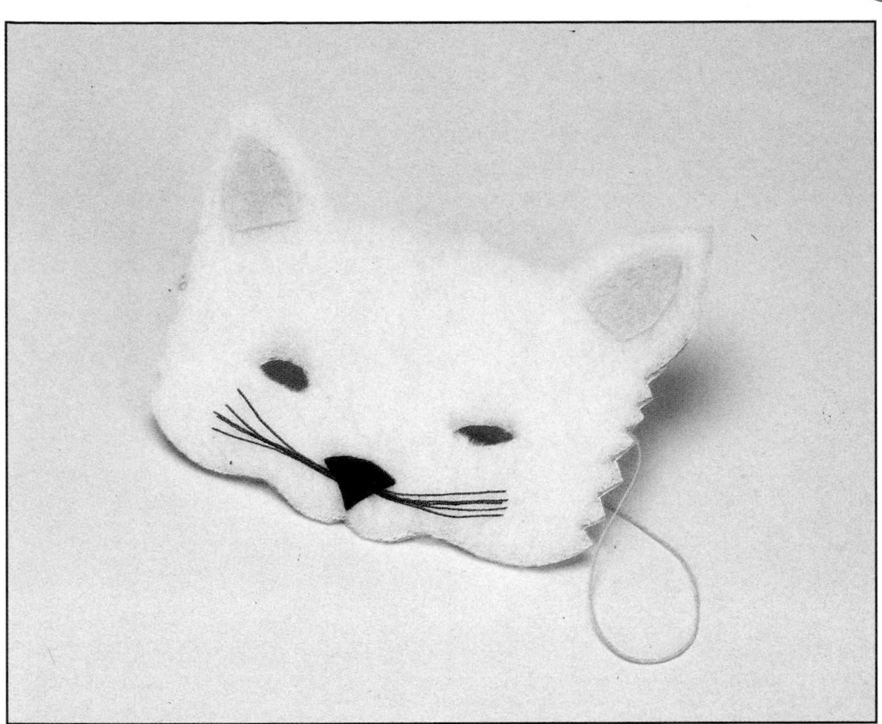

This appealing children's mask is covered in soft fake fur. Using the template on page 92 cut out the cat shape in thin cardboard, fake fur and white sticky-backed plastic. In all three, cut out the eyes.

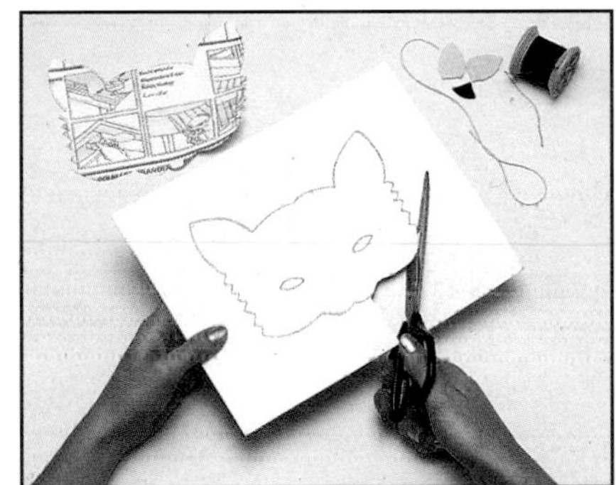

Glue the fur piece to the cardboard one. When the glue has dried, trim the edges, then cut a nose in black felt and two ears in pink felt. To make the whiskers, put some glue onto a piece of cardboard and pull black thread through it as shown. When the thread dries it will be stiff.

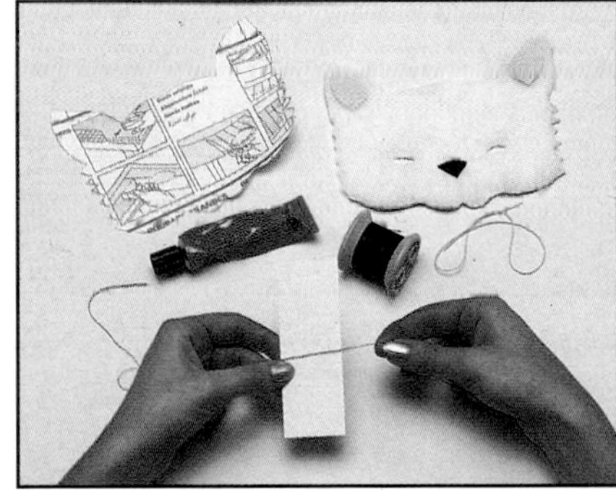

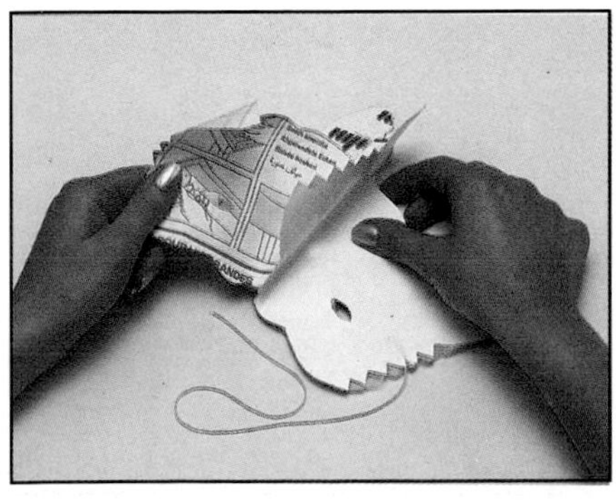

Glue the ears in place, then cut the thread into lengths of about 10cm (4in). Lay them where the nose is to be placed. Put some glue onto the nose and place it over the ends of the whiskers. Tape a piece of elastic to each side of the mask on the wrong side. Finally, peel the backing off the plastic and stick it to the underside of the mask.

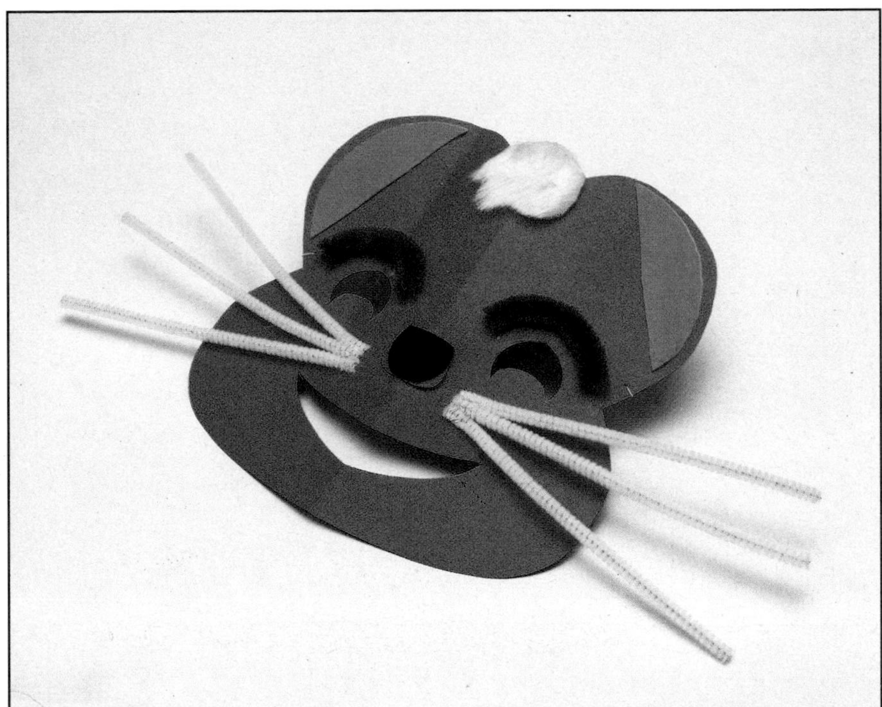

This mask is simple enough for small children to put together; the only tricky bit is drawing the pattern. First take a 20cm (8in) square of stiff paper. Fold it in half, and open it out, then fold it in half the other way. Now draw the shape of the face on one side as shown, including the mouth and nose.

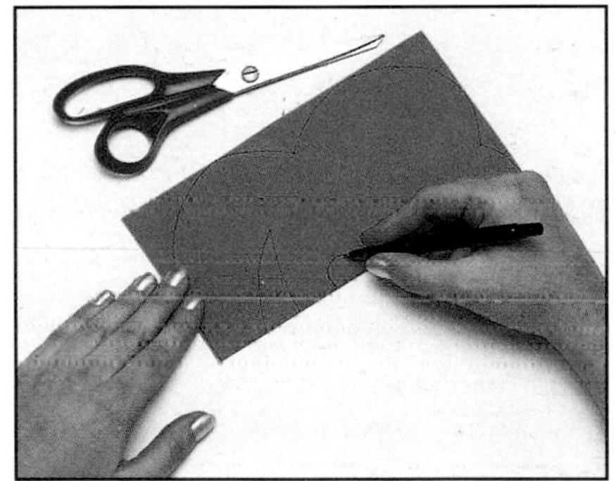

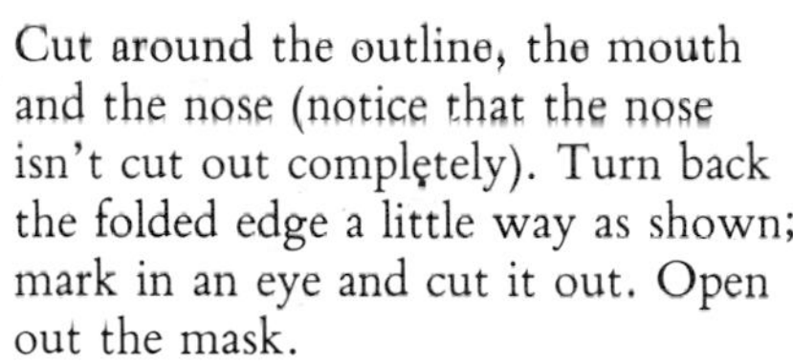

Cut around the outline, the mouth and the nose (notice that the nose isn't cut out completely). Turn back the folded edge a little way as shown; mark in an eye and cut it out. Open out the mask.

Cut out some pink felt ears and a black felt nose. Cut some white pipe cleaner whiskers and brown pipe cleaner eyebrows. Glue them all in place. Finally attach a piece of shirring elastic to either side, knotting it at the back.

 GIFTS AND FAVOURS 

Gifts and favours complement any festivity, can show off your creativity and flair, and may be taken home by your guests as a momento of the party. Flowers, sweets or presents in beautiful little packages are a generous touch that is certain to please. The craft ideas in this section show you how to create many kinds of parcels and decorate them to suit your party and table theme. Some of the designs featured include boxes, baskets, envelopes and small bags. Also included are instructions on making crackers, no longer just seen at Christmas but at all times of the year and on all occasions.

The floral theme of this table setting is reminiscent of afternoon tea in an old-fashioned country garden and was inspired by the rose-patterned china. In keeping with the floral theme, the conical envelope is made from decorated giftwrap, sealed with a flower motif. Here, it holds sweets, but any small gift will work well.

FLORAL ENVELOPE

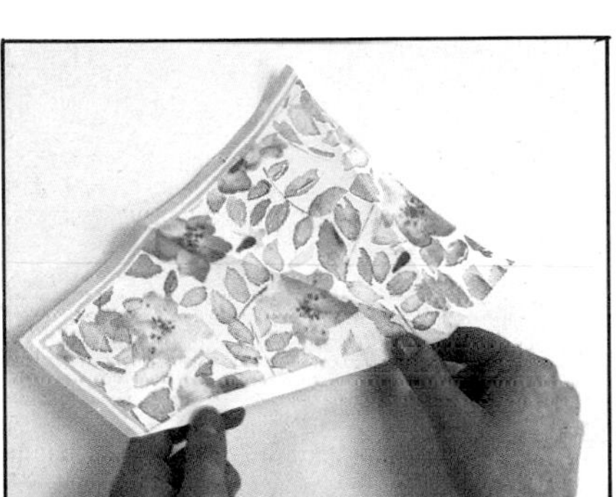

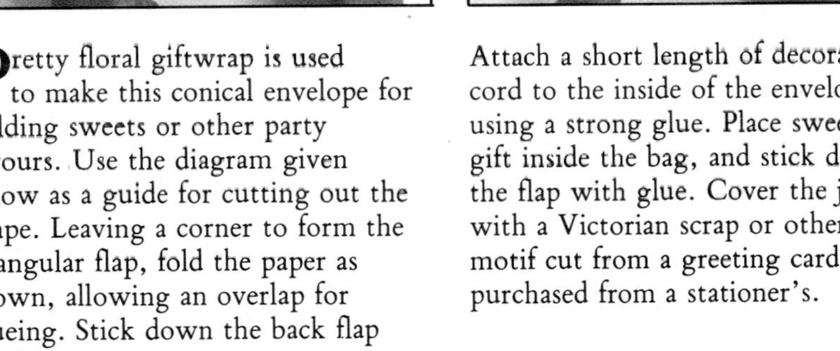

Pretty floral giftwrap is used to make this conical envelope for holding sweets or other party favours. Use the diagram given below as a guide for cutting out the shape. Leaving a corner to form the triangular flap, fold the paper as shown, allowing an overlap for glueing. Stick down the back flap neatly.

Attach a short length of decorative cord to the inside of the envelope, using a strong glue. Place sweets or a gift inside the bag, and stick down the flap with glue. Cover the join with a Victorian scrap or other floral motif cut from a greeting card or purchased from a stationer's.

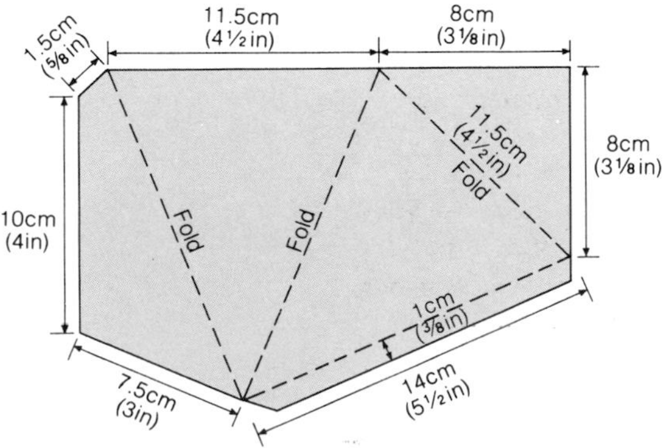

GIFT BASKETS

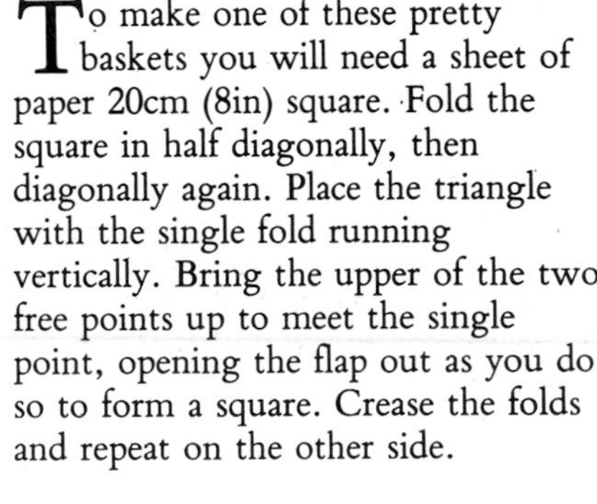

To make one of these pretty baskets you will need a sheet of paper 20cm (8in) square. Fold the square in half diagonally, then diagonally again. Place the triangle with the single fold running vertically. Bring the upper of the two free points up to meet the single point, opening the flap out as you do so to form a square. Crease the folds and repeat on the other side.

Position the newly formed square with the free edges pointing away from you. Fold the top free corner down to meet the opposite corner, then fold it back on itself to the horizontal centre line. Fold the flap in half once more. Repeat on the other side as shown. Turn the top left flap over to the right side, then fold it back on itself so that the corner meets the vertical centre line.

Fold the left hand corner in towards the vertical centre line also. Turn the basket over and repeat on the other side as shown. Open out the shape slightly and fold the top two flaps down inside the basket. Flatten the base. Cut a thin strip of paper for a handle and slip the ends into the slots on each side of the basket rim. Staple in place and decorate the basket with ribbons or lace.

SQUARE GIFT BOX

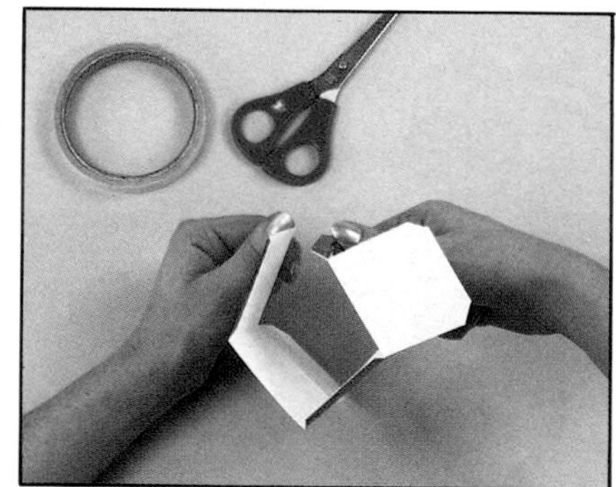

This elegant little box is ideal for wrapping a special gift. First draw the diagram to the specified measurements, then trace it. Tape the tracing to the wrong side of medium-weight cardboard with masking tape and draw over the outline with a ballpoint pen to make a light indentation in the cardboard. Cut around the outline.

Score the fold lines carefully with scissor points and fold the box accordingly. Apply glue to the flaps and join the box together as shown. Allow it to dry thoroughly before using it.

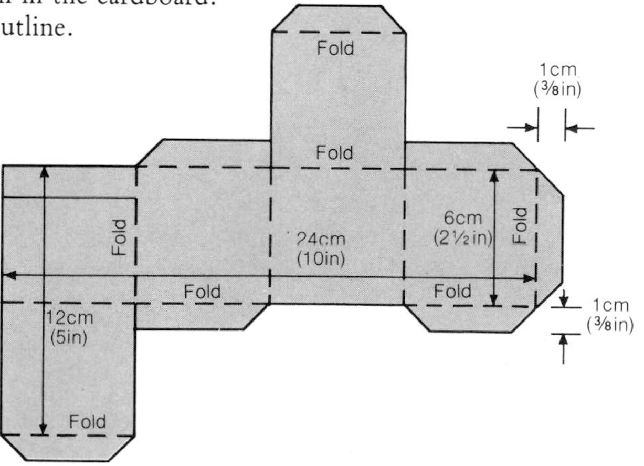

GIFT-WRAPPED SOAPS

Pretty fabric makes the perfect wrapping for fine scented soap; watch for suitable remnants in fabric departments. Cut a 15cm (6in) square of fabric, using pinking shears for a decorative edge and to prevent fraying.

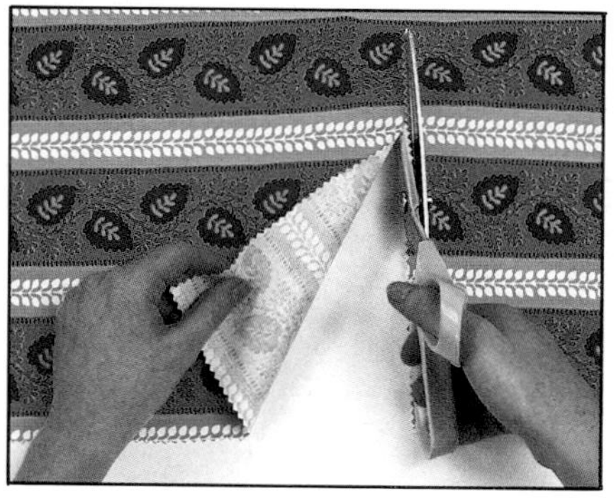

For a gift bag, place the soap in the centre of the square of fabric. Gather the corners together in the centre. Tie a contrasting ribbon around the fabric and into a bow. For an envelope, fold the four corners of the square over the soap to overlap in the centre.

Hold the flaps of the envelope in place and tie them up with a contrasting ribbon. Finish off with a large bow.

LAVENDER GIFT BAG

FLORAL FAVOUR

Sweet-smelling lavender sachets can be taken home by your guests and used to scent bureau drawers. You will need some dried lavender, a square of muslin, two squares of net (one white and one lilac) and a length of ribbon. To dry your own lavender, pick the stems just before the flowers open, and hang them up in a warm, dry place.

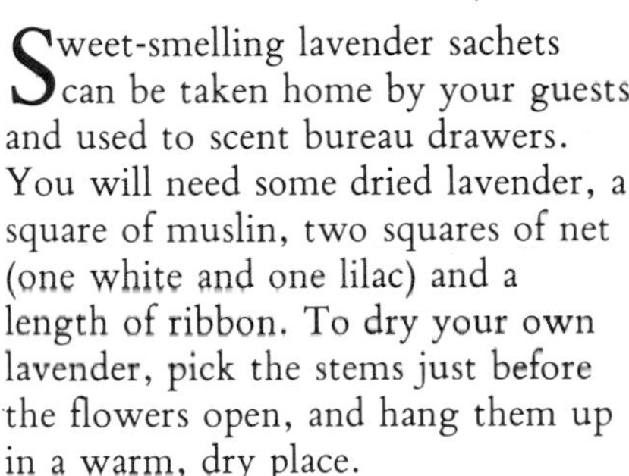

Lay the square of white net on top of the lilac square. On top of this place the square of muslin and then some lavender flowers stripped off the stem. Gather all the layers together in two hands and bunch them together in the centre.

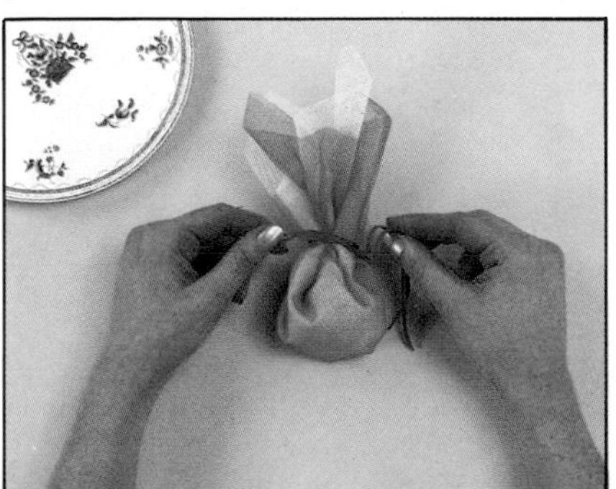

Tie the ribbon around the fabric and into a bow. Trim off any excess ribbon, and place the bag on a plate. Add a couple of fresh flowers or sprigs of lavender as further decoration.

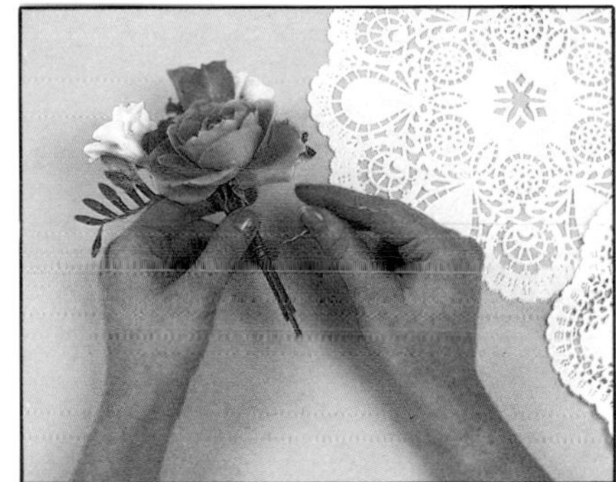

This pretty favour will scent a summer table and can be taken home by a guest after the meal. Group together five or six flowers to form a small posy. Holding them firmly in one hand, tie the stems together with a length of fuse wire.

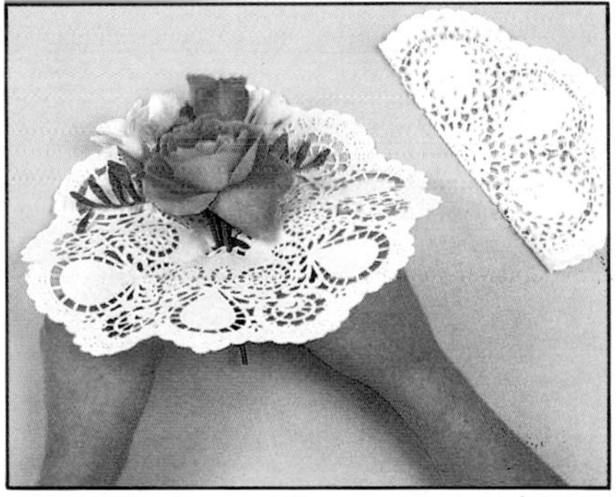

Fold the smaller of two doilies in half and set it aside. With a pair of scissors snip a small hole in the centre of the larger doily and push the stems of the posy through it.

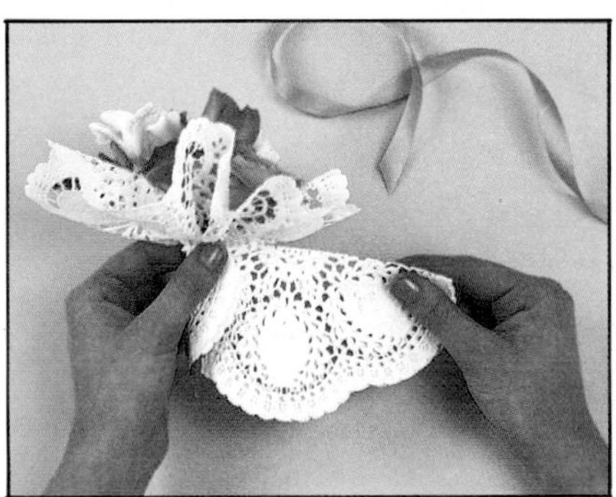

Gather the large doily together around the flower-heads and hold it firmly in place. With the other hand, wrap the folded doily around the stems, making sure it overlaps the excess gathers of the large doily. Use a pin or tape to hold it in place. Tie a piece of satin ribbon around the posy to conceal the joins.

GIFT BOX POM-POM

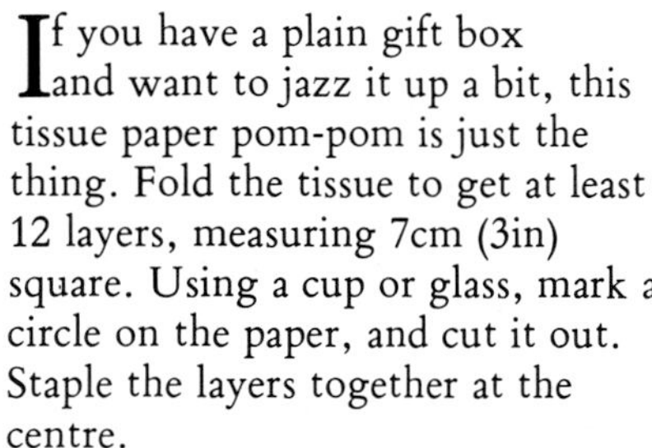

If you have a plain gift box and want to jazz it up a bit, this tissue paper pom-pom is just the thing. Fold the tissue to get at least 12 layers, measuring 7cm (3in) square. Using a cup or glass, mark a circle on the paper, and cut it out. Staple the layers together at the centre.

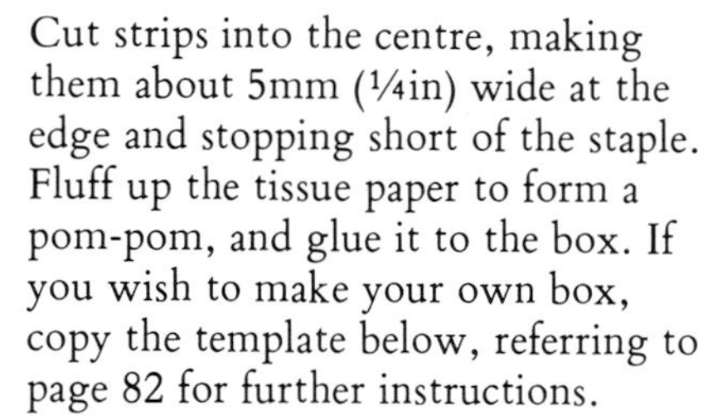

Cut strips into the centre, making them about 5mm (¼in) wide at the edge and stopping short of the staple. Fluff up the tissue paper to form a pom-pom, and glue it to the box. If you wish to make your own box, copy the template below, referring to page 82 for further instructions.

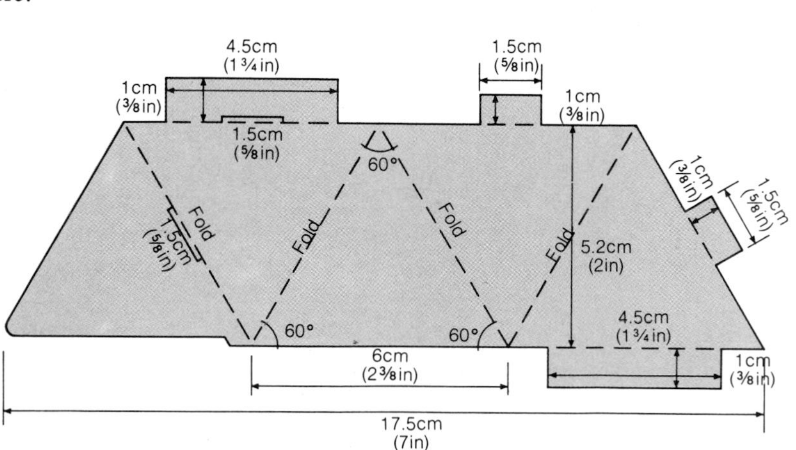

VALENTINE GIFT BOXES

Decorating your own gift boxes for sweets or a tiny present adds a festive touch to a special occasion. These red and black boxes contain chocolate hearts for a Valentine's Day dinner. For the smaller box, first paint a plain heart-shaped wooden box red. Use a fine-bristle artist's brush to add black dots all over the outside of the box.

Place one or more chocolates in the box, along with some red ribbon for padding. Tie the lid in place with thin black ribbon.

Add an individual touch to a plain red cardboard box by lining it with black tissue and tying black and white spotted ribbon around it.

CANDY CONE

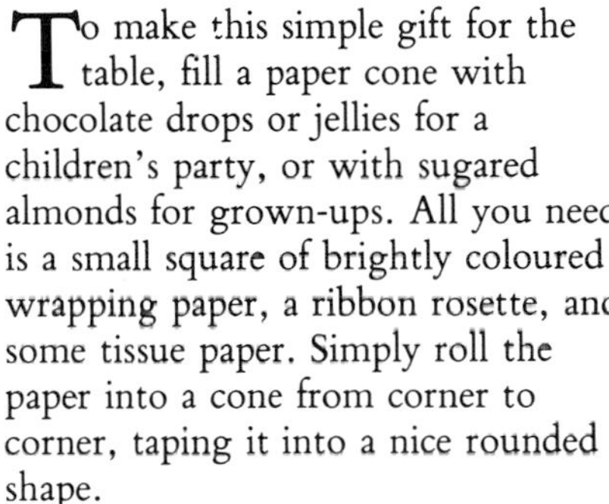

To make this simple gift for the table, fill a paper cone with chocolate drops or jellies for a children's party, or with sugared almonds for grown-ups. All you need is a small square of brightly coloured wrapping paper, a ribbon rosette, and some tissue paper. Simply roll the paper into a cone from corner to corner, taping it into a nice rounded shape.

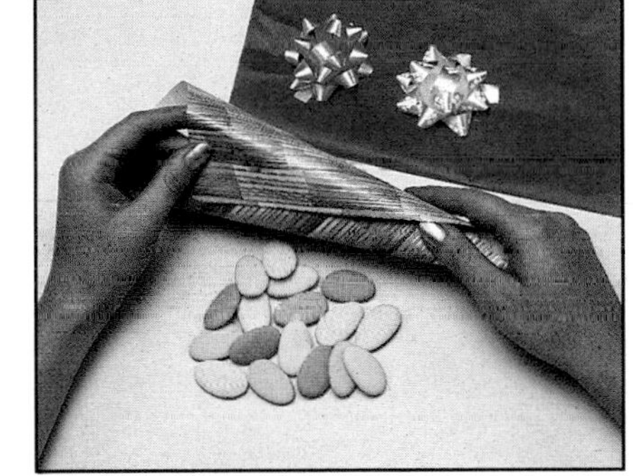

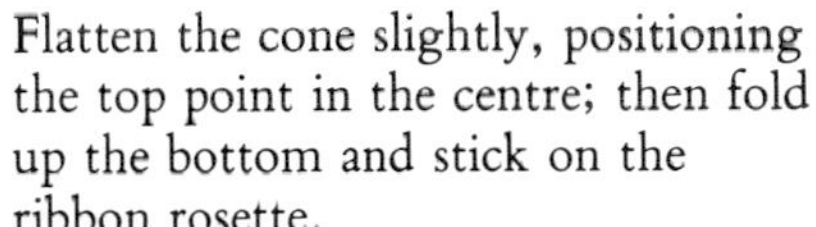

Flatten the cone slightly, positioning the top point in the centre; then fold up the bottom and stick on the ribbon rosette.

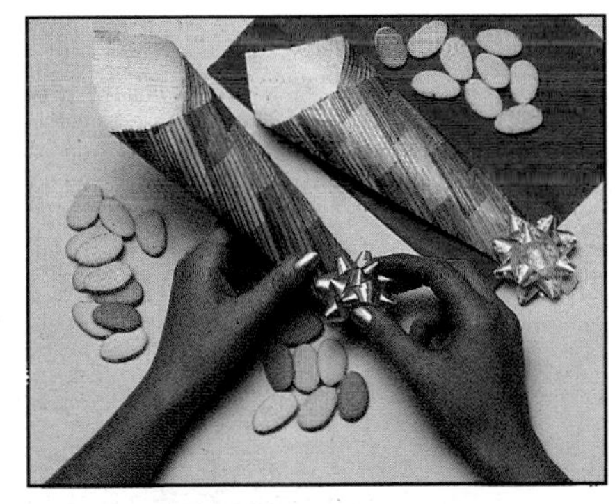

Scrunch up a little bit of tissue paper and slip it inside the cone to hold it in shape, then fill the top with sweets so that they spill out onto the point. You could attach a place card to each cone and use the cones to mark place settings at a large party.

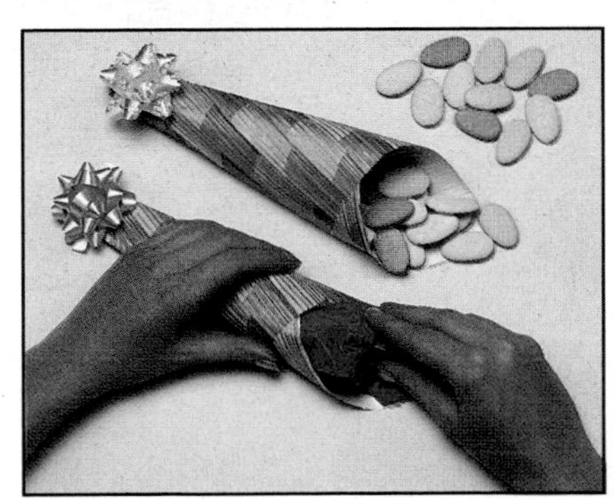

CHOCOLATE SHELL SURPRISE

Here's a pretty — and witty — way to serve shell-or fish-shaped chocolates. (You can either buy these from some confectioners, or make them yourself using special moulds.) Cut a large doily in half. Put one half aside, and cut the other one in half again to make a quarter section; discard the remaining quarter.

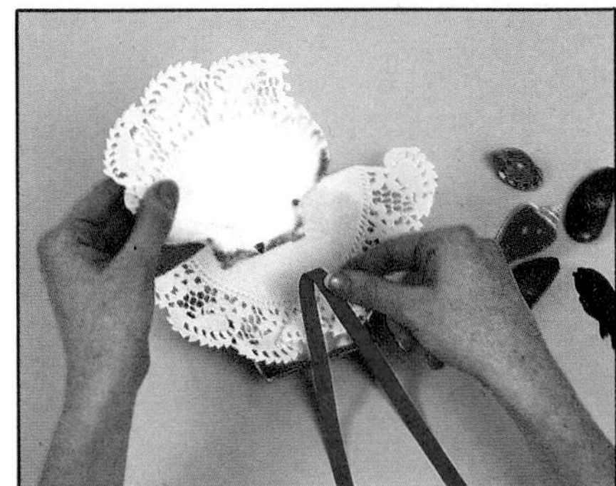

Take two scallop shells, one slightly larger than the other. Place the half doily on top of the larger shell, straight edge away from you. Put the quarter doily into the smaller shell, fancy edge away from you. Trim the ends of a 25 to 30cm (10 to 12in) length of blue satin ribbon; fold the ribbon in two and place it in the large scallop shell.

Holding the ribbon in position, place the small shell in the larger one; straighten the edges of the doilies if necessary. Fill the small shell with a mixture of real shells and chocolate shells and fish shapes.

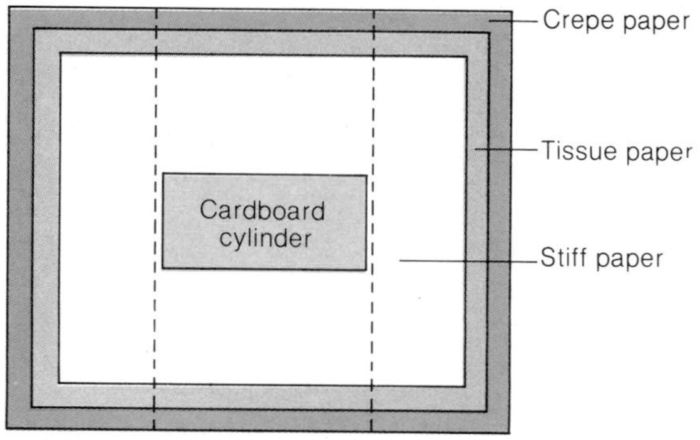

TRADITIONAL CRACKERS

Crackers are always a must at the dinner table at Christmas. The diagram above shows the materials required for a cracker: crepe paper for the outside, tissue paper for the lining, and stiff paper and a cardboard cylinder to hold the cracker in shape.

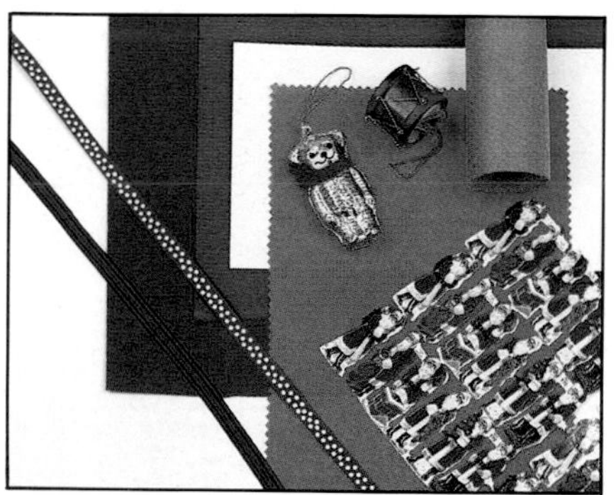

Cut the paper layers as indicated above. Roll them around the tube, and stick them in place securely with either glue or tape. A friction strip can be placed between the stiff paper and cylinder to provide a 'bang' when the cracker is pulled.

Gather the paper together at one end and tie it with ribbon. Leave the other end open to drop in the gift, hat and joke of your choice. Tie this end and trim the ribbons neatly.

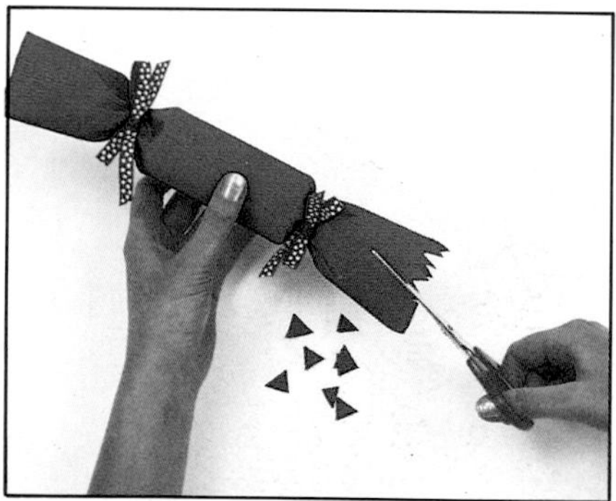

Cut a zigzag edge in the paper at both ends; or leave the ends plain, if you prefer.

Add the final decorative touches — in this case, contrasting layers of crepe paper and a paper motif.

RED HOT CRACKERS

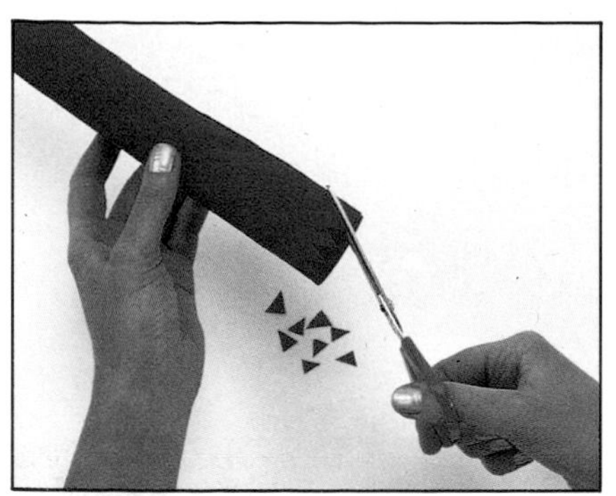

Stylish black and white paper decorates these modern bright red crackers. Follow the instructions on page 86 for assembling the basic cracker, using red crepe paper for the outer layer. Cut a decorative edging, if desired, at both ends.

Cut a rectangular piece of black and white gift wrap or other patterned paper, long enough to go around the cylinder with a small overlap. Cut the long edges to match the ends of the cracker. Wrap the strip around the cracker and glue along the join.

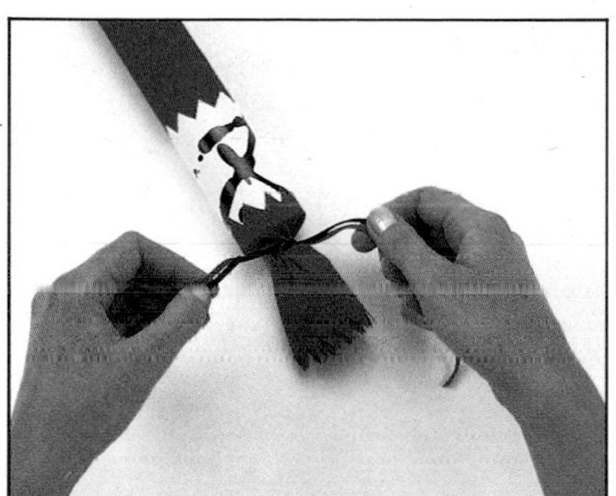

Tie one end with two lengths of fine ribbon in black, white and/or red. Insert the gift into the cylinder and tie the other end. Add place cards or write names on the crackers if appropriate.

VICTORIAN CRACKER

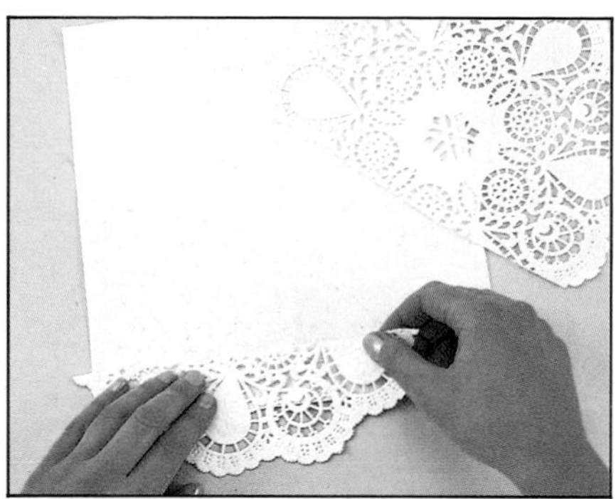

This old-fashioned cracker makes a charming addition to the table. Follow the basic step-by-step guide for making a cracker on page 86, cutting the outer crepe paper layer 5cm (2in) short of the recommended size. Make up the difference by attaching strips of paper doilies as shown, using double-sided tape or glue to secure the strips at each end.

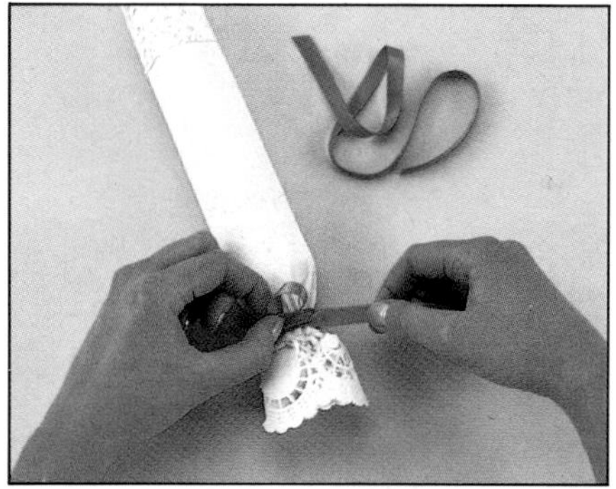

Cover the join of doily and crepe paper at one end with a length of ribbon in a contrasting colour, tied in a bow. Insert the chosen motto and small gifts in the cylinder. Tie the other end as before, and trim the ribbon ends neatly.

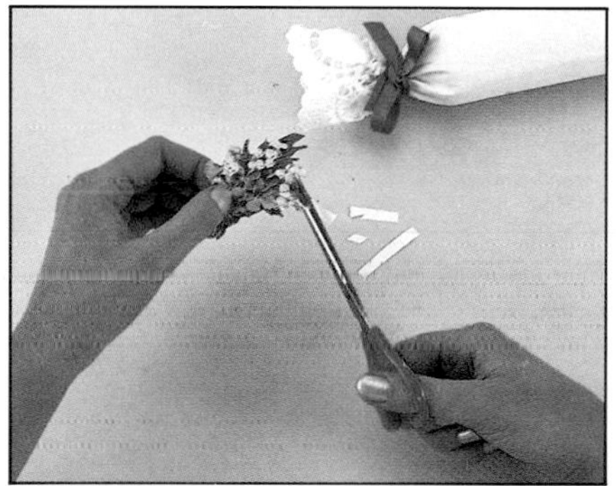

Cut out a traditional Victorian scrap or motif from an old Christmas card or other greeting card, and glue it to the cracker. Alternatively, you may be able to purchase attractive Victorian-style motifs from a stationer's.

GLAMOUR CRACKER

This beautiful cracker is not designed to be pulled but to be taken home as a memento. First take a tube of cardboard and wrap white crepe paper around it. Insert short cardboard tubes into each end, leaving gaps of 5cm (2in) between the main and end sections. Cover the central and end sections on the outside with silver foil paper, and stick pink foil paper to the inside of the end sections.

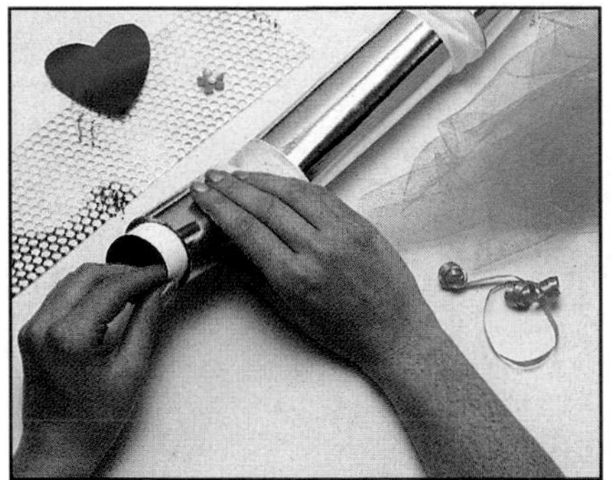

Wind a length of silver sequin waste around the centre. Next take two strips of pink net and draw a piece of thread through the centre of each to gather it. Tie them at each end with a strip of curling gift wrap ribbon. (Curl the ribbon by running the blunt edge of a pair of scissors along it.)

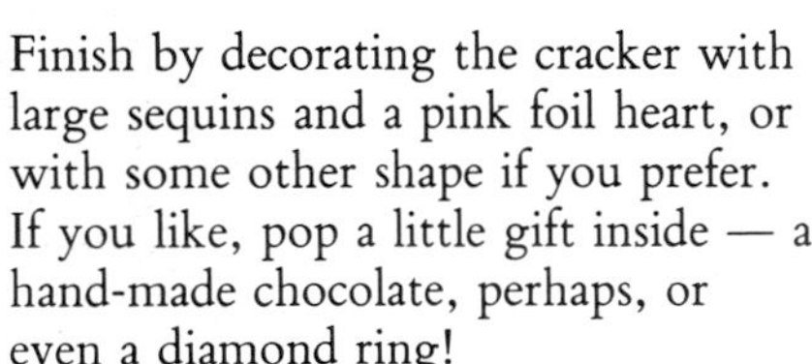

Finish by decorating the cracker with large sequins and a pink foil heart, or with some other shape if you prefer. If you like, pop a little gift inside — a hand-made chocolate, perhaps, or even a diamond ring!

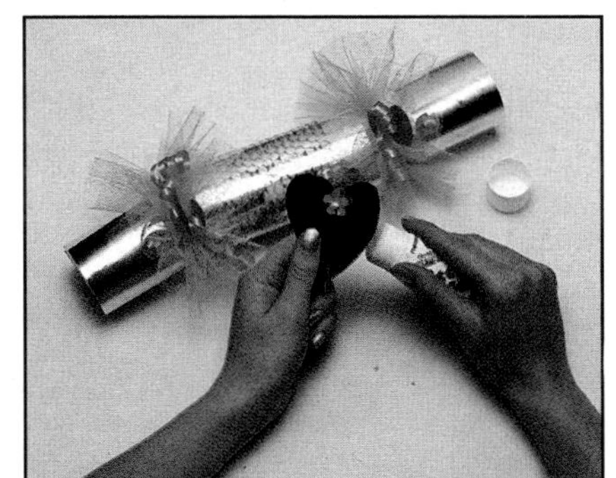

EASTER BUNNY

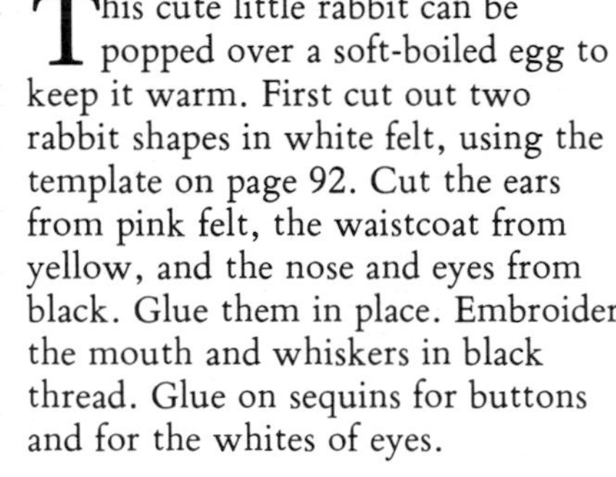

This cute little rabbit can be popped over a soft-boiled egg to keep it warm. First cut out two rabbit shapes in white felt, using the template on page 92. Cut the ears from pink felt, the waistcoat from yellow, and the nose and eyes from black. Glue them in place. Embroider the mouth and whiskers in black thread. Glue on sequins for buttons and for the whites of eyes.

Take a piece of ribbon 5cm (2in) long and glue the ends together to form a loop. Tie a piece of thread tightly around the middle of the ribbon to form a bow, and sew it to the rabbit between the mouth and the top of the waistcoat.

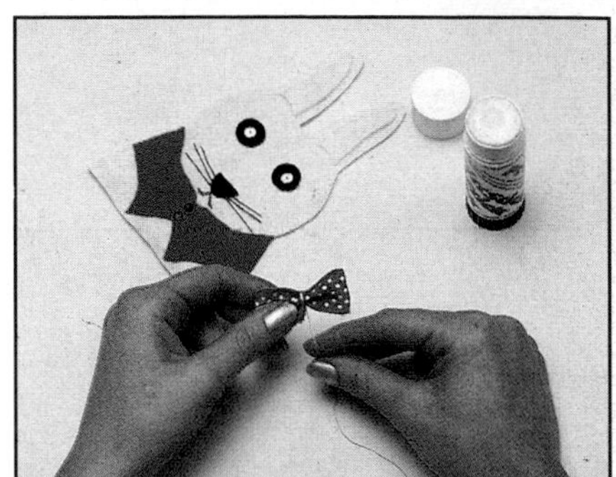

With wrong sides facing, sew the front and back together along the edge, using blanket stitch.

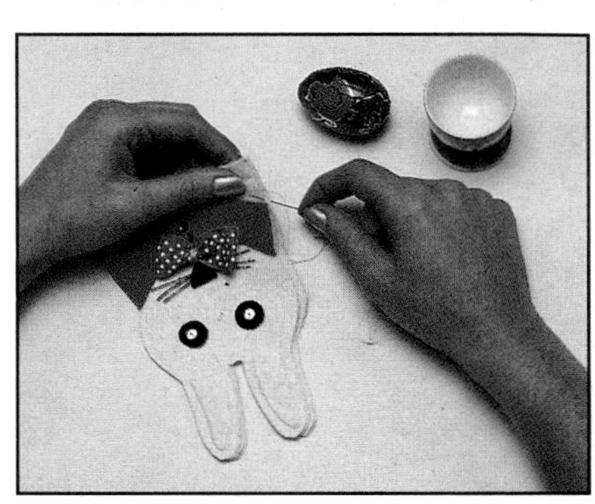

NET PARCELS

These are cute little gifts to place beside each setting on the table. Begin by cutting out a circle of net, using a standard sized dinner plate as a guide.

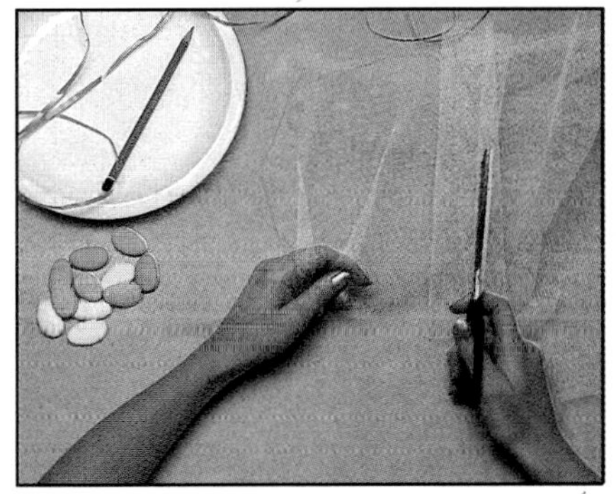

Place a few pastel-coloured sugared almonds into the net, and bunch it into a parcel with an elastic (rubber) band to hold it together.

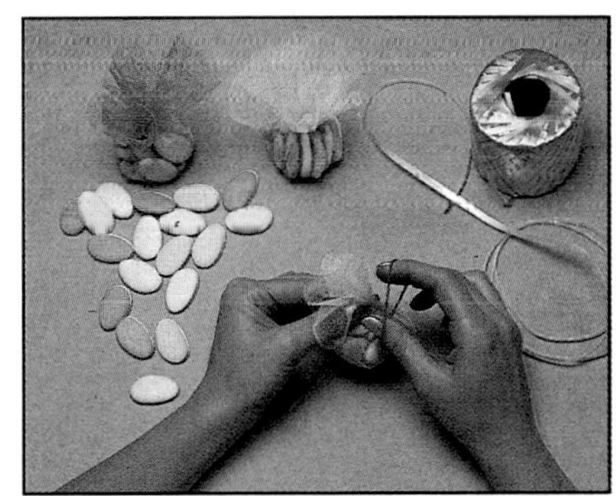

Now just trim the parcel with curling gift wrap ribbon. (Curl the ribbon by running the blunt edge of a pair of scissors along it.) You could slip a name tag over the ribbon before tying it and use the parcel as an unusual place marker.

FASHION FLOWERS

These most unusual flowers are made from coloured nylon stockings or tights (pantyhose). First cut some pieces of copper wire 20cm (8in) long. Bend each into a petal shape with pliers. You need five petals for each flower. Cut the nylons into pieces and stretch them over the wire very tightly, binding them on with green tape.

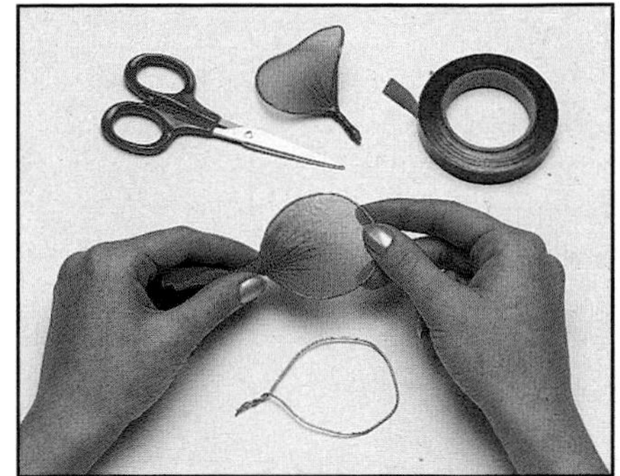

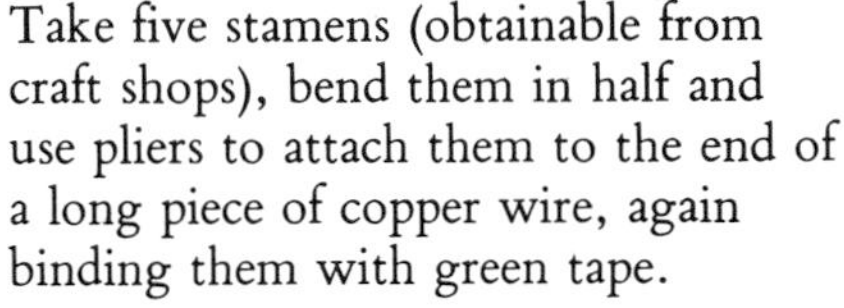

Take five stamens (obtainable from craft shops), bend them in half and use pliers to attach them to the end of a long piece of copper wire, again binding them with green tape.

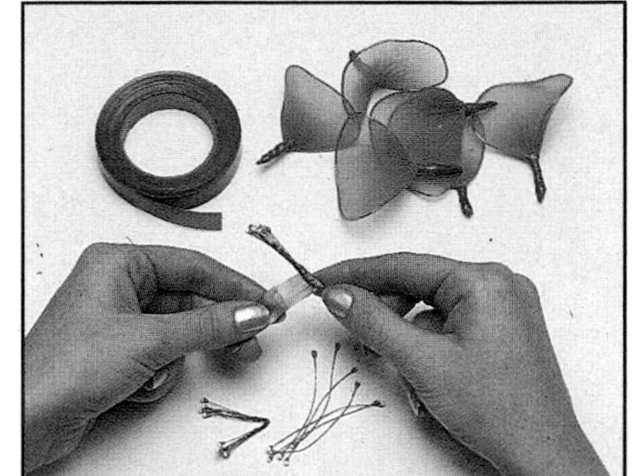

Now arrange the petals around the stamens. Start by placing the middle two opposite each other. Bind them, then add the other three around them. When all the petals are in place, tape around the top of the stem and continue down it to the end. When you have made several blooms, wrap them in shiny paper and tie a net bow around the outside.

TEMPLATES AND TECHNIQUES

Some of the projects in this book are based on the templates given on the next three pages. These have been reduced in size, in order to fit the space available; so you will first need to enlarge them. If, for example, each square of the printed grid is said to represent 5cm (2in), you should draw your own grid, making each square measure 5cm x 5cm (2in x 2in). Then, using the grid lines as a guide, copy the shape onto your full-size grid.

On pages 93-94, you will find step-by-step instructions for some basic 'ingredients' required in many party decorations. These include tassels and pom-poms for trimming hats and other decorations, paper flowers for displays or garlands, and papier-mâché which has been used for hats and masks in this book.

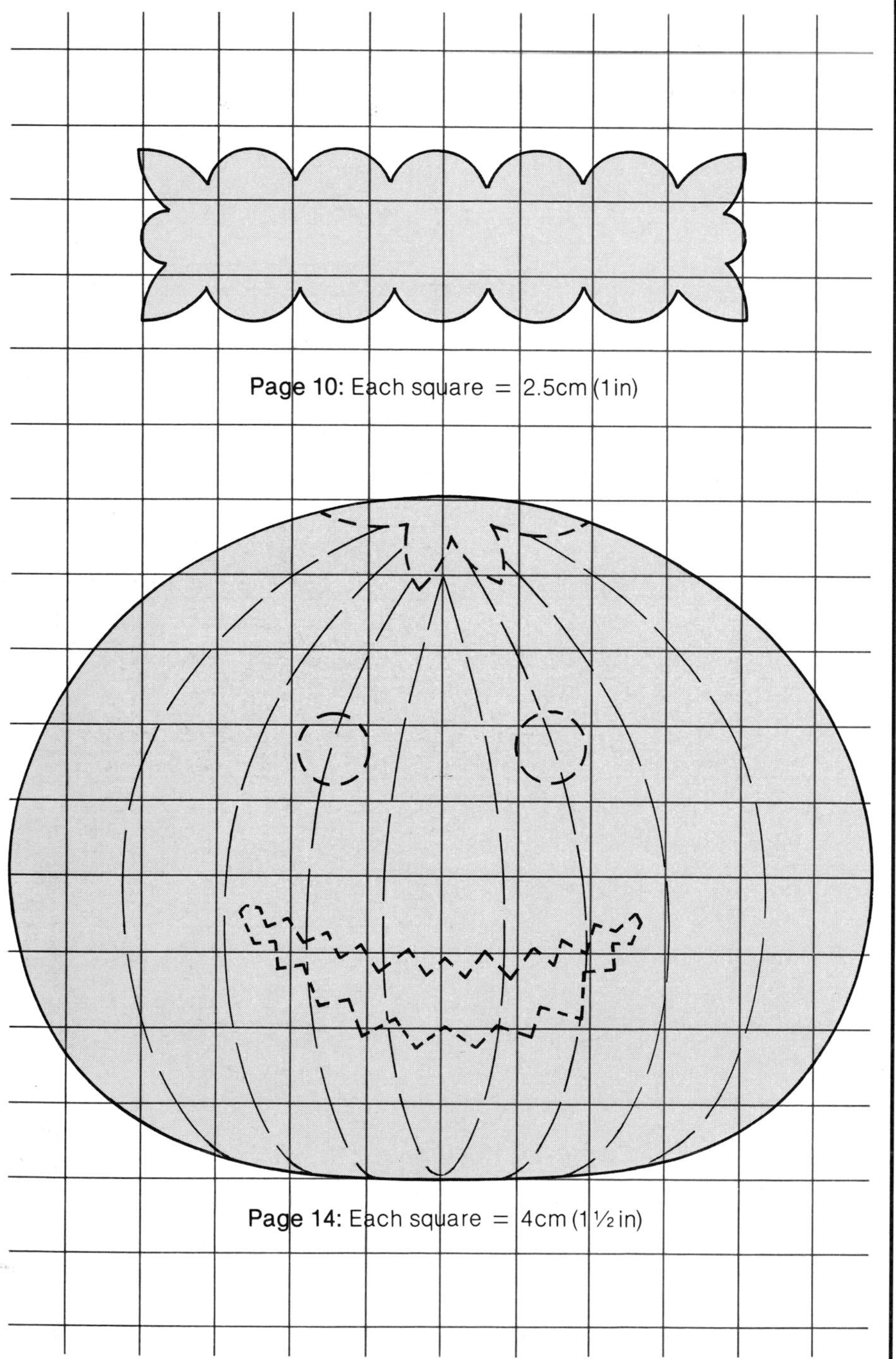

Page 10: Each square = 2.5cm (1in)

Page 14: Each square = 4cm (1½in)

Page 13: Each square = 2.5cm (1in)

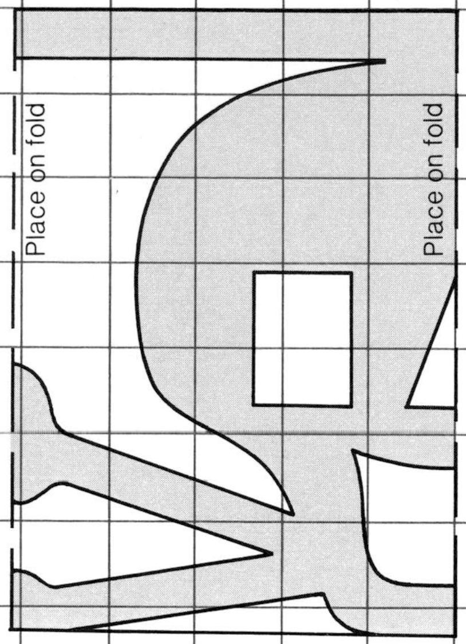

Place on fold

Place on fold

Page 13: Each square = 2.5cm (1in)
Page 18: Each square = 1.5cm (⅝in)

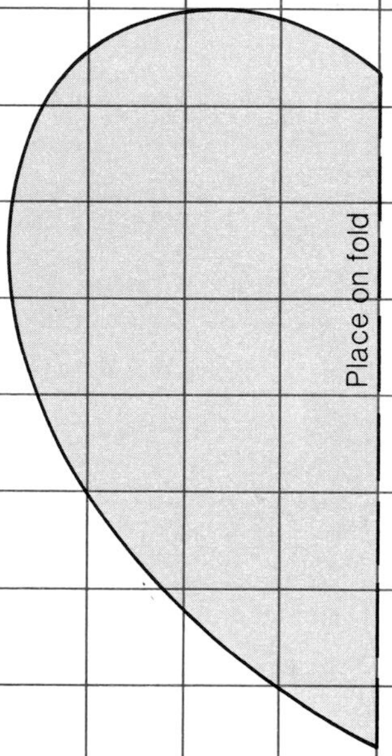

Place on fold

Page 18: Each square = 2cm (¾in)

Page 19: Each square = 2cm (¾in)

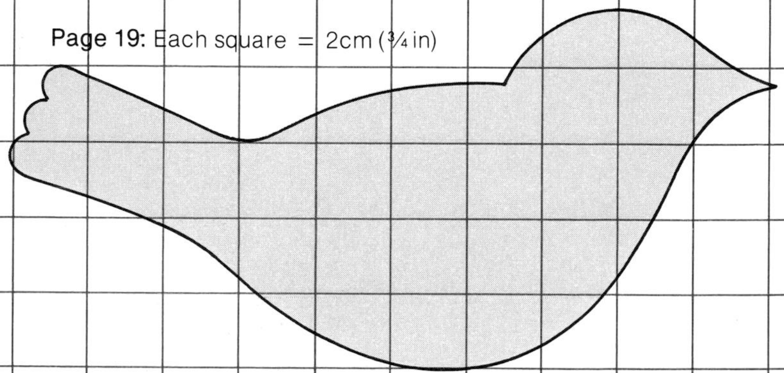

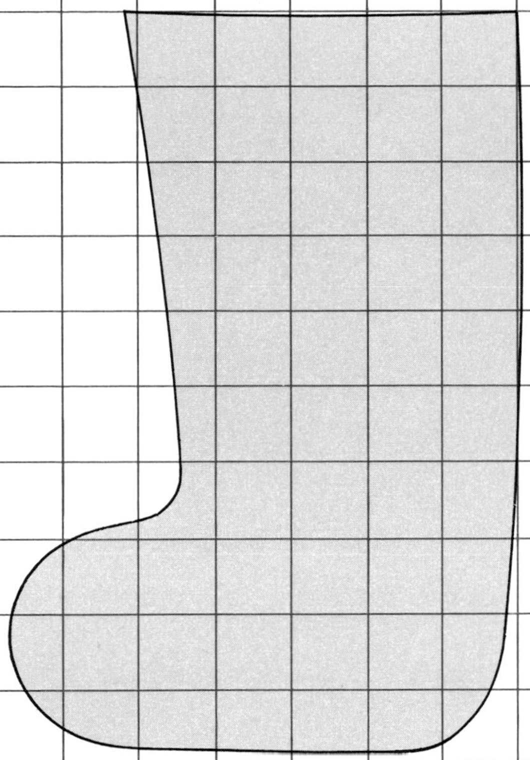

Page 27: Each square = 2cm (¾ in)

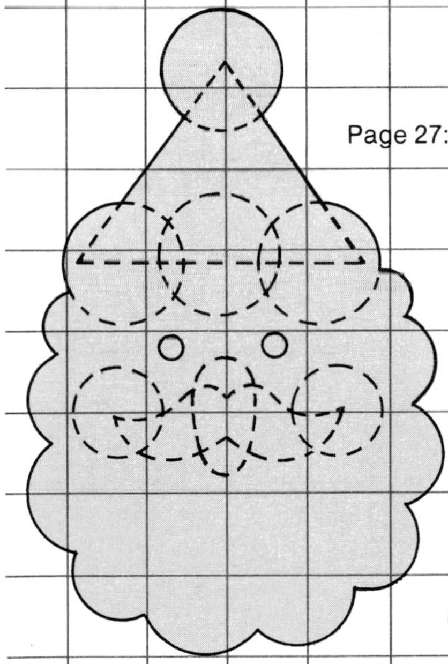

Page 27: Each square = 2cm (¾ in)

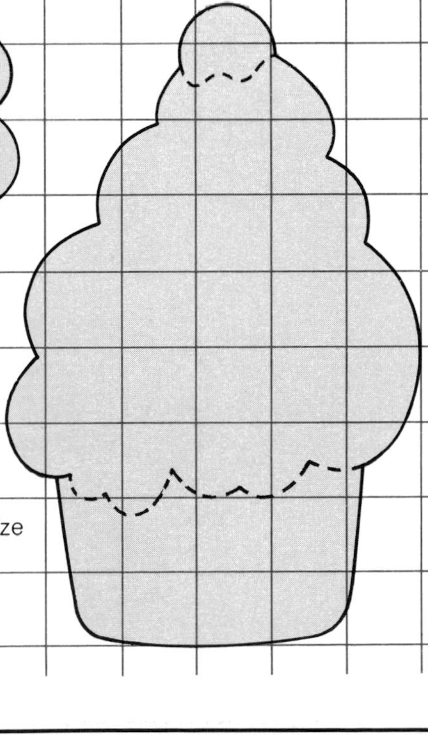

Page 63: Cut same size

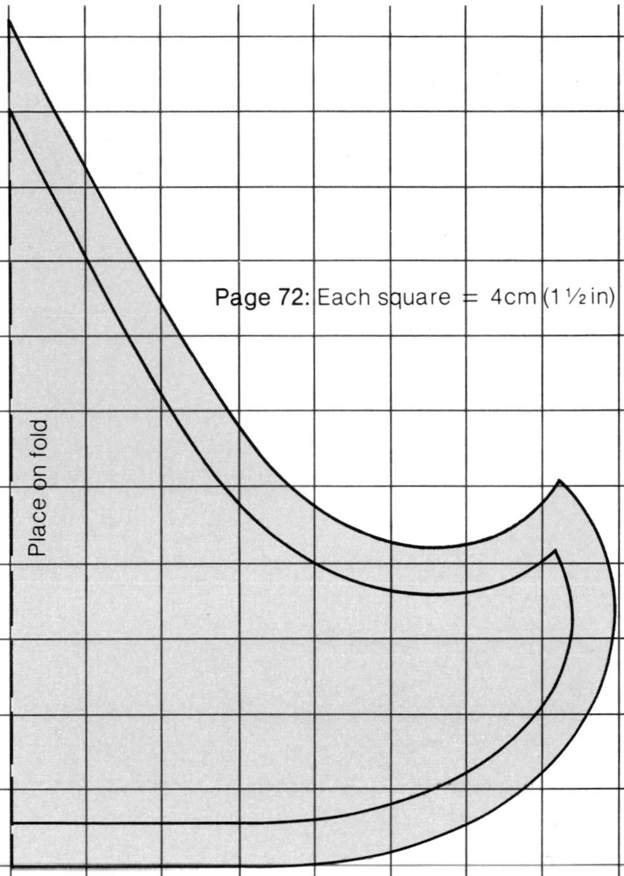

Page 72: Each square = 4cm (1 ½ in)

Place on fold

Page 73: Each square = 4cm (1 ½ in)

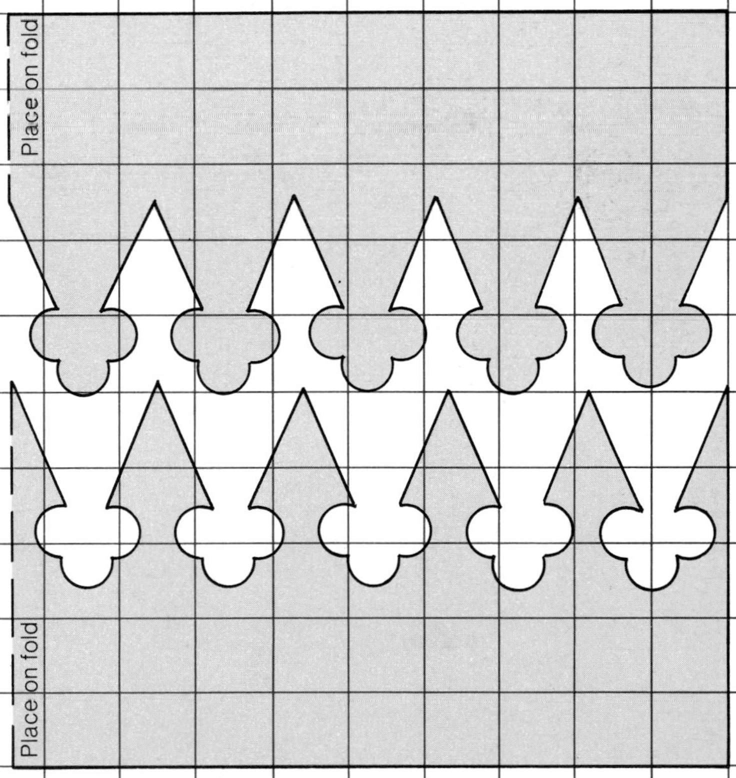

Place on fold

Place on fold

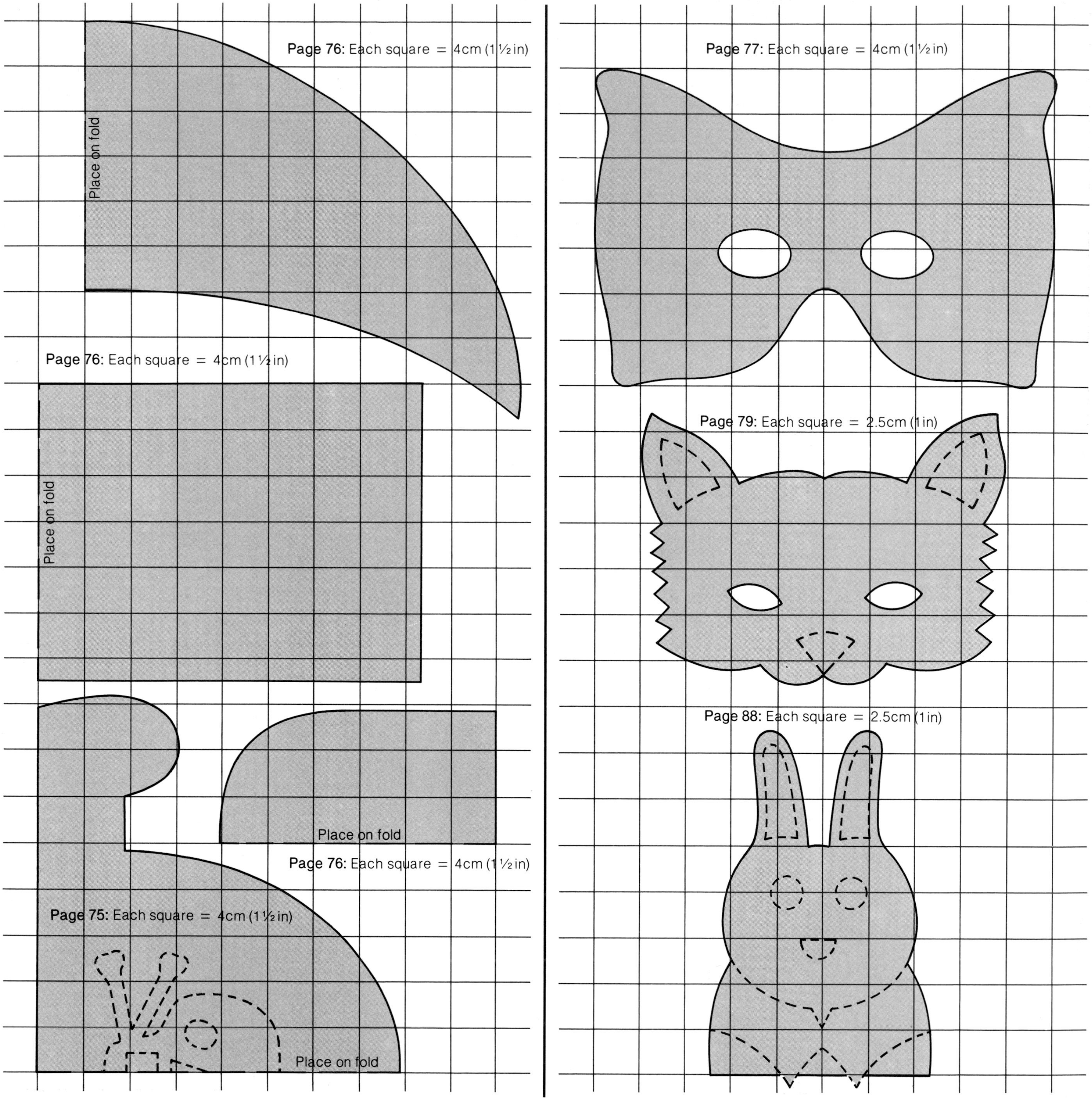

Page 76: Each square = 4cm (1½in)

Place on fold

Page 76: Each square = 4cm (1½in)

Place on fold

Place on fold

Page 76: Each square = 4cm (1½in)

Page 75: Each square = 4cm (1½in)

Place on fold

Page 77: Each square = 4cm (1½in)

Page 79: Each square = 2.5cm (1in)

Page 88: Each square = 2.5cm (1in)

TASSELS

Tassels are useful for trimming hats or the edges of hanging decorations, and they are very easy to make. Cut several strands of yarn or cord; the more you cut, the fuller the tassel will be. The strands should be twice the finished length of the tassel. Tie them firmly in the centre. Leave the tying strands uncut, and fold the tassel strands in half.

Now wind a cord several times around all the strands, about 2.5cm (1in) from the top (or less, for a small tassel.) Tie it firmly and cut off the ends.

Trim the ends off the tassel so that they are all the same length. Use the top cord to attach it to whatever you are trimming.

POM-POMS

These jolly trimmings, ideal for party hats, can be made of yarn left over from knitting projects. First cut two circles of cardboard with a diameter the size you wish the finished pom-pom to be. Cut a fairly large hole in the centre. Now wind yarn (doubled, to speed up the work) over the cardboard rings until you can barely push the yarn through any more.

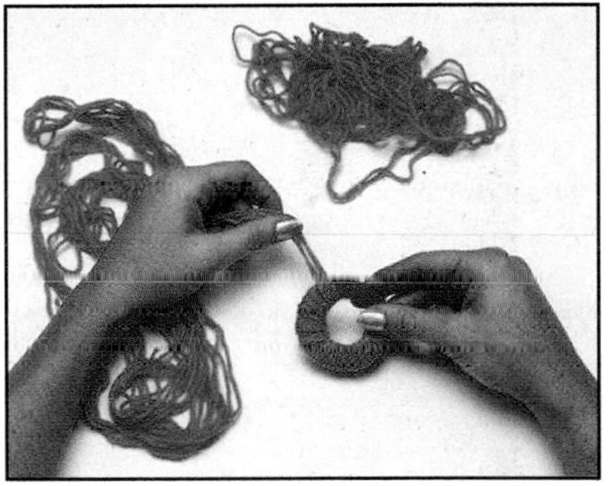

The more yarn you use, the bushier the pom-pom. When you have finished, tie off the end of the yarn. Snip through all the yarn around the outer edge of the cardboard rings.

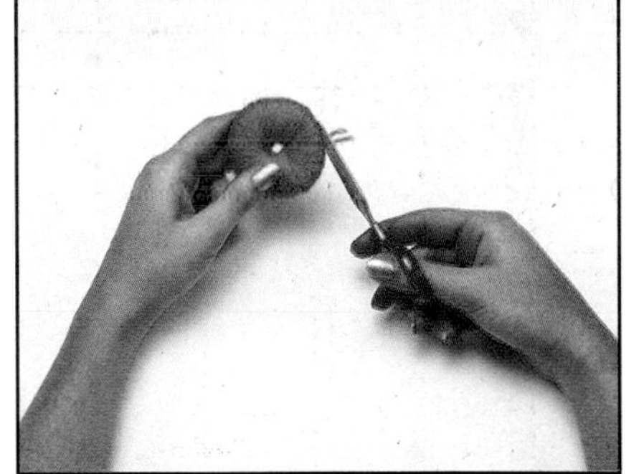

Wind a piece of yarn between the cardboard rings around all the strands. Pull firmly and make a strong knot, leaving long ends. Now take out the rings. Finish by trimming off any straggling ends of yarn.

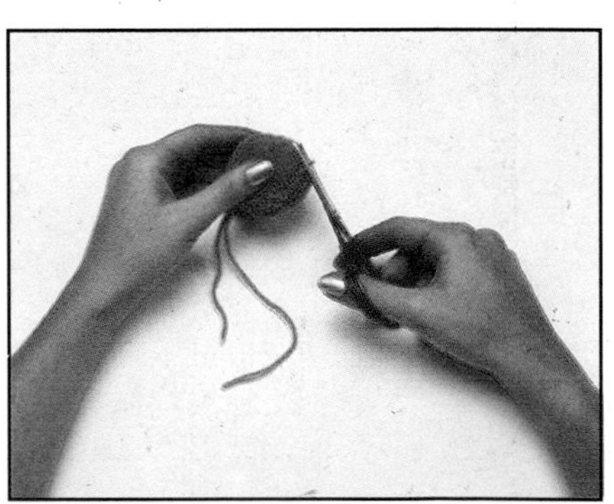

PAPIER-MÂCHÉ

This is something we probably all learned at school but many of us have long forgotten! First you need to choose a bowl or some other receptacle that is roughly the shape you wish to achieve. Tear up lots of newspaper into narrow strips, and then make up a flour and water paste, not too stiff, not too runny. You will soon discover the correct consistency when you get started.

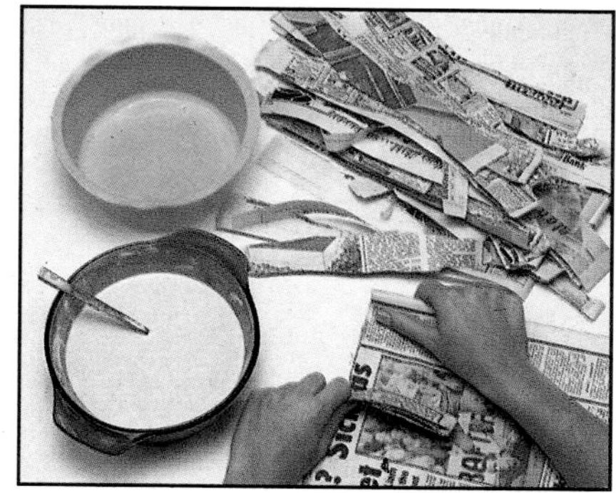

Dip the newspaper into the paste and start placing it on the bowl, working your way around it until the whole surface is covered. Keep working over it, in all directions, until you have built up at least six layers. This will give you a firm mould. Make sure to keep it smooth as you go along.

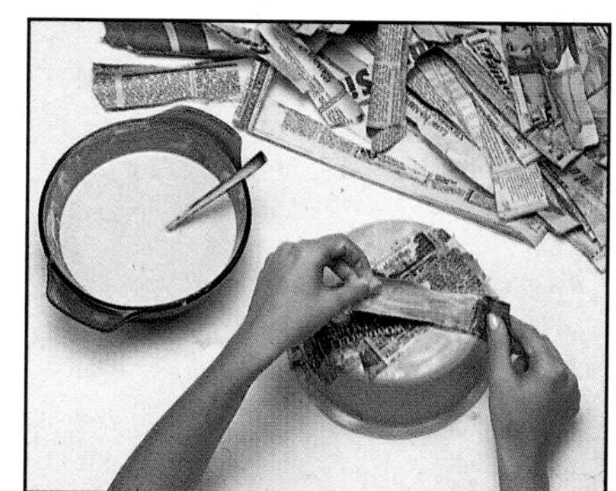

When you have finished, leave the papier-mâché to dry in a warm dry place. It will take about 24 hours to dry completely — more if it is particularly thick. When it is ready, ease it off the bowl. You may have to sand down the rough edges, but this is best done after the first coat of paint, as this will show up any lumps and bumps.

PAPER FLOWERS

These little carnation-shaped flowers are useful for adorning all sorts of decorations, or can be used by themselves to make a lovely floral centrepiece. Take an ordinary paper tissue and cut it in half lengthwise. Concertina-fold it down its length, as shown, then tie it in the middle with a piece of wire or twine.

Fold the tissue in half, and wrap one end of the wire firmly around the base to hold the shape in position. (The other end serves as the stem.)

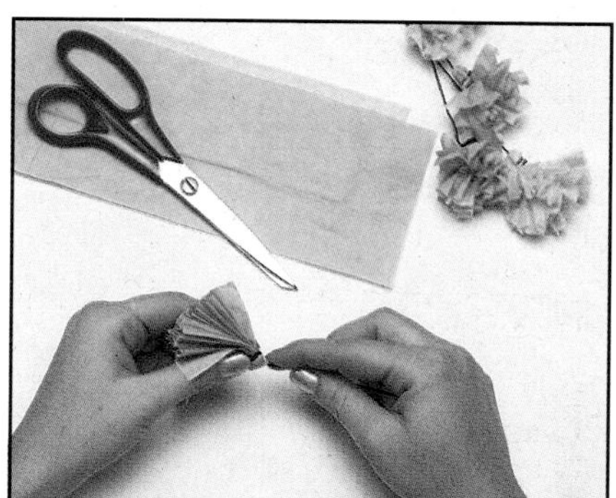

Now simply fluff out the paper, teasing it with your fingers until it resembles a carnation.

INDEX

A

Abstract Tablecloth **45**
Anniversaries **58**
Apricots and Cream **29**
Autumn Gold **43**

B

Balloon decorations **15**
Baubles **21, 40**
Bells **21**
Bird designs **19**
Birds on the Wing **19**
Bishop's Hat, The **48**
Bonnet **76**
Bootee Garland **7**
Branching Out **39**
Buffet Envelope **55**
Burn's Night **67**
Butterfly, The **49**

C

Candle Centrepiece **38**
Candle Cluster **34**
Candle Fold **51**
Candles **33, 34, 38, 41**
Candy Crackers **9**
Candy Cone **85**
Cat mask **79**
Centrepieces **28-43**
Charlie Clown **78**
Cheeky Chicks **19**
Chocolate Shell Surprise **85**
Christenings **7**
Christmas decorations **12, 16, 20, 22, 23, 24, 25, 26, 27, 38, 42, 67, 69, 86**
Circular Napkin **56**
Clowning Around **73**
Clown's hat **73**
Clown's mask **78**
Collage Place Card **63**
Colour-Flecked Placemat **70**
Colourful Cupcakes **63**
Colourful Kite **15**
Cone Candle Stand **33**
Co-ordinating Candlesticks **34**
Crackers **9, 26, 43, 86, 87, 88**
Crepe Paper Chain **11**
Crown **73**
Crowning Glory **73**
Curious Cat **79**
Cutout Place Card **65**

D

Decorated Napkins **59**
Double Jabot **30**

E

Easter Bunny **88**
Easter decorations **65, 88**
Easter Place Marker **65**
Edible decorations **29, 30, 32, 40, 41, 43**
Egg warmer **88**
Eight-Pointed Star **20**
Etched Melon Fruit Bowl **30**
Everlasting Wreath **23**
Expanding Chain **10**

F

Fancy Foil **21**
Fans **17**
Fantastic **15**
Fascinating Fez **75**
Fashion Flowers **89**
Favours **80-89**
Felt Christmas Tree **22**
Fez **75**
Fleur-de-lys **52**
Fleur-de-lys Tablecloth **46**
Floral designs **6, 31, 33, 35, 37, 38, 39, 41, 46, 54, 58, 59, 62, 80, 81, 83, 89, 94**
Floral Envelope **81**
Floral Favour **83**
Floral Napkin Ring **59**
Floral Place Card **62**
Floral table setting **80**
Flower-Strewn Tablecloth **46**
Flowers and Frills **41**
Forest Foliage **38**
Four Feathers **53**
Free-Style Place Card **61**
Fresh from the Garden **6**
Frosted Fruit **32**
Fun Fairy Cakes **41**

G

Garlands **6-13**
Gift Baskets **81**
Gift Box Pom-Pom **84**
Gift-Wrapped Soaps **82**
Gifts 80-89
Gingerbread Man Envelope **66**
Glamour Cracker **88**
Glitter Tree Placemat **69**
Go For Gold **69**
Gold and Silver Crackers **43**
Graceful Bells **21**
Graduation **7**
Graduation Garland **7**

H

Halloween decorations **13, 14, 36**
Hand-Painted Fruit Basket **32**
Hanging Decorations **14-27**
Hanging Evergreen Wreath **25**
Happy Face **14**
Harlequin Masks **77**
Harlequin Party Mask **35**
Harlequin Place Card **61**
Harlequin Placemat **71**
Harlequin table setting **60**
Harvest-Time Basket **37**
Hats **72-76**
Heart Strings **18**
Hearts Delight **13**
Highland Holly **12**
Hogmanay **67**
Holiday Centrepiece **40**
Hoop-La! **24**
Host of Daffodils, A **39**
Hot Lips **12**

I

Instant Placemat **70**
Ivy Candle-Ring **33**

J

Jack-O'-Lantern **36**
Jester's hat **72**
Jokey Jester **72**
Jolly Roger **75**

K

Kite Place Cards **64**
Kites **15, 64**

L

Lace-Trimmed Placemat **68**
Lacy Napkin Bow **58**
Lacy Napkin Folder **54**
Lady's Slipper **52**
Lavender Gift Bag **83**
Layered Fruit Salad **30**
Little Boxes **26**
Little Crackers **26**
Lotus Blossom **53**

M

Marzipan Fruit Parcels **40**
Masks **72, 77-79**
Masque Ball **77**
Medieval Lady **76**
Mischievous Mouse **79**
Mobiles **18, 19**
Mouse mask **79**

NO

Napkin Rings **57, 58, 59**
Napkins **44, 48-59**
Nest of Eggs **29**
Net Napkin Ring **56**
Net Parcels **89**
Oriental Fan **50**
Outlook Fine **16**

PQ

Paper Chains **10, 11**
Paper Flowers **94**
Papier-Mâché **94**
Pastel Napkin Box **54**
Picnic Tres Chic **71**
Pierrot Hat **74**
Pirate Hat **75**
Place cards **60-67**
Placemats **60, 68-71**
Pocket Napkin **55**
Pom-Poms **93**
Potato Print 'Placemat' **45**
Pretend Balloons **15**
Pretty Pleats **15**
Pretty PVC Placemat **68**
Princess, The **49**
Pumpkin Lantern **36**
Pure and Simple **48**
Pure Elegance **51**

R

Rag-Rolled Tablecloth **47**
Ribbon Tree **42**
Ribbon-Trimmed Tablecloth **47**
Ribbons and Curls **35**
Ricepaper Fans Place Card **62**
Red Hot Crackers **87**

S

Santa Faces **27**
Scalloped Squares **10**
Shiny Foil Chain **11**
Skull and Crossbones **13**
Snowflake **16**
Square Gift Box **82**
Stars **20**
Stencil Shell Napkin **57**
Stocking Fillers **27**
Summer Beauty **31**
Swags of Net **9**
Swaying Palms **18**
Sweets Galore **8**

T

Table centrepieces **28-43**
Tablecloths **44-47**
Tartan Place Card **67**
Tassel Napkin Ring **57**
Tassels **93**
Techniques **90, 93-94**
Teddy Bears' Picnic **64**
Teddy Place Marker **67**
Templates **90-92**
Thanksgiving decorations **37, 44, 58**
Thanksgiving Napkin **58**
Thanksgiving table setting **44**
Total Disguise **78**
Traditional Crackers **86**
Twinkle Twinkle **20**

UV

Valentine Gift Boxes **84**
Valentine Place Card **66**
Valentine's Day decorations **12, 13, 18, 66, 84, 88**
Victorian Bonnet **76**
Victorian Cracker **87**

WXYZ

Warm Welcome **24**
Wedding table setting **28**
Weddings **9, 28, 58**
Wicked Witch **74**
Witch's hat **74**
Wreaths **23, 24, 25**

ACKNOWLEDGEMENTS

The author and pulishers would like to thank the following for their help in compiling this book:

Valley Industries Ltd., 5 Heathermount Drive, Crowthorne, Berkshire
Porth Decorative Products Ltd., Tonypandy, Mid Glamorgan, Wales
Philip and Tacey Ltd., North Way, Andover, Hants
Offray Ribbons Ltd., Ashbury, Rosecrea, Co. Tipperary, Ireland (UK office: Fir Tree Place, Church Rd., Ashford, Middlesex)
Naylor Ball Design Partnership, 177 Waller Rd., London SE14
Fablon, the House of Mayfair, Cramlington, Northumberland
Heal's, 196 Tottenham Court Road, London W1
Lakeland Plastics, Alexander Buildings, Windermere, Cumbria
Paperchase, 213 Tottenham Court Road, London W1
Pebeo water-based, textured and fabric paints from: Artemis Products Ltd., 684 Mitcham Road, Croydon
Viners Cutlery, Cranborne House, Cranborne Road, Potters Bar, Hertfordshire

Special thanks also go to Marion Dale and Pearl Piggot